WOULD YOU RATHER

Drinking Edition

VOLUME 2

Welcome to **Would You Rather: Drinking Edition - Volume 2**, the sequel you didn't know you needed but absolutely deserve. If you loved the wild, outrageous fun of our first volume, buckle up–because this one's even crazier, riskier, and more unpredictable.

Whether you're hosting a house party, pregaming for a night out, or just looking to stir up some chaos with friends, this book is your ultimate drinking game companion. Packed with scandalous questions, awkward dilemmas, and no-win situations, it's designed to push boundaries, spark hilarious debates, and test just how far you're willing to go for a laugh (or a drink).

What's Inside?

13 Ridiculously Fun Rounds – From Dirty Decisions to Cringe Confessions and Drunken Debacles, each round is packed with 18 tough-as-hell questions guaranteed to make you sweat–and sip!

New Drinking Rules – With updated rules for players and game-masters, expect even more chaos, power plays, and penalties! <u>No one's</u> getting out of this game sober.

Round Winner's Choices – Winners don't just get bragging rights– they also get control of the drinks with hilarious new options!

Lucid Ponderings

Rules

Basic Gameplay

- Gather your group, grab your drinks, and decide who will be the first **game-master**–the person in charge of reading the questions and keeping track of points for the first round.
- Make sure everyone has a drink ready, as sips, gulps, and shots might be required based on the rules!
- Before starting, agree on any **house rules**–for example, whether interruptions are allowed, if there's a time limit for answers, or how wild stories can get!

The Role of the Game-Master – Players take turns being the game-master after each round. The game-master reads the questions aloud from the book and listens to everyone's answers. They're also responsible for tracking points and enforcing the drinking rules.

Answering the Questions – Moving clockwise, each player takes turns explaining their answer to the group. Answers can be **funny**, **logical**, **ridiculous**, **creative**, or completely absurd–it's up to the player's creativity!

Judging the Winner – After hearing all the answers, the game-master decides which player gave the best response for that question based on **humor**, **logic**, or **creativity**.

- The winner's name is written in the Winner Box for that question, along with a quick note about why they won (e.g., funniest, most shocking, most relatable).
- The winner earns **one** point for that question, which is recorded in the Score Table at the end of the round.
- Once all questions in the round have been answered, the game-master tallies up the scores in the Points Table and declares the **Round Winner**–the player with the most points in that round.
- The round winner gets to pick a **Round Winner's Choice** option which is listed on the last page of the rules.
- The next round begins with a new game-master, and the fun continues!

Game-Master Drinking Rules

1. **The Forgetful Sip:** If the game-master forgets to ask a question or skips a player, they take a sip.

2. **Delayed Reaction:** If the game-master laughs or reacts before everyone has answered the question, they take a sip.

3. **Timekeeper's Toll:** If the game-master allows a player to take too long to answer (you can set a reasonable time limit like 60 seconds), they take a sip.

4. **Question Repeat:** If the game-master repeats a question that has already been asked in the same game session, they take a sip.

5. **Misinterpretation Misdemeanor:** If the game-master incorrectly summarizes or misinterprets a player's answer, leading to a misunderstanding, they take a sip.

6. **Unanimity Unraveled:** If everyone chooses the same answer and the game-master fails to notice, they take a sip.

7. **The Distraction Debacle:** If the game-master gets distracted (e.g., by their phone, someone not in the game) and needs to be reminded to continue the game, they take a sip.

8. **Messy Math** – If the game-master messes up the score tally or forgets to record a winner, they take one sip for each mistake.

9. **Judge's Bias** – If the game-master picks the same winner for two questions in a row, they take two sips to prove they aren't playing favorites.

Player Drinking Rules

- If a player's explanation for their choice is particularly **creative**, **logical** or **humorous**, the rest of the group takes a sip.

1. **Confidence Crash** – If a player changes their answer mid-explanation, they take **three** sips.
2. **Echo Effect** – If a player repeats someone else's answer without adding something new, they take **two** sips.
3. **Laugh Attack** – If a player laughs at their own answer before sharing it, they take **one** sip.
4. **Rule Rebel** – If a player ignores or breaks a rule, they take **two** sips.
5. **Speechless Slip** – If a player is unable to give an answer, they **finish** their drink.
6. **Stumble Sip** – If a player stutters, pauses for too long, or says "um" more than three times while explaining their answer, they take **one** sip.
7. **Sarcasm Slam** – If a player uses sarcasm in their answer and someone calls them out, they take **two** sips.
8. **Interruptions Are Expensive** – If a player interrupts someone else's turn, they must take one sip **immediately** and another sip **when it's their turn** for the whole round.

Round Winner's Choice

1. **Down it!:** The round winner picks up to **three** people to finish their drink.

2. **Question Master:** The round winner becomes the next game-master, granting them the power to choose the next set of "Would You Rather" questions.

3. **Rule Maker:** The winner gets to create a new, unique rule for the next round. This could be a fun twist on answering questions or a new drinking guideline.

4. **Immunity Grant:** The winner can grant immunity to themselves or another player, protecting them from any drinking penalties **ONLY** in the next round.

5. **Storyteller Spotlight:** The winner can choose a player to tell a short **funny, embarrassing** or **interesting** story about themselves. The rest of the group has to drink slowly and continuously (so the drink has to be on their lips and flowing into their mouth) whilst that person tells their story. If someone laughs, gasps or stops drinking, that person must finish their entire drink.

6. **Mystery Mixer** – The winner picks **two** players who must combine their drinks (or mix in a mystery ingredient) and finish the mixture before the first question ends on the next round.

7. **The Drunk Whisperer** – The winner picks any player and can make them speak in whispers only until the end of the next round. If they forget, they take two sips each time they slip up.

Can't remember?

Seriously? No surprise there—**Snap a pic** of the rules now before your memory gets any fuzzier. (Future-you will thank you.)

Loved This Book? Show Us Some Love Back!

Enjoyed the laughs, the debates, and maybe a few too many drinks? We've got more where that came from—so why not support us with just a few taps?

How? Glad you asked!

Scan the QR code to visit our Amazon page and hit that Follow button. This tells Amazon, "Hey, these guys are awesome!"–and trust us, it helps more than you know.

Oh, and if you're feeling extra generous, drop us a cheeky review! Your feedback keeps the drinks flowing and the fun going. 🍸🍺
Cheers, and thanks for being part of the madness!

Lucid Ponderings

Amazon UK

Amazon US

Thank You!

Also, whilst we love these drinking games as much as you guys, please keep the following in mind.

Moderation and Safety

Drink Responsibly: Players should be mindful of their alcohol consumption and know their limits.

Stay Hydrated: Encourage players to drink water throughout the game to stay hydrated.

Know Your Limits: Encourage players to opt out of a drink if they feel they've had enough–no judgments, just fun.

Non-Alcoholic Options: Suggest having fun mocktails or soft drinks available for those who prefer not to drink or need a break.

Check-Ins: Recommend that players check in with each other to make sure everyone's feeling good throughout the game.

Plan for Safety: Ensure a safe way home for those who have been drinking.

Round I

Game-Master:

Dirty Decisions

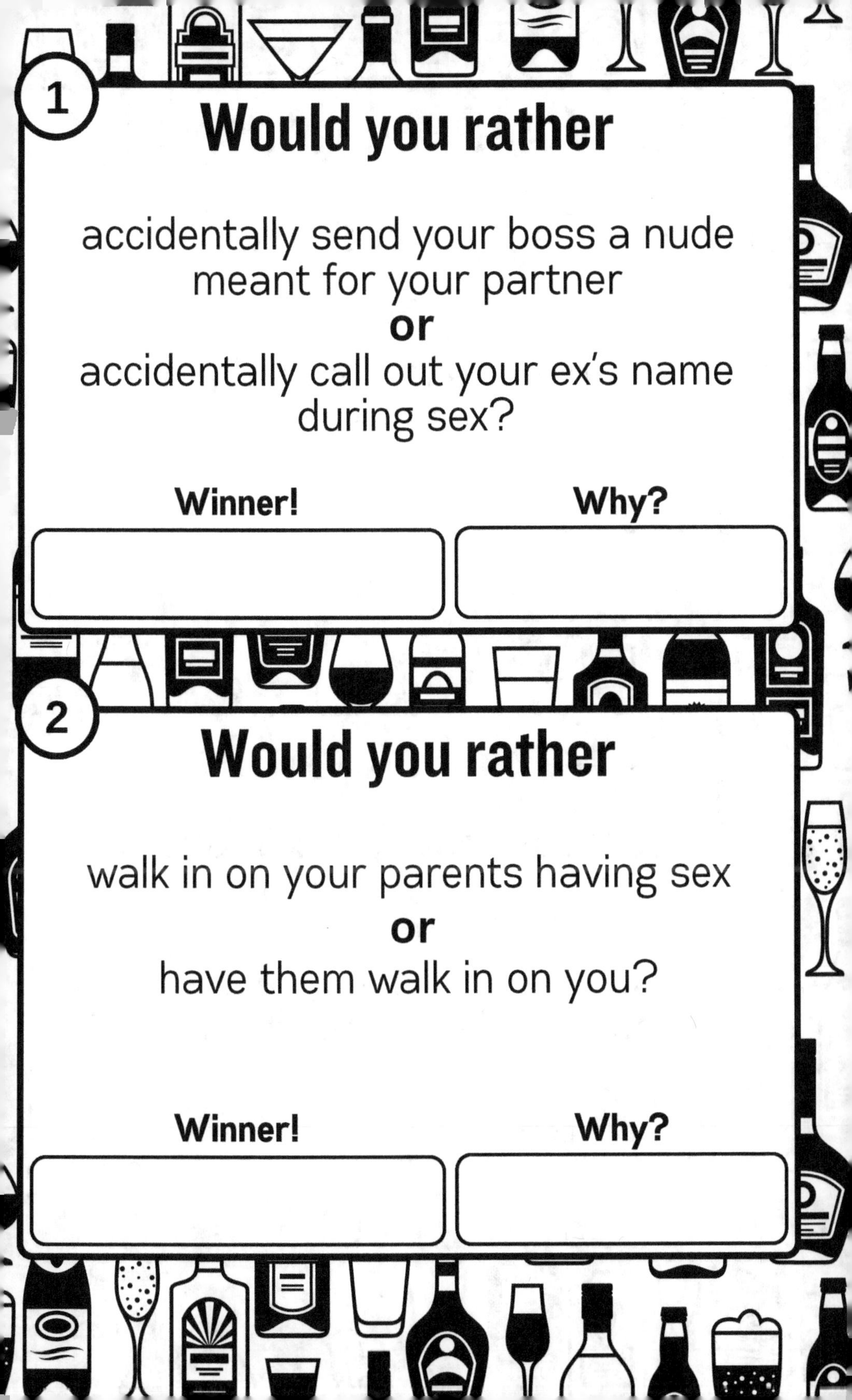

1

Would you rather

accidentally send your boss a nude
meant for your partner
or
accidentally call out your ex's name
during sex?

Winner!   Why?

2

Would you rather

walk in on your parents having sex
or
have them walk in on you?

Winner!   Why?

3

Would you rather

have your sex tape accidentally go viral

or

have to explain your most embarrassing kink on live TV?

Winner!

Why?

4

Would you rather

get caught having sex in public

or

have your partner announce every detail of your sex life at a family dinner?

Winner!

Why?

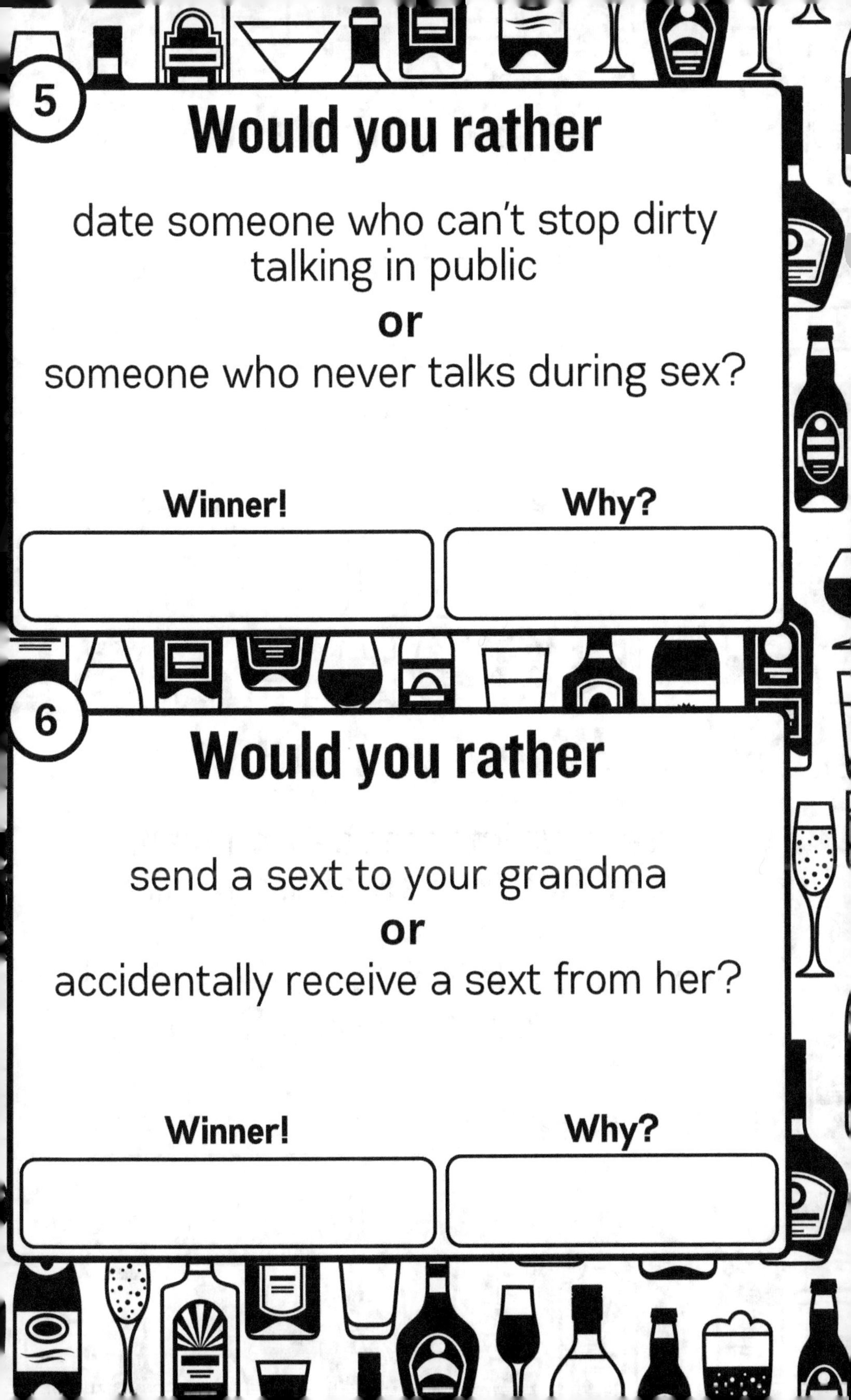

5

Would you rather

date someone who can't stop dirty talking in public
or
someone who never talks during sex?

Winner!

Why?

6

Would you rather

send a sext to your grandma
or
accidentally receive a sext from her?

Winner!

Why?

7

Would you rather

wear lingerie to work every day
or
have to send a dirty text to your boss
once a week?

Winner!

Why?

8

Would you rather

have your internet search history
exposed to your entire family
or
have your bedroom fantasies leaked to
your coworkers?

Winner!

Why?

9

Would you rather

have your sex playlist randomly play
during a work Zoom meeting
or
have your webcam accidentally turn on
while you're getting undressed?

Winner!

Why?

10

Would you rather

hook up with someone who's really into
roleplay but only as a baby
or
someone who insists on making animal
noises during sex?

Winner!

Why?

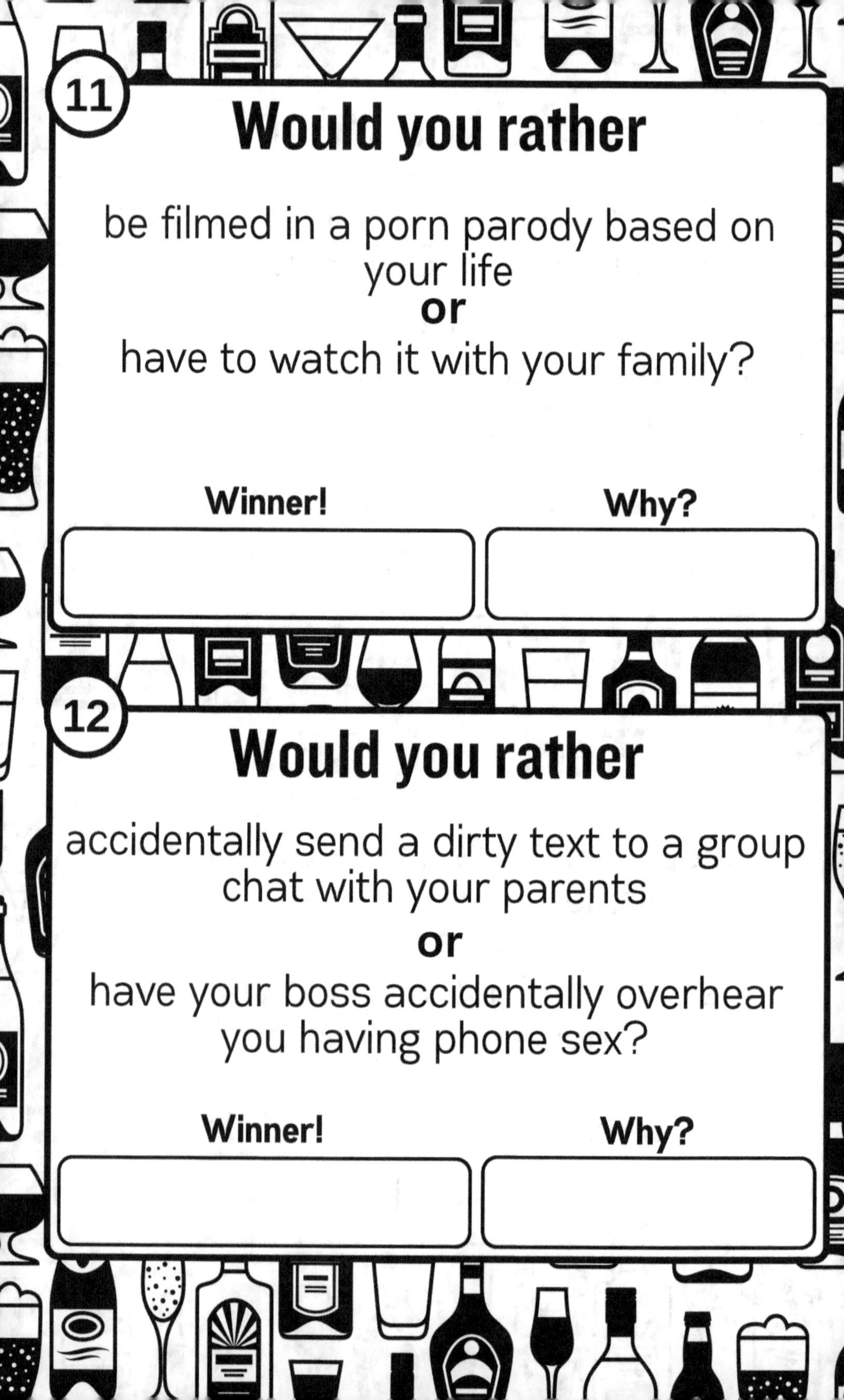

11
Would you rather

be filmed in a porn parody based on your life
or
have to watch it with your family?

Winner!
Why?

12
Would you rather

accidentally send a dirty text to a group chat with your parents
or
have your boss accidentally overhear you having phone sex?

Winner!
Why?

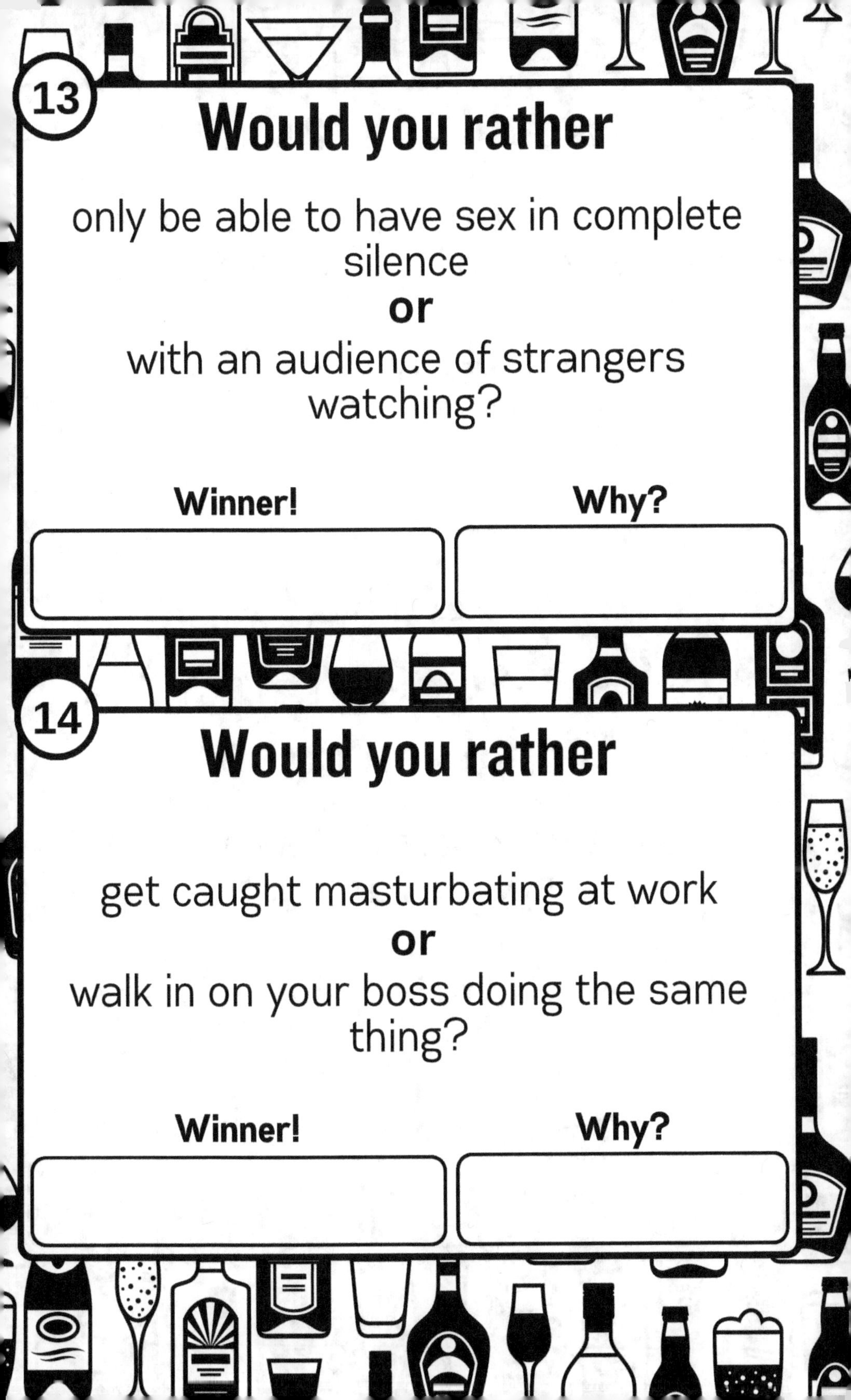

13
Would you rather
only be able to have sex in complete silence
or
with an audience of strangers watching?
Winner!
Why?
14
Would you rather
get caught masturbating at work
or
walk in on your boss doing the same thing?
Winner!
Why?

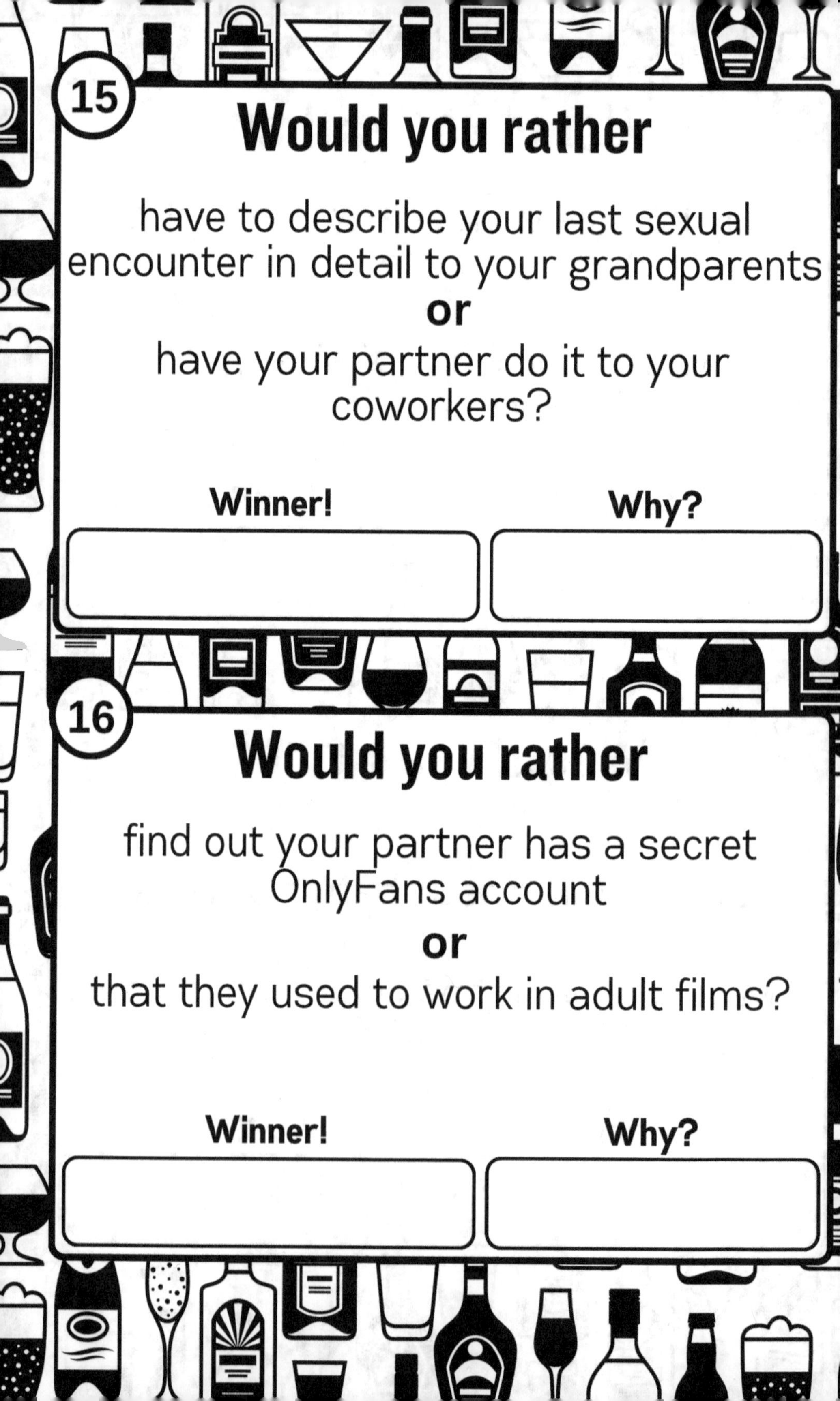

15
Would you rather

have to describe your last sexual encounter in detail to your grandparents
or
have your partner do it to your coworkers?

Winner!

Why?

16
Would you rather

find out your partner has a secret OnlyFans account
or
that they used to work in adult films?

Winner!

Why?

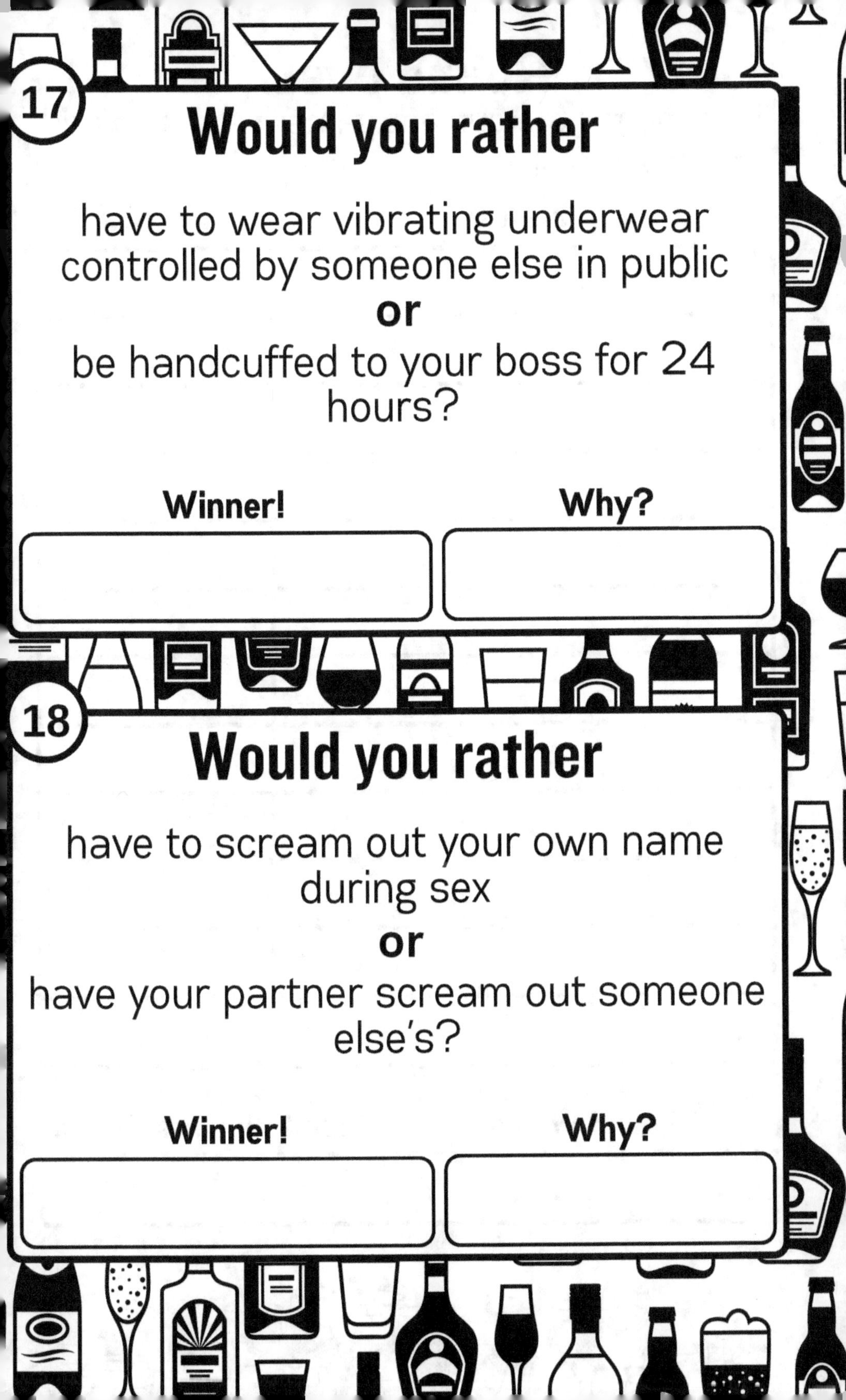

17

Would you rather

have to wear vibrating underwear controlled by someone else in public

or

be handcuffed to your boss for 24 hours?

Winner!

Why?

18

Would you rather

have to scream out your own name during sex

or

have your partner scream out someone else's?

Winner!

Why?

Round over!

It's time for the current game-master to add up the scores!

Name	Points

Round Winner	Round Winners Choice

Round 2

Game-Master:

Random Mayhem

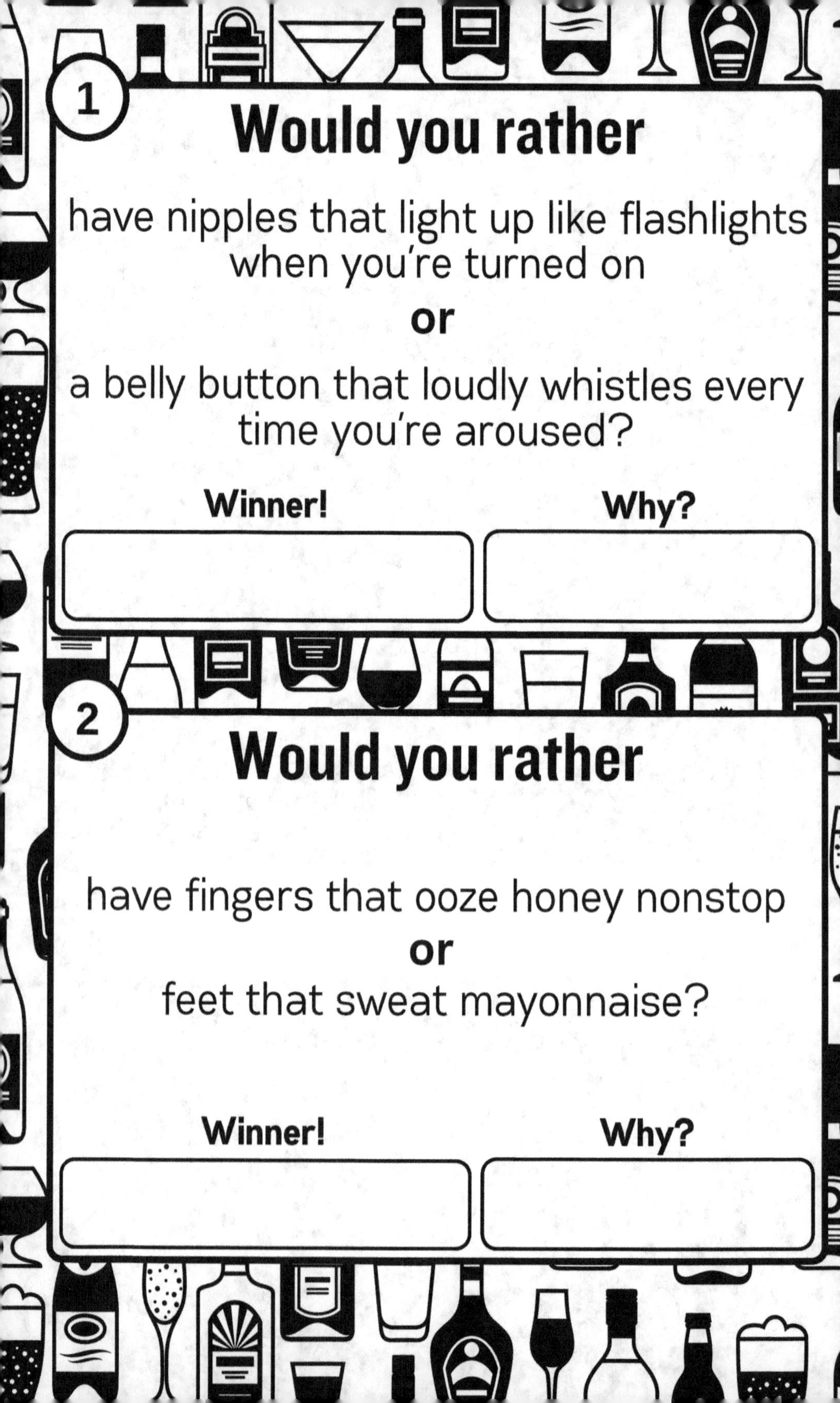

1
Would you rather
have nipples that light up like flashlights when you're turned on
or
a belly button that loudly whistles every time you're aroused?
Winner!
Why?
2
Would you rather
have fingers that ooze honey nonstop
or
feet that sweat mayonnaise?
Winner!
Why?

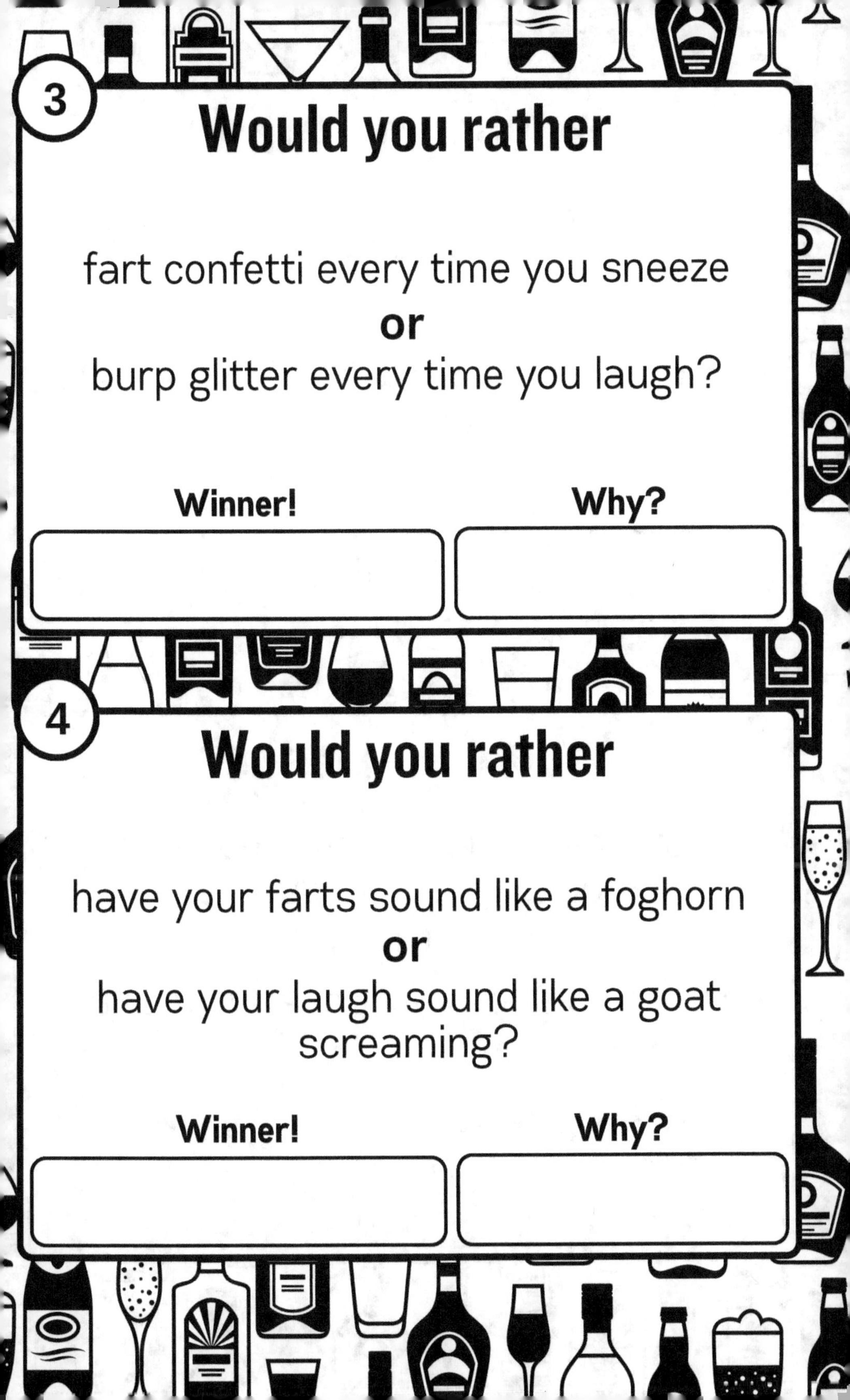

3

Would you rather

fart confetti every time you sneeze
or
burp glitter every time you laugh?

Winner!

Why?

4

Would you rather

have your farts sound like a foghorn
or
have your laugh sound like a goat screaming?

Winner!

Why?

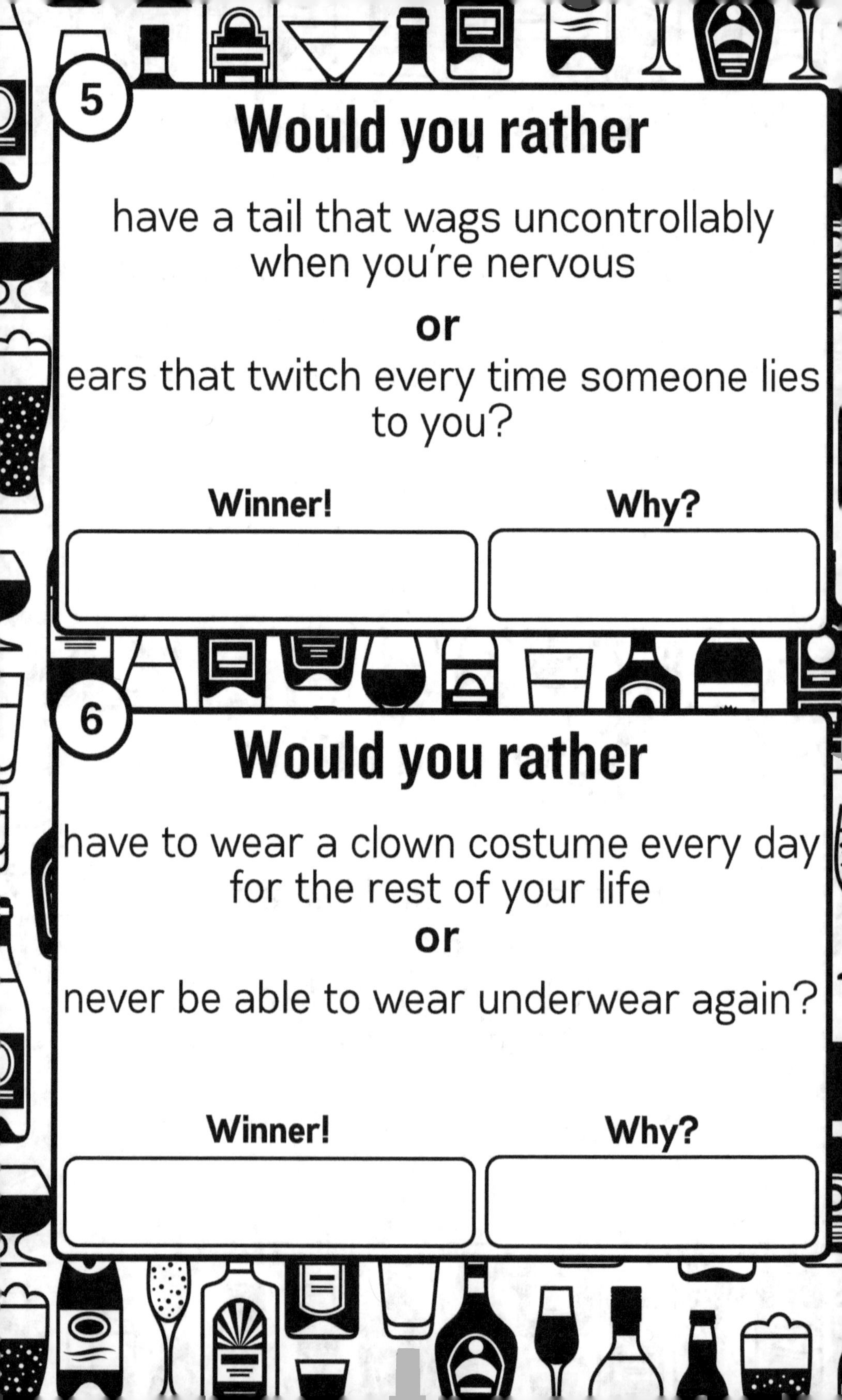

5

Would you rather

have a tail that wags uncontrollably
when you're nervous

or

ears that twitch every time someone lies
to you?

Winner!

Why?

6

Would you rather

have to wear a clown costume every day
for the rest of your life
or

never be able to wear underwear again?

Winner!

Why?

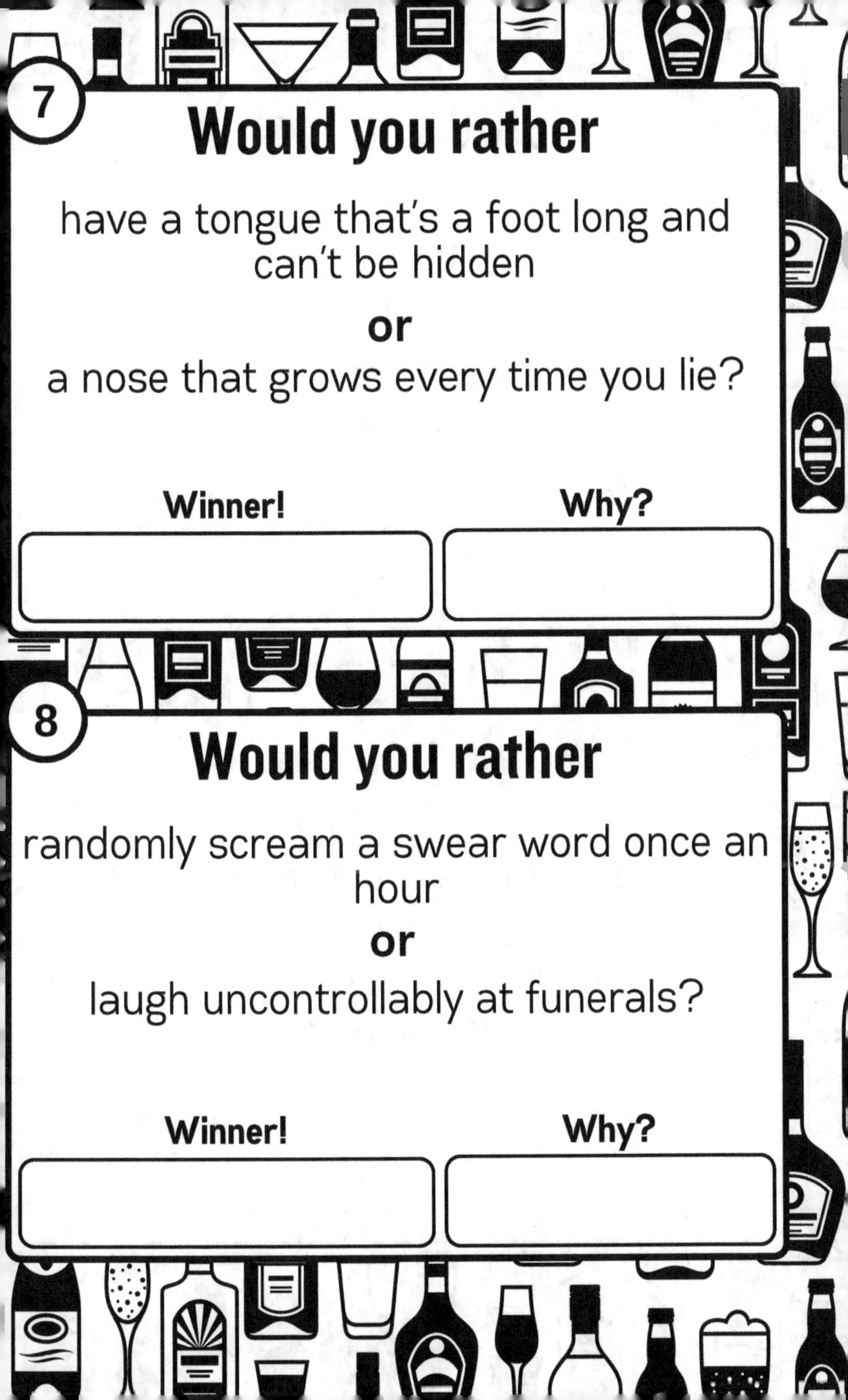

7
Would you rather
have a tongue that's a foot long and can't be hidden
or
a nose that grows every time you lie?
Winner!
Why?
8
Would you rather
randomly scream a swear word once an hour
or
laugh uncontrollably at funerals?
Winner!
Why?

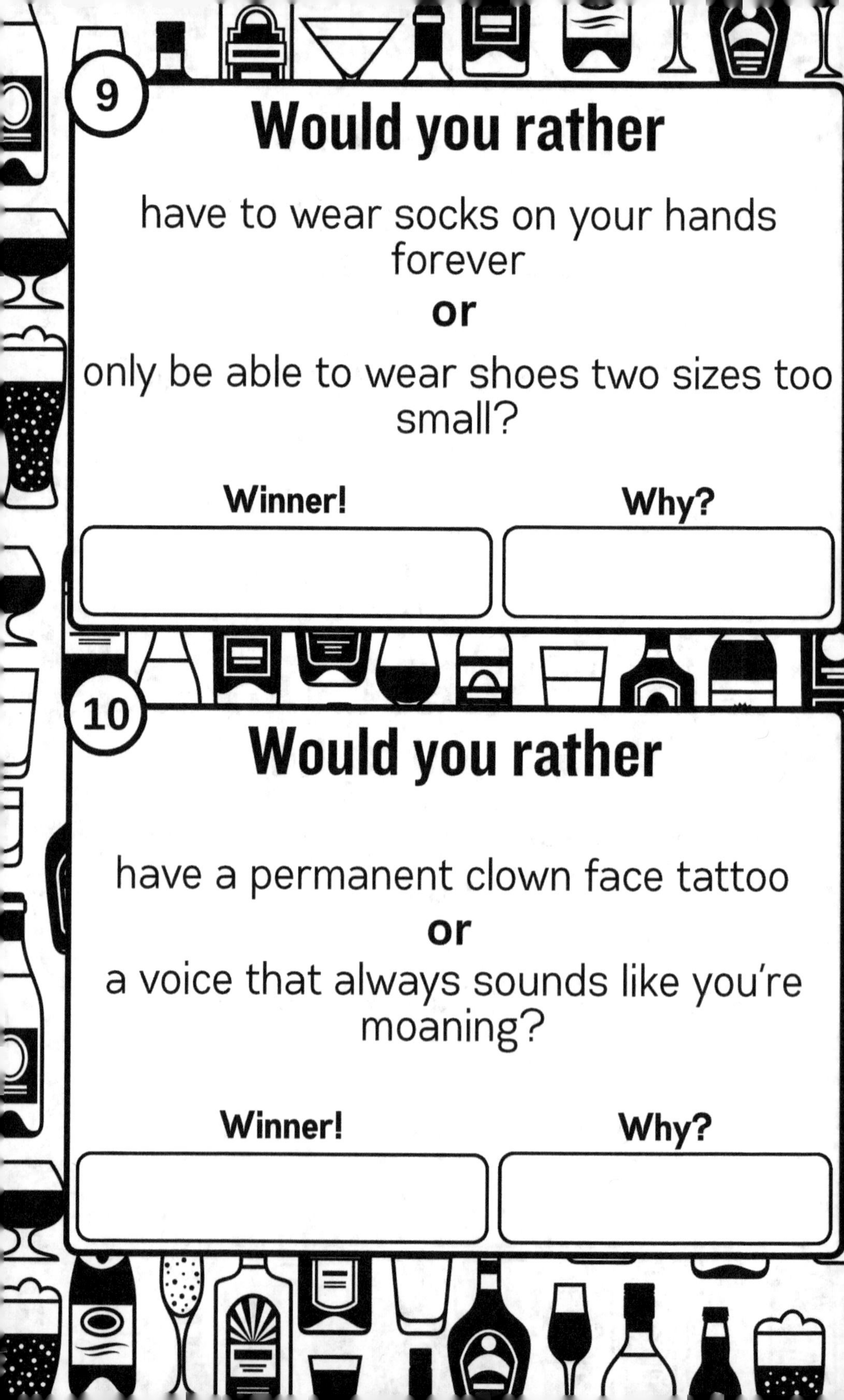

9

Would you rather

have to wear socks on your hands forever

or

only be able to wear shoes two sizes too small?

Winner!

Why?

10

Would you rather

have a permanent clown face tattoo

or

a voice that always sounds like you're moaning?

Winner!

Why?

11
Would you rather
have legs that collapse like a folding chair every time someone says your name
or
arms that flail like inflatable tube men whenever you're surprised?
Winner!
Why?
12
Would you rather
have to walk backward everywhere you go
or
crawl on all fours whenever you're inside a building?
Winner!
Why?

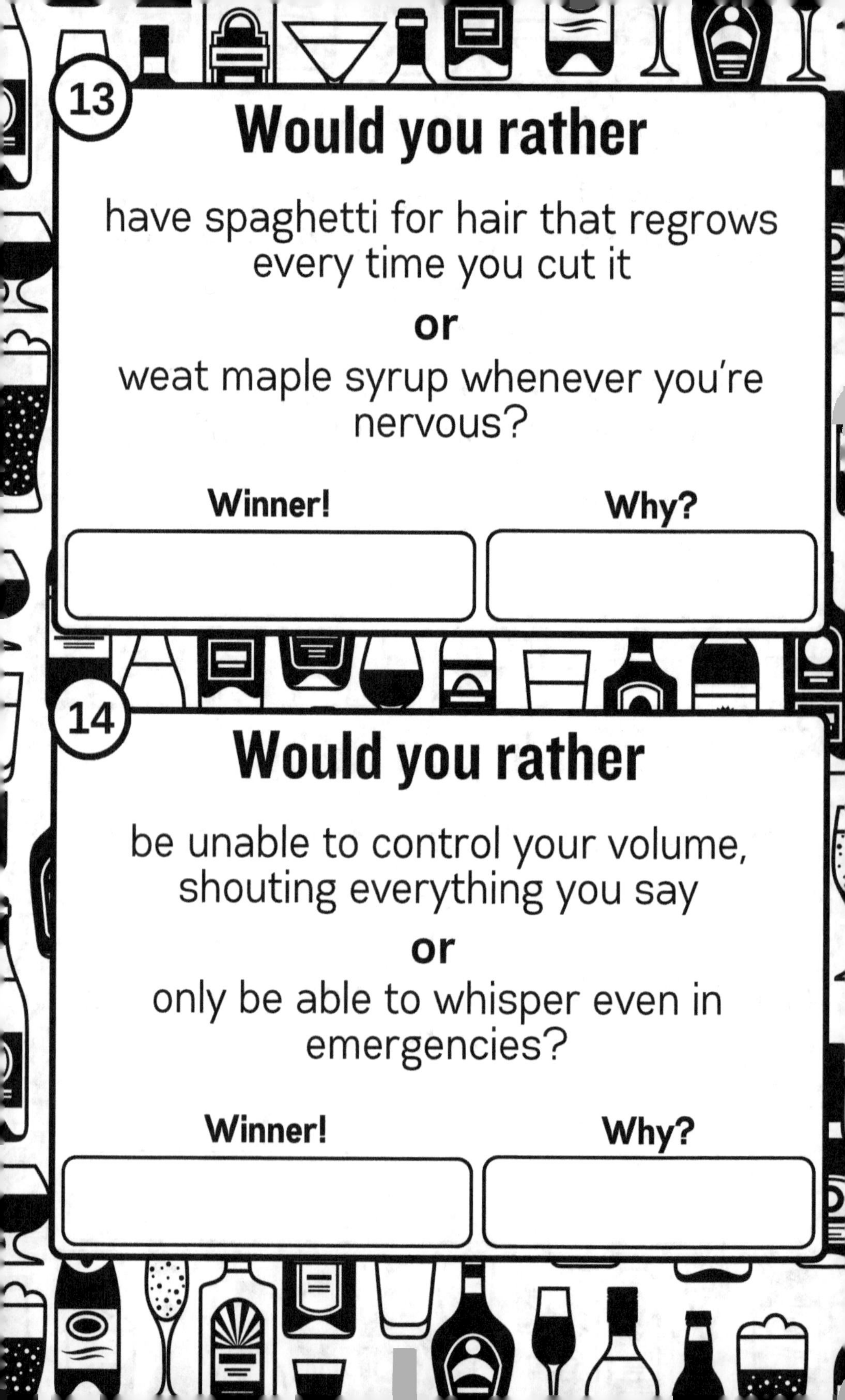

13

Would you rather

have spaghetti for hair that regrows
every time you cut it

or

weat maple syrup whenever you're
nervous?

Winner!   **Why?**

14

Would you rather

be unable to control your volume,
shouting everything you say

or

only be able to whisper even in
emergencies?

Winner!   **Why?**

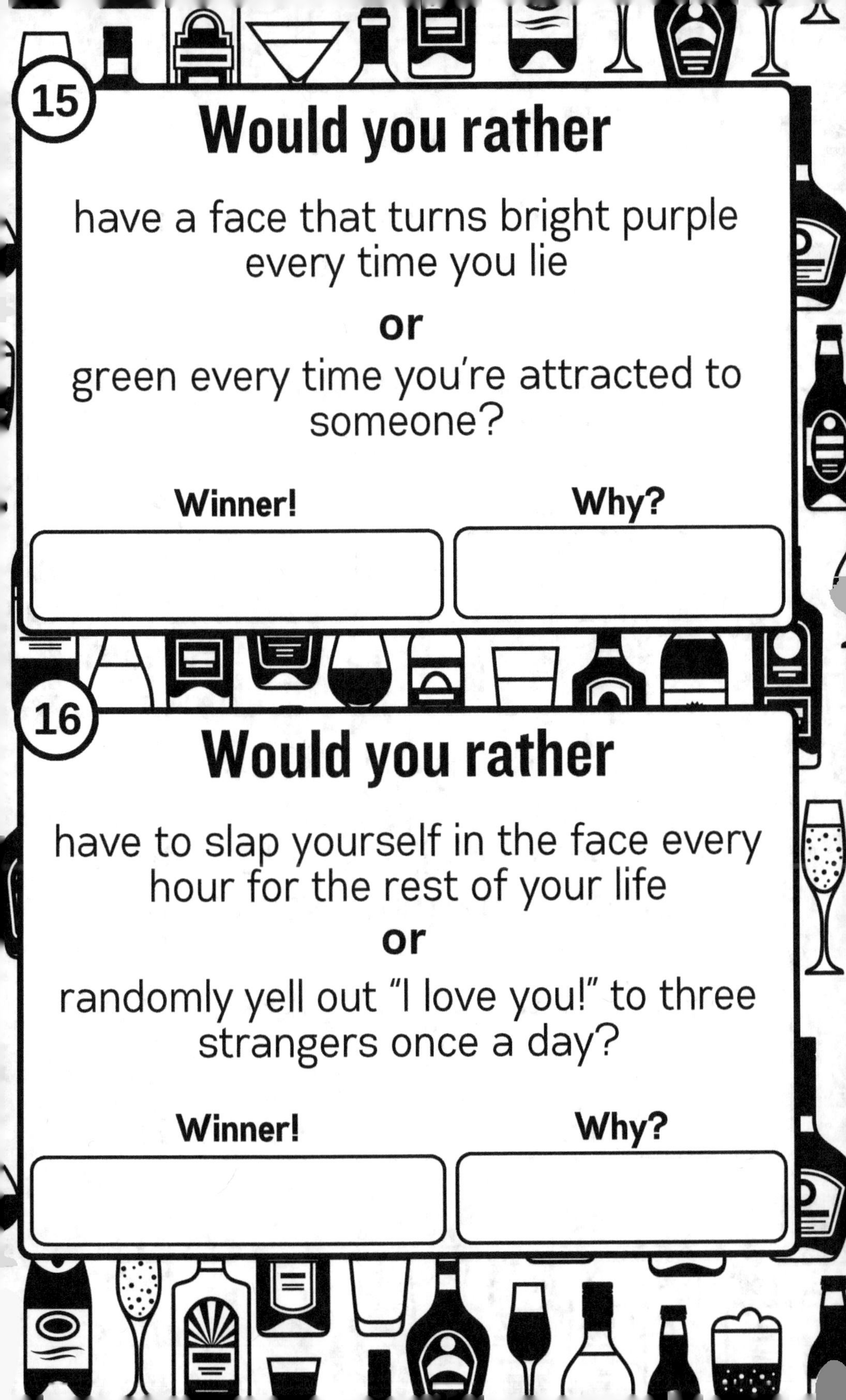
15
Would you rather
have a face that turns bright purple every time you lie
or
green every time you're attracted to someone?
Winner!
Why?
16
Would you rather
have to slap yourself in the face every hour for the rest of your life
or
randomly yell out "I love you!" to three strangers once a day?
Winner!
Why?

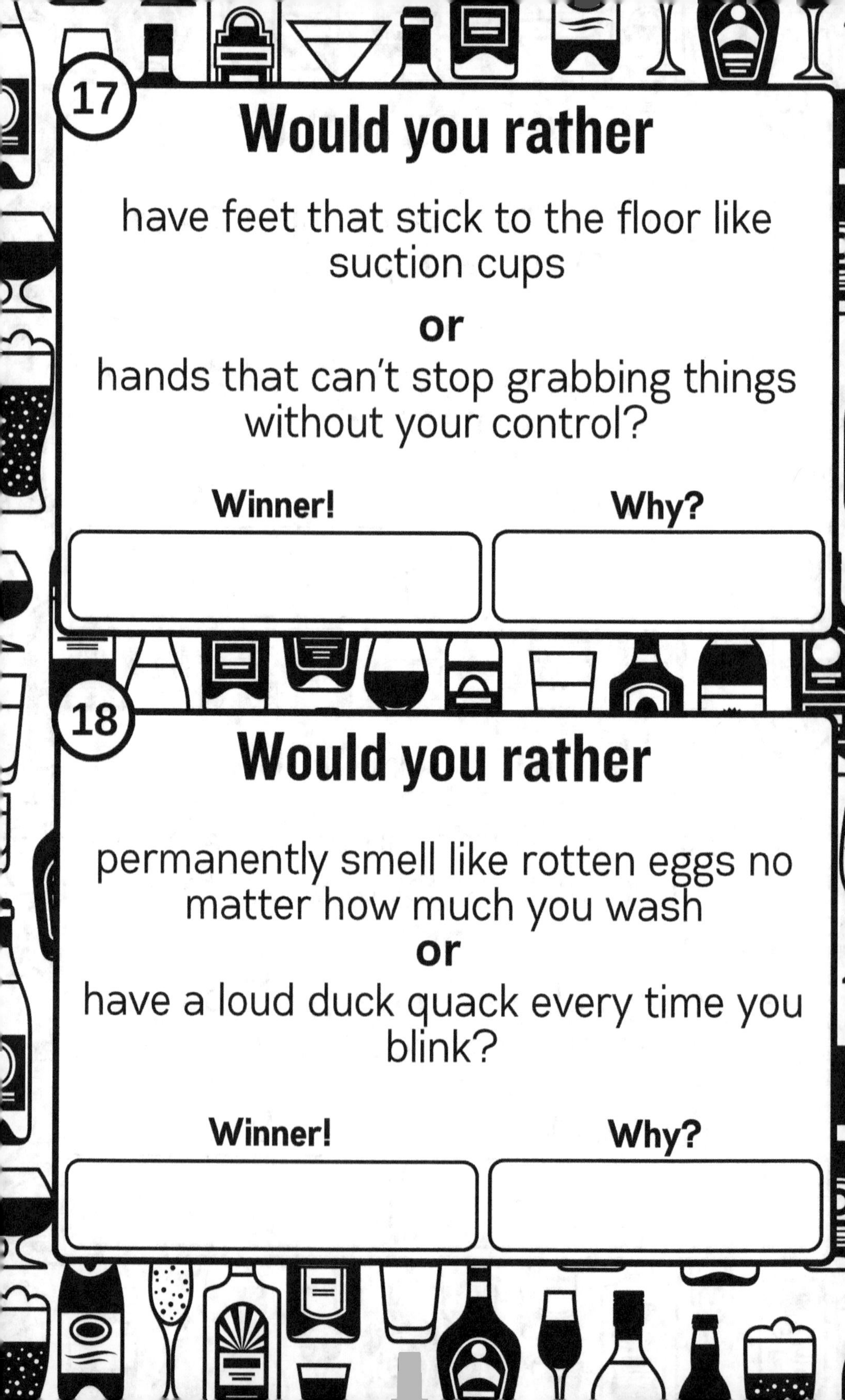

17

Would you rather

have feet that stick to the floor like suction cups

or

hands that can't stop grabbing things without your control?

Winner!

Why?

18

Would you rather

permanently smell like rotten eggs no matter how much you wash

or

have a loud duck quack every time you blink?

Winner!

Why?

Round over!

It's time for the current game-master to add up the scores!

Name	Points

Round Winner	Round Winners Choice

Round 3

Game-Master:

Weird Kinks

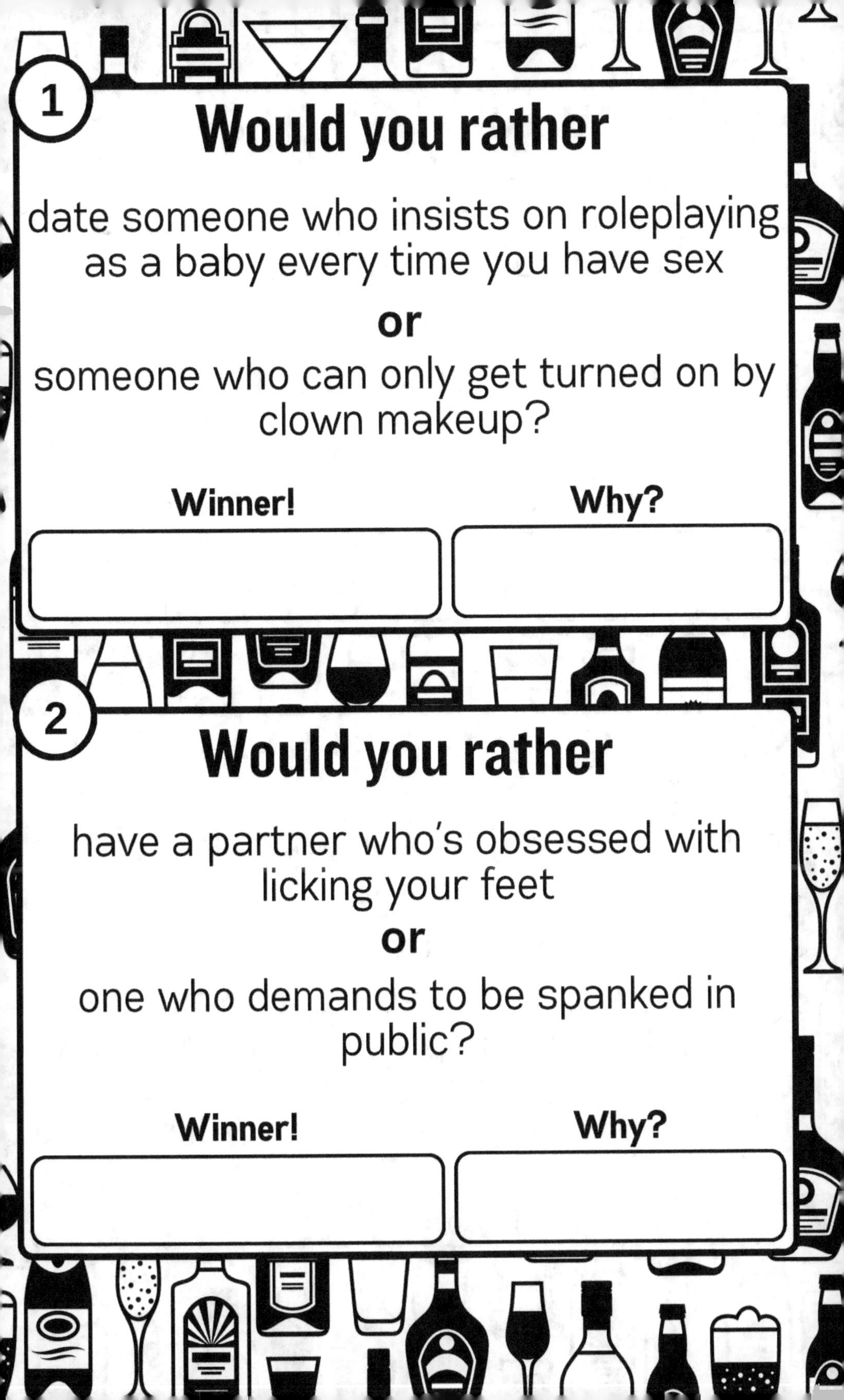

1

Would you rather

date someone who insists on roleplaying as a baby every time you have sex

or

someone who can only get turned on by clown makeup?

Winner!

Why?

2

Would you rather

have a partner who's obsessed with licking your feet

or

one who demands to be spanked in public?

Winner!

Why?

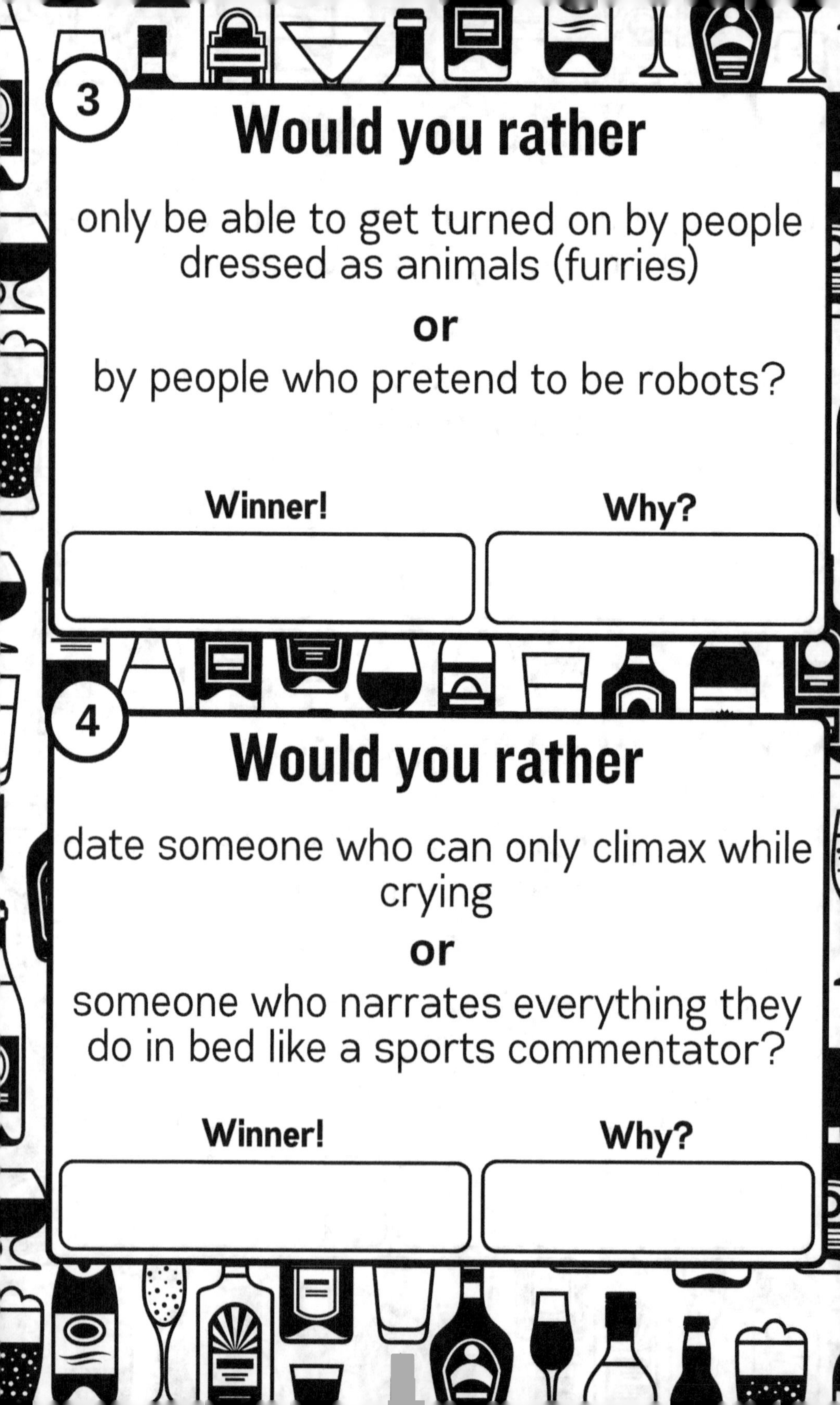
3
Would you rather
only be able to get turned on by people dressed as animals (furries)
or
by people who pretend to be robots?
Winner!
Why?
4
Would you rather
date someone who can only climax while crying
or
someone who narrates everything they do in bed like a sports commentator?
Winner!
Why?

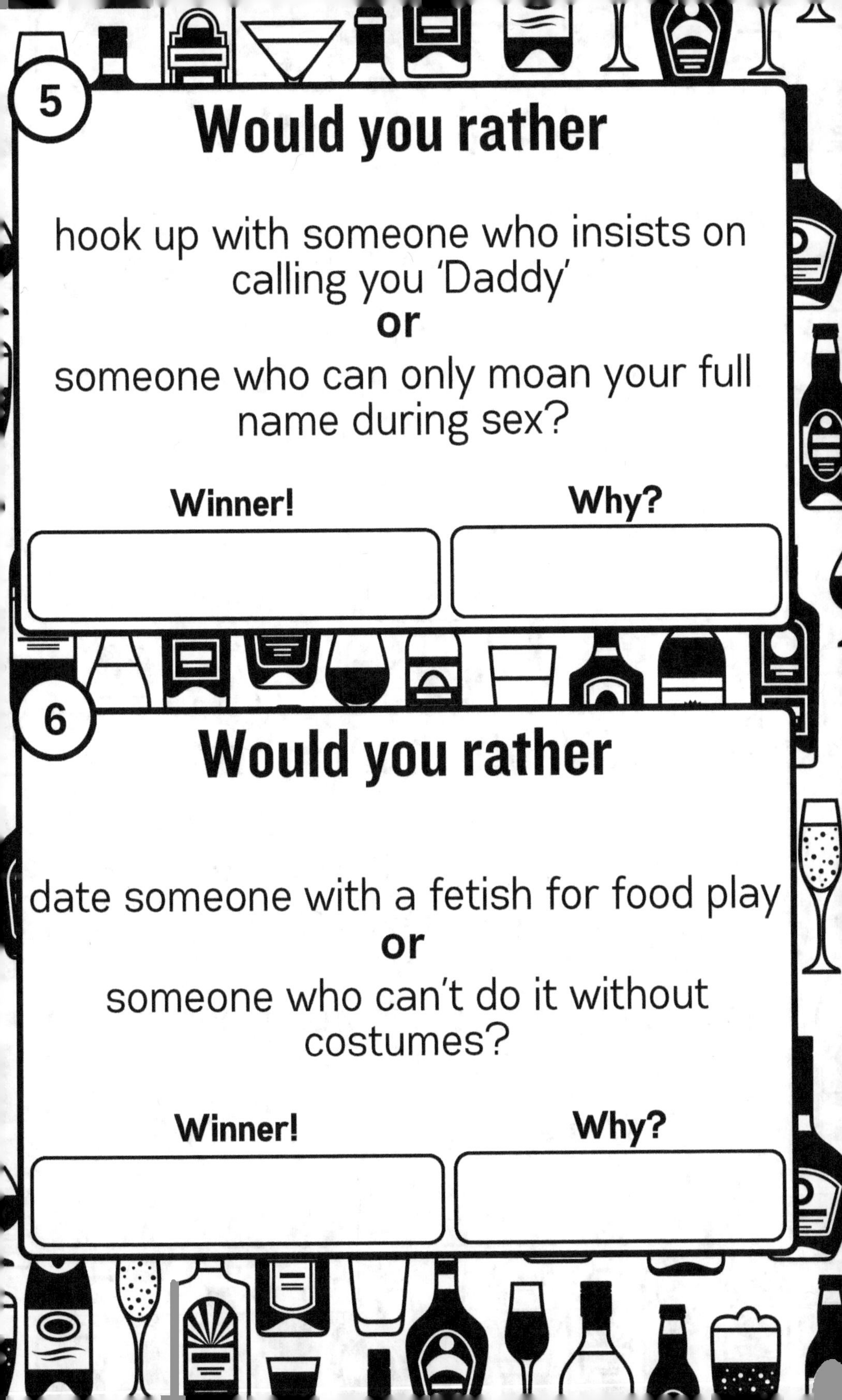

5 Would you rather

hook up with someone who insists on calling you 'Daddy'

or

someone who can only moan your full name during sex?

Winner!   **Why?**

6 Would you rather

date someone with a fetish for food play

or

someone who can't do it without costumes?

Winner!   **Why?**

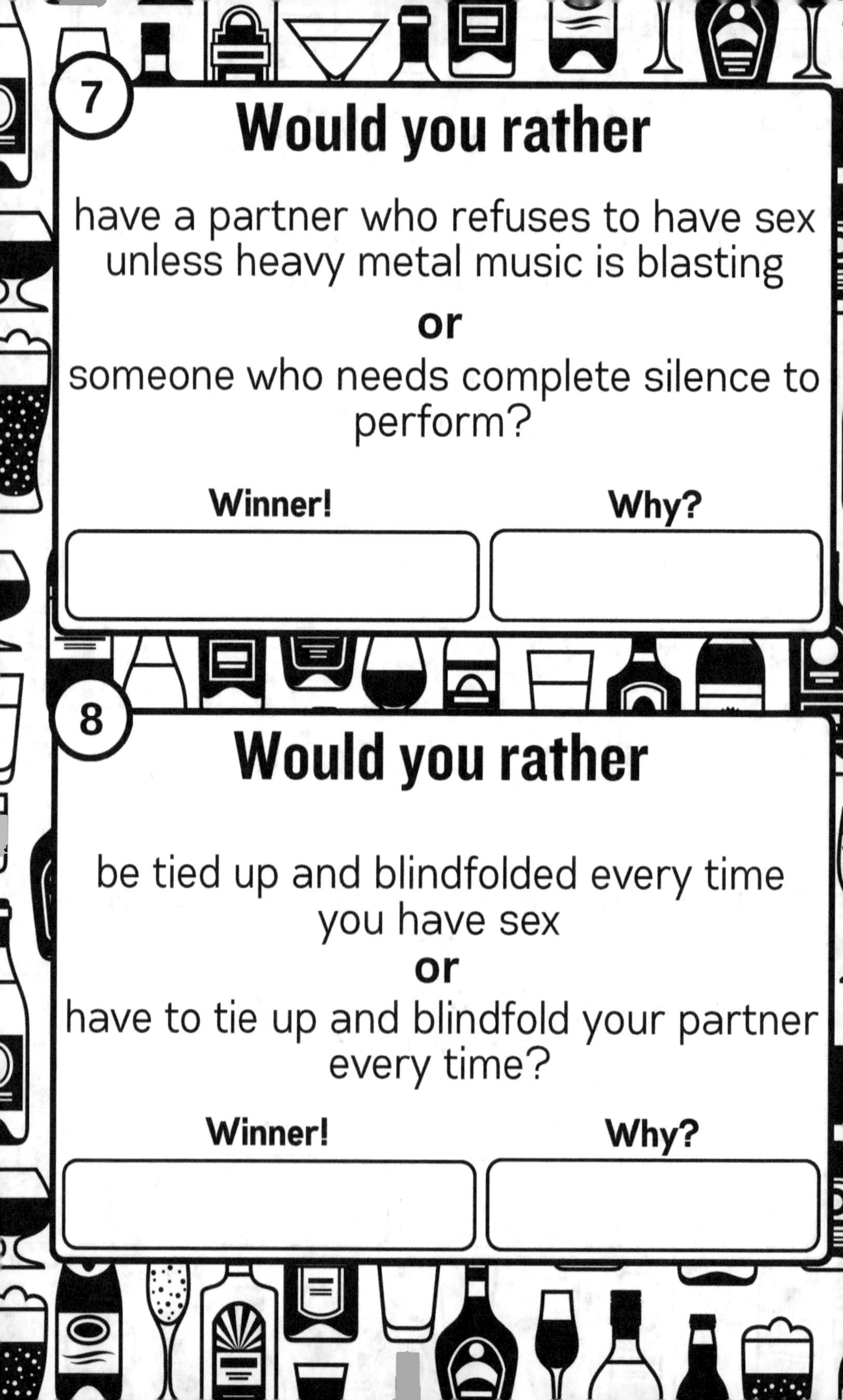

7

Would you rather

have a partner who refuses to have sex unless heavy metal music is blasting

or

someone who needs complete silence to perform?

Winner!

Why?

8

Would you rather

be tied up and blindfolded every time you have sex

or

have to tie up and blindfold your partner every time?

Winner!

Why?

9

Would you rather

have a partner who can only orgasm
when you yell insults at them
or
someone who can only climax if you
compliment them non-stop?

Winner!

Why?

10

Would you rather

date someone who wants to film every
sexual encounter
or
someone who insists on live-streaming it
to anonymous strangers?

Winner!

Why?

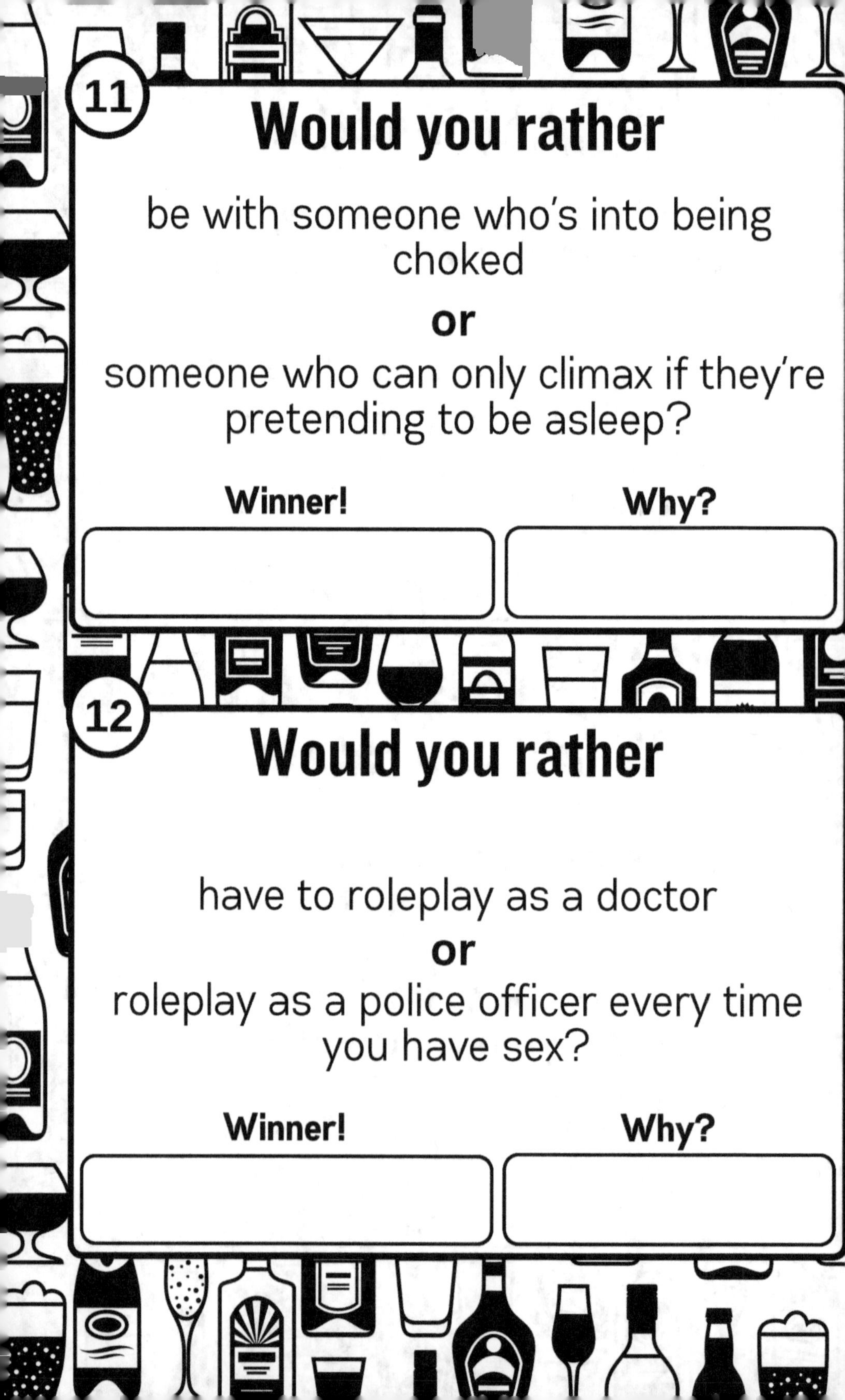

11

Would you rather

be with someone who's into being choked

or

someone who can only climax if they're pretending to be asleep?

Winner! **Why?**

12

Would you rather

have to roleplay as a doctor
or
roleplay as a police officer every time you have sex?

Winner! **Why?**

13
Would you rather
date someone who insists on wearing a furry tail plug in public
or
someone who has a fetish for dressing like a baby?
Winner!
Why?
14
Would you rather
be with someone who can't have sex without dirty talk
or
someone who can only have sex if they stay completely silent?
Winner!
Why?

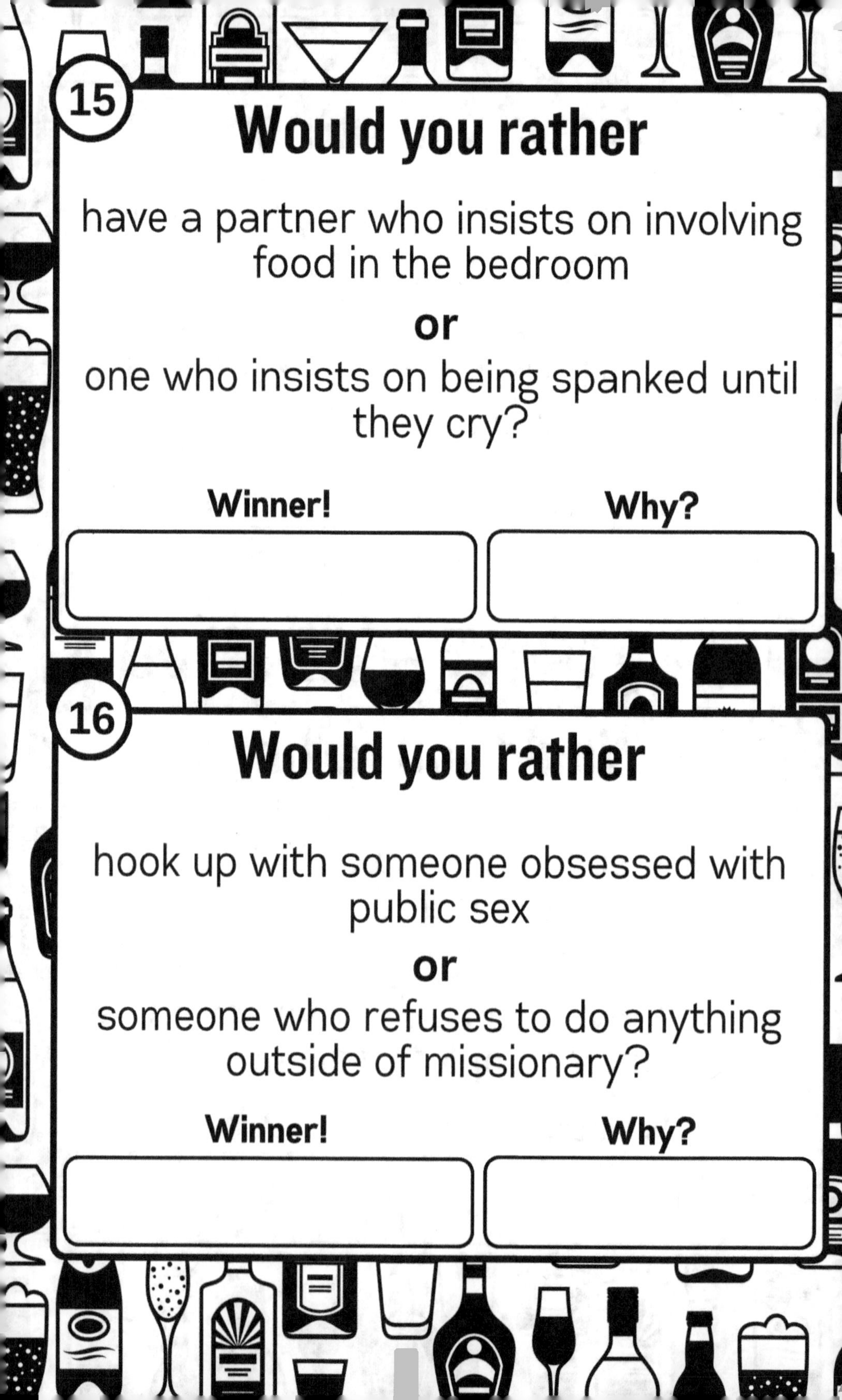

15

Would you rather

have a partner who insists on involving food in the bedroom

or

one who insists on being spanked until they cry?

Winner!

Why?

16

Would you rather

hook up with someone obsessed with public sex

or

someone who refuses to do anything outside of missionary?

Winner!

Why?

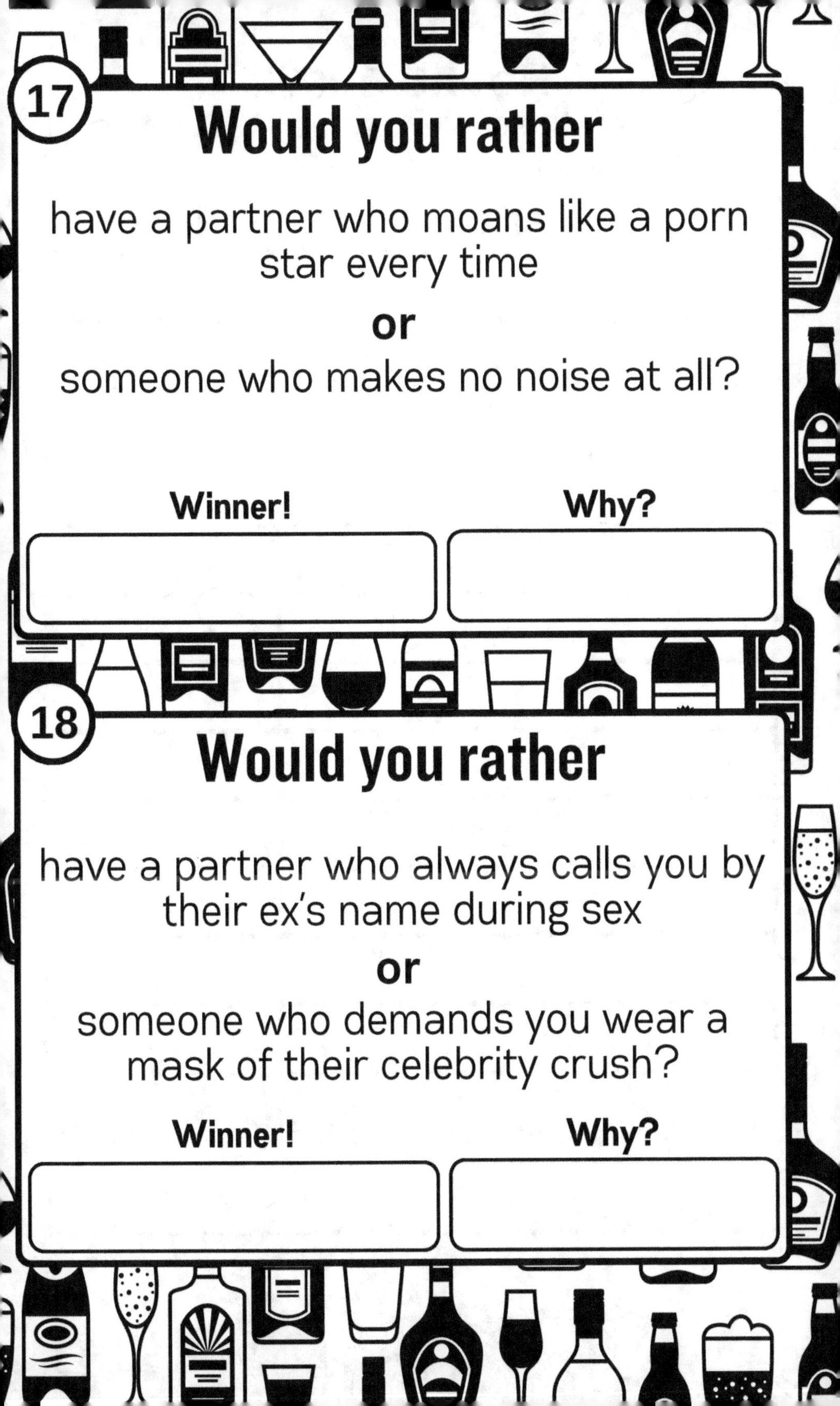

17

Would you rather

have a partner who moans like a porn star every time

or

someone who makes no noise at all?

Winner!

Why?

18

Would you rather

have a partner who always calls you by their ex's name during sex

or

someone who demands you wear a mask of their celebrity crush?

Winner!

Why?

Round over!

It's time for the current game-master to add up the scores!

Name	Points

Round Winner	Round Winners Choice

Game-Master:

Career Nightmares

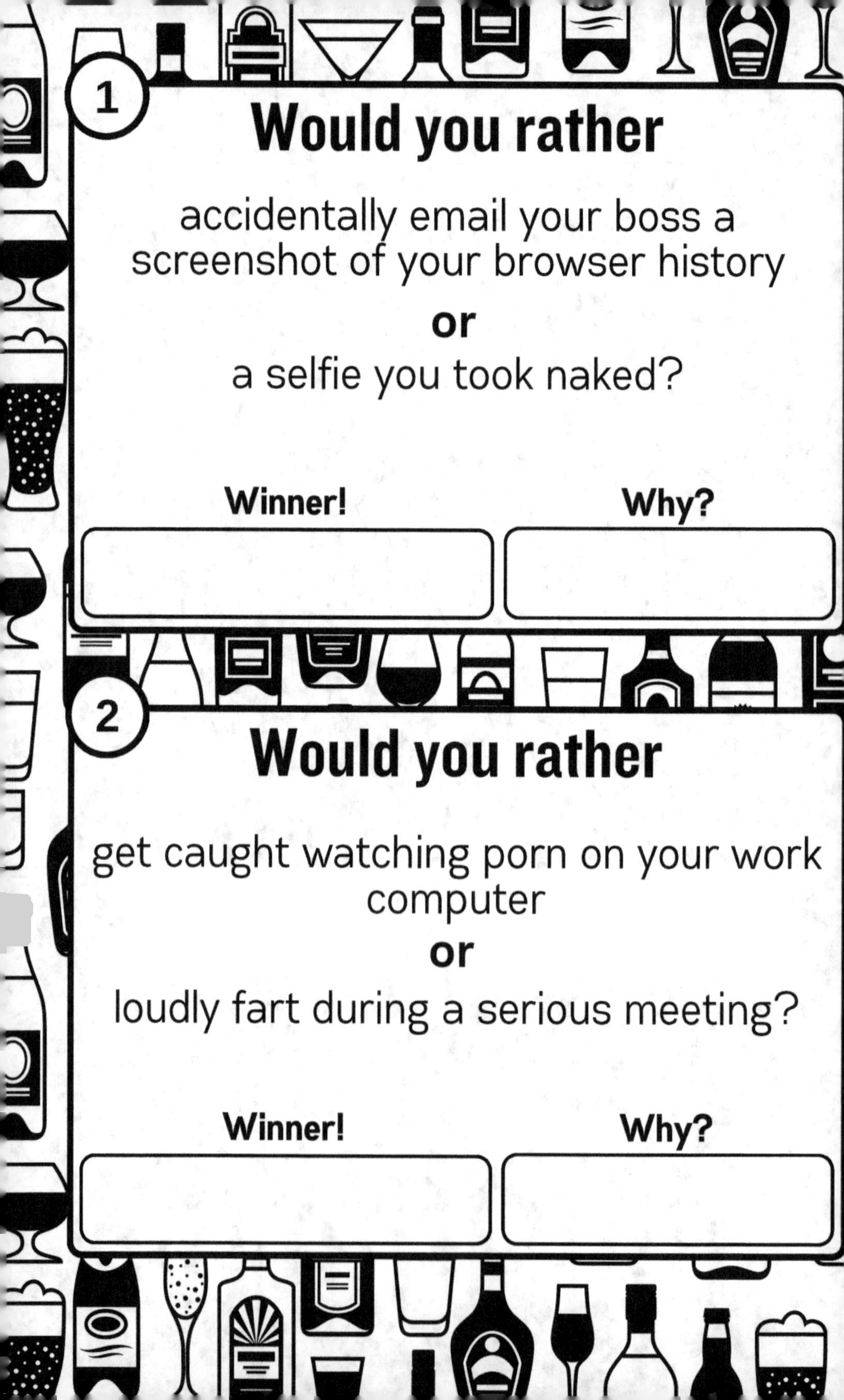

1

Would you rather

accidentally email your boss a screenshot of your browser history

or

a selfie you took naked?

Winner!

Why?

2

Would you rather

get caught watching porn on your work computer

or

loudly fart during a serious meeting?

Winner!

Why?

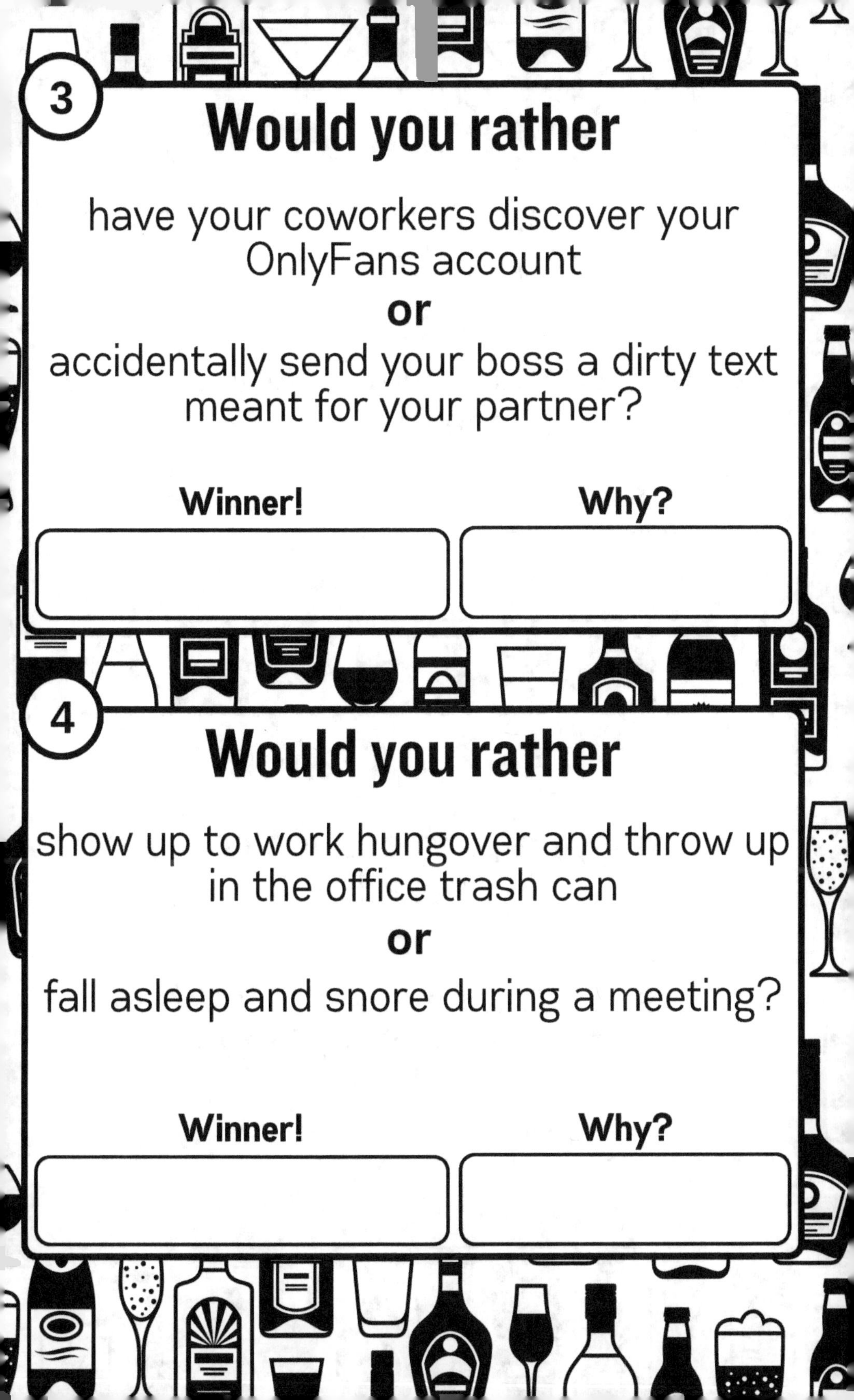
3
Would you rather
have your coworkers discover your OnlyFans account
or
accidentally send your boss a dirty text meant for your partner?
Winner!
Why?
4
Would you rather
show up to work hungover and throw up in the office trash can
or
fall asleep and snore during a meeting?
Winner!
Why?

5
Would you rather
have your boss walk in on you hooking up in the break room
or
accidentally call them 'Daddy' during a meeting?
Winner!
Why?
6
Would you rather
have to give a presentation completely naked
or
wear a shirt that says 'Ask Me About My STD' for an entire workday?
Winner!
Why?

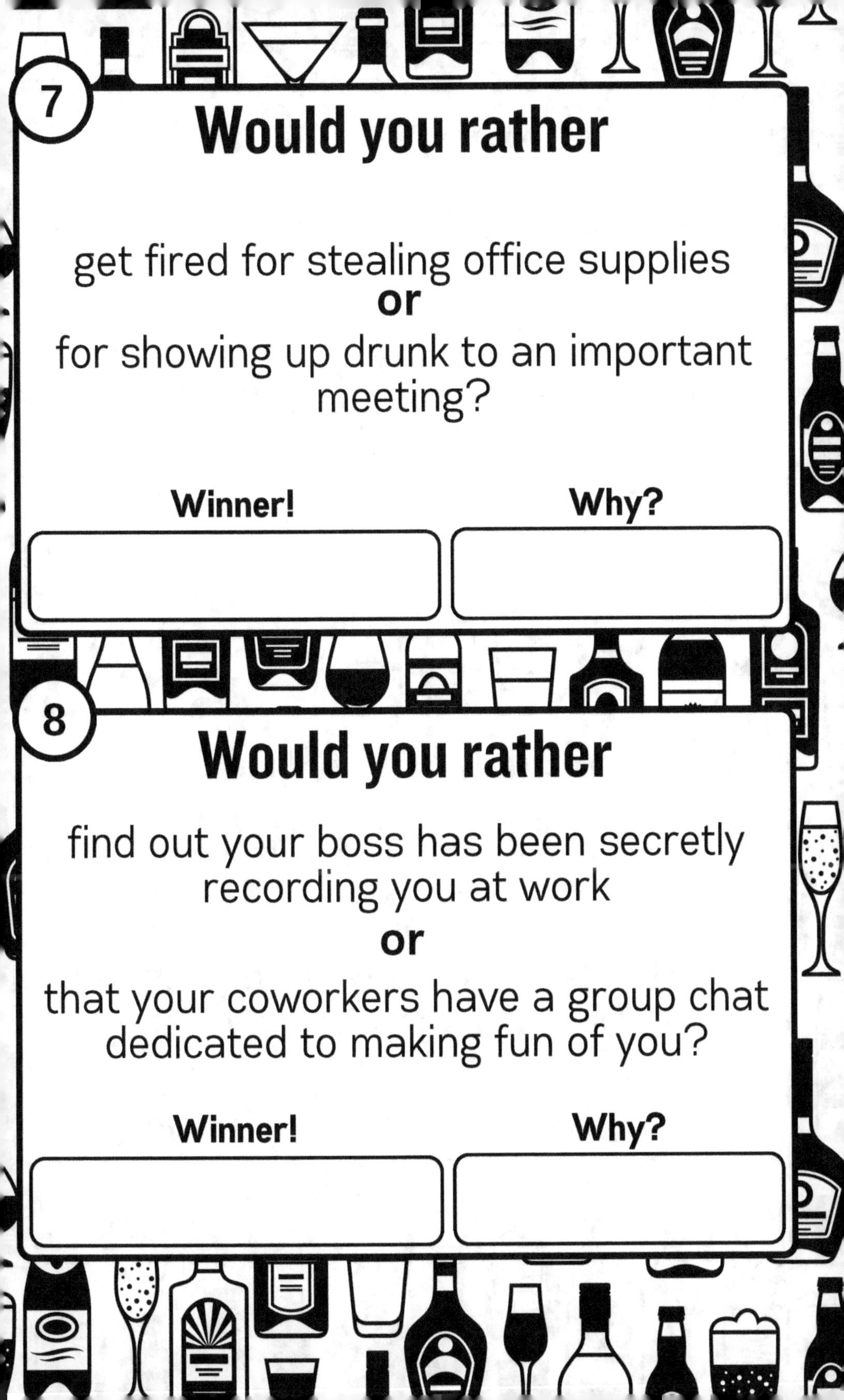

7

Would you rather

get fired for stealing office supplies
or
for showing up drunk to an important meeting?

Winner!

Why?

8

Would you rather

find out your boss has been secretly recording you at work
or
that your coworkers have a group chat dedicated to making fun of you?

Winner!

Why?

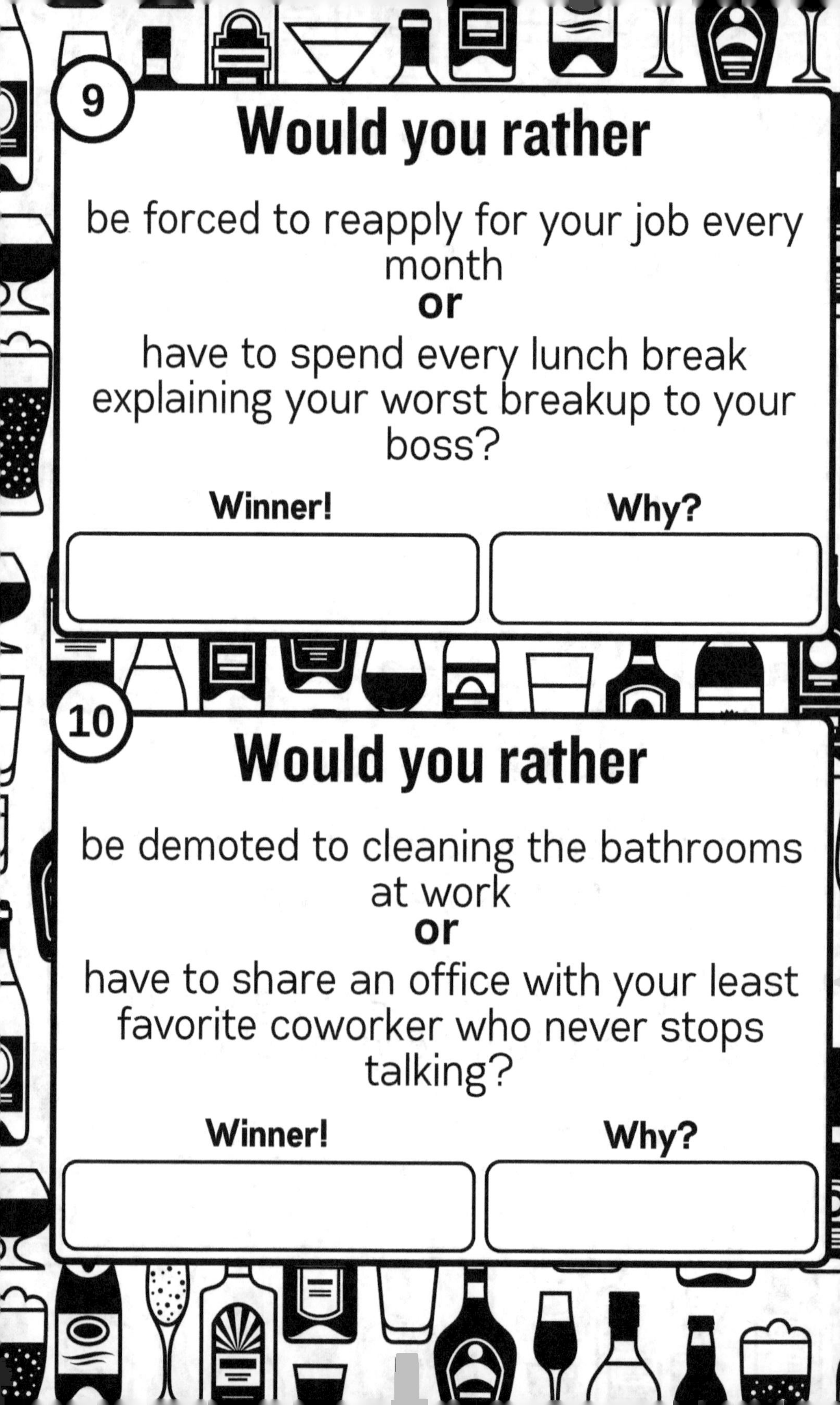

9

Would you rather

be forced to reapply for your job every month
or
have to spend every lunch break explaining your worst breakup to your boss?

Winner!

Why?

10

Would you rather

be demoted to cleaning the bathrooms at work
or
have to share an office with your least favorite coworker who never stops talking?

Winner!

Why?

11

Would you rather

have your boss read your diary out loud
to the whole office
or
play a video of your most embarrassing
drunk moment in the break room?

Winner!

Why?

12

Would you rather

get caught making out with a coworker
at the office party
or
drunkenly confess your love to your
boss?

Winner!

Why?

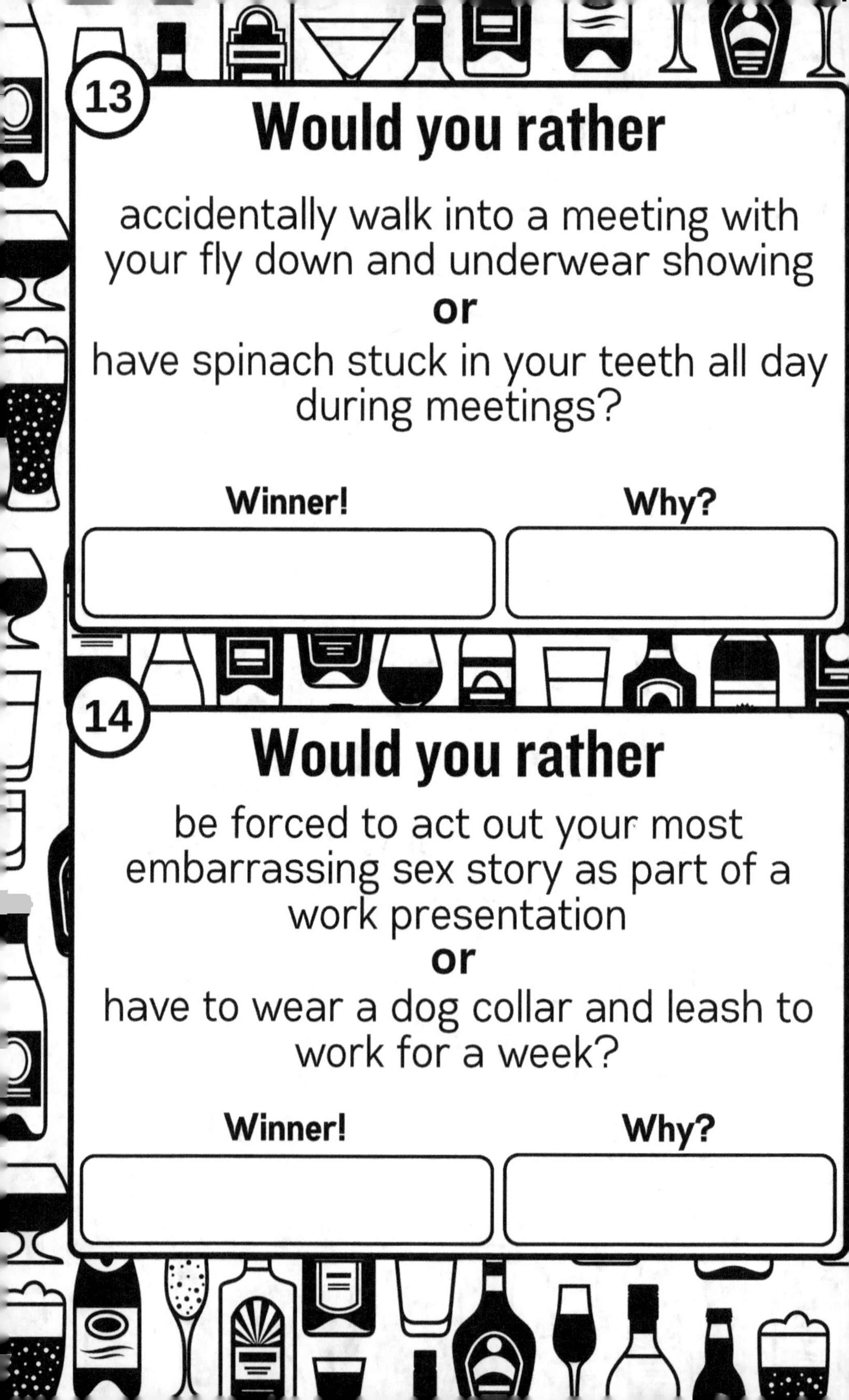

13

Would you rather

accidentally walk into a meeting with your fly down and underwear showing

or

have spinach stuck in your teeth all day during meetings?

Winner!

Why?

14

Would you rather

be forced to act out your most embarrassing sex story as part of a work presentation

or

have to wear a dog collar and leash to work for a week?

Winner!

Why?

15

Would you rather

have your partner call you 20 times during a meeting to fight about your relationship

or

have your mom send you a text about your sex life that pops up on the projector screen?

Winner!   **Why?**

16

Would you rather

have to wear a shirt that says "I Got Fired" for a month

or

have your worst coworker promoted to be your boss?

Winner!   **Why?**

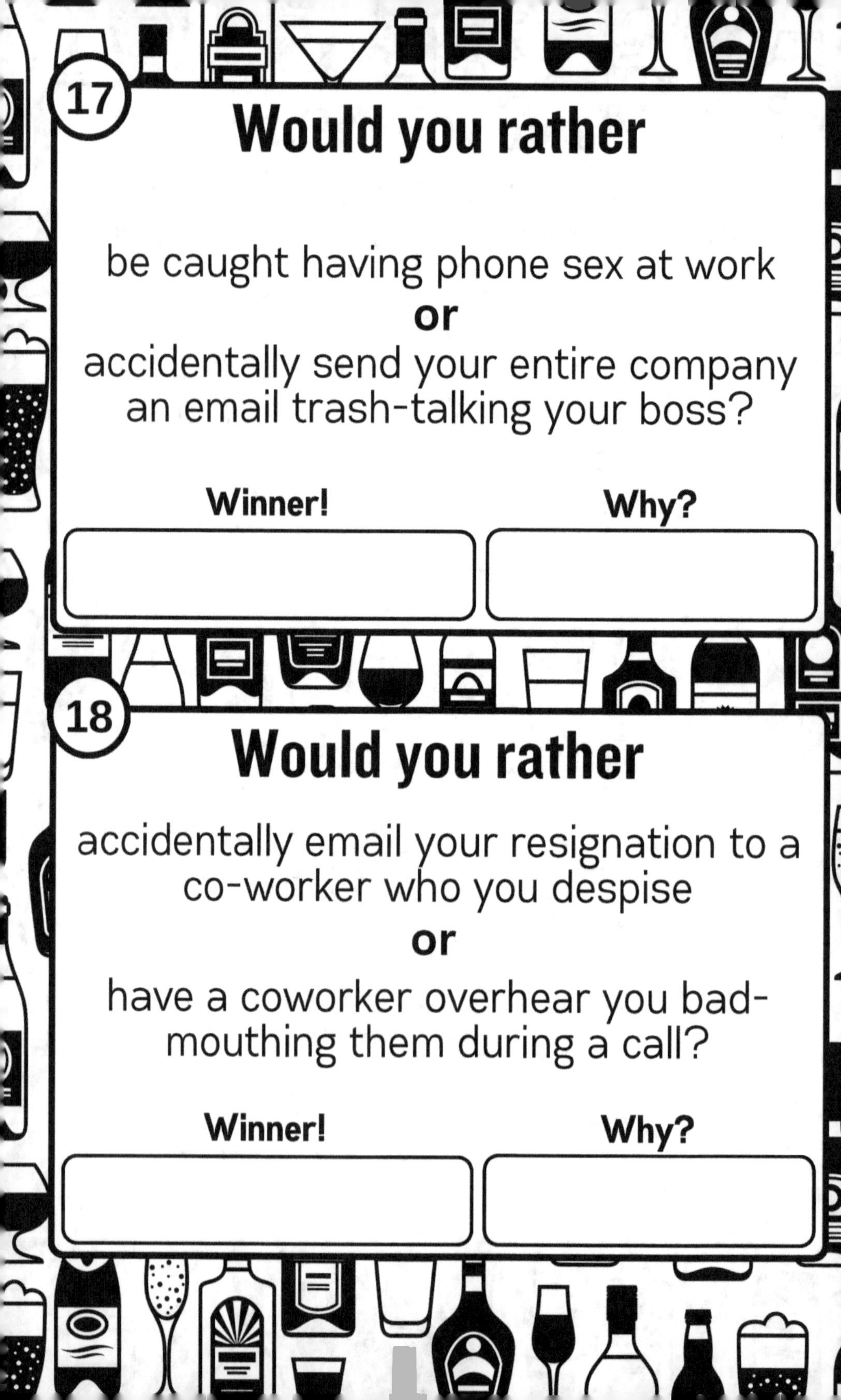

17
Would you rather

be caught having phone sex at work
or
accidentally send your entire company
an email trash-talking your boss?

Winner!   Why?

18
Would you rather

accidentally email your resignation to a
co-worker who you despise
or
have a coworker overhear you bad-
mouthing them during a call?

Winner!   Why?

Round over!

It's time for the current game-master to add up the scores!

Name	Points

Round Winner	Round Winners Choice

Round 5

Game-Master:

Money Mayhem

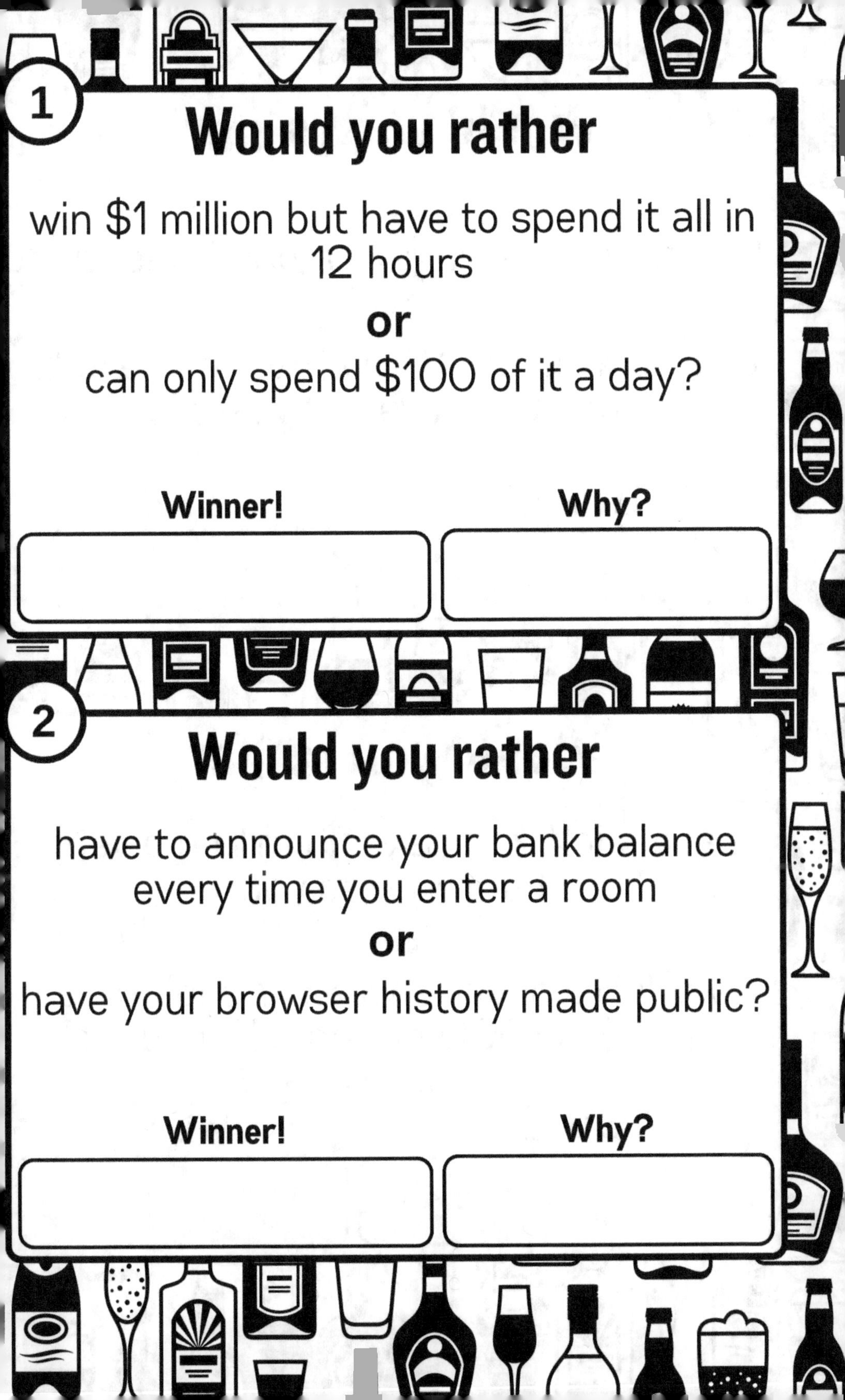

1
Would you rather

win $1 million but have to spend it all in 12 hours

or

can only spend $100 of it a day?

Winner!

Why?

2
Would you rather

have to announce your bank balance every time you enter a room

or

have your browser history made public?

Winner!

Why?

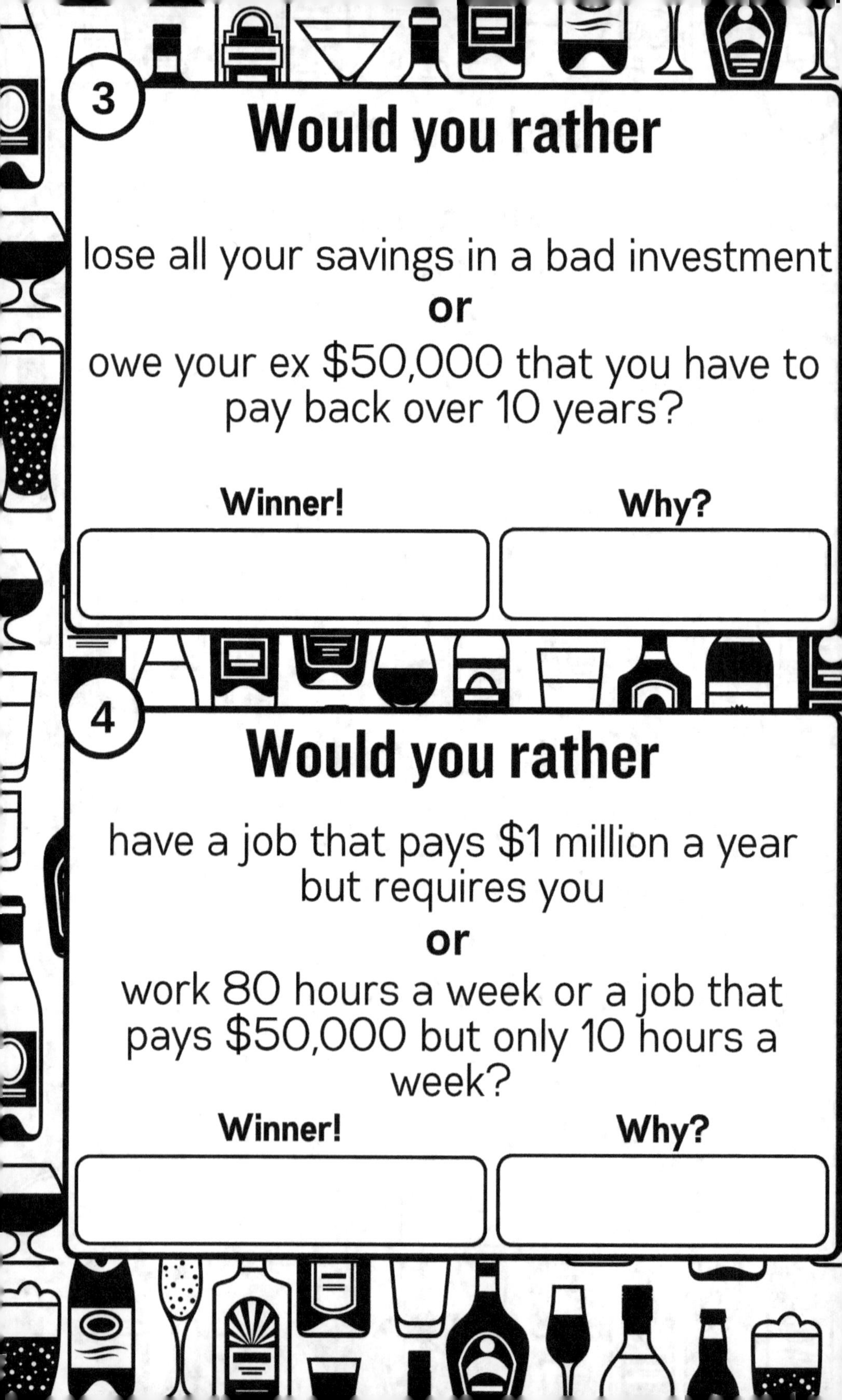
3
Would you rather

lose all your savings in a bad investment
or
owe your ex $50,000 that you have to
pay back over 10 years?

Winner!   Why?

4
Would you rather

have a job that pays $1 million a year
but requires you
or
work 80 hours a week or a job that
pays $50,000 but only 10 hours a
week?

Winner!   Why?

5

Would you rather

accidentally transfer $5,000 to your worst enemy

or

lose $500 every time you swear?

Winner!

Why?

6

Would you rather

have unlimited money but can never have sex again

or

be broke but have the best sex of your life every day?

Winner!

Why?

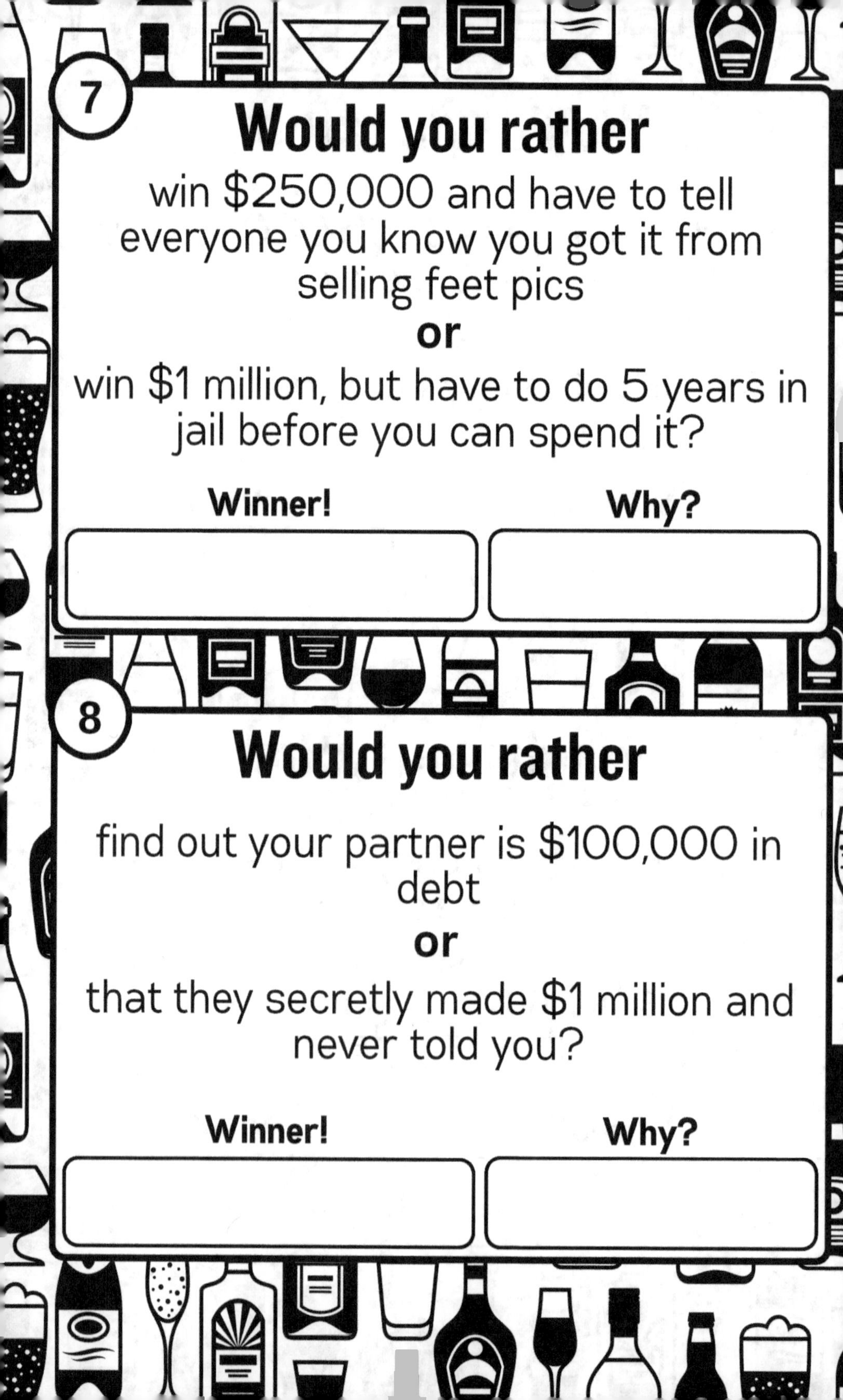
7
Would you rather
win $250,000 and have to tell everyone you know you got it from selling feet pics
or
win $1 million, but have to do 5 years in jail before you can spend it?
Winner!
Why?
8
Would you rather
find out your partner is $100,000 in debt
or
that they secretly made $1 million and never told you?
Winner!
Why?

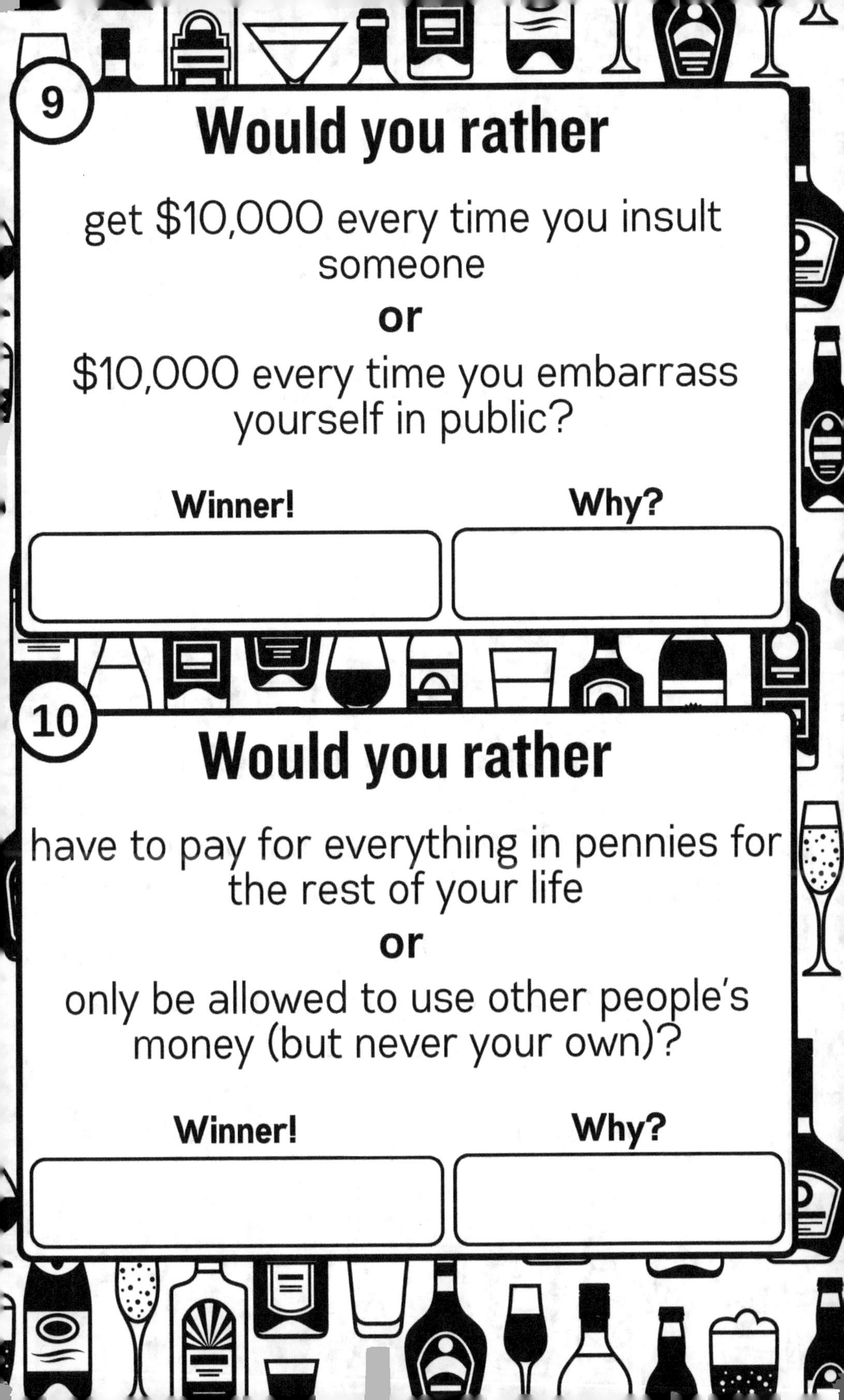

9

Would you rather

get $10,000 every time you insult someone

or

$10,000 every time you embarrass yourself in public?

Winner!   Why?

10

Would you rather

have to pay for everything in pennies for the rest of your life

or

only be allowed to use other people's money (but never your own)?

Winner!   Why?

11
Would you rather

have your credit card declined every time you try to impress someone
or
always have to ask someone else to pay for you?

Winner!
Why?

12
Would you rather

get paid $1 million to quit your job immediately and never work again
or
keep your current job forever at your current salary?

Winner!
Why?

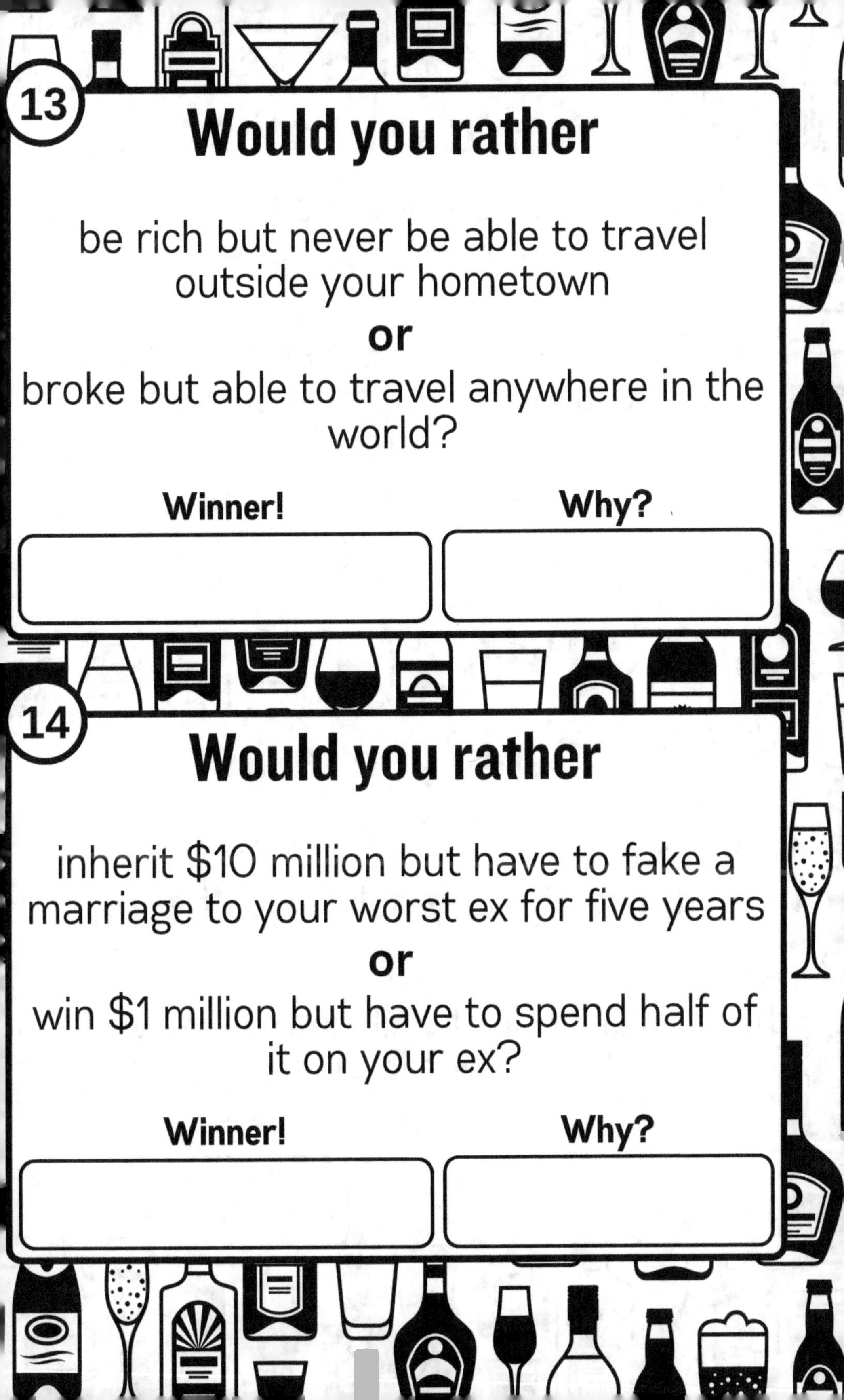

13

Would you rather

be rich but never be able to travel outside your hometown

or

broke but able to travel anywhere in the world?

Winner!

Why?

14

Would you rather

inherit $10 million but have to fake a marriage to your worst ex for five years

or

win $1 million but have to spend half of it on your ex?

Winner!

Why?

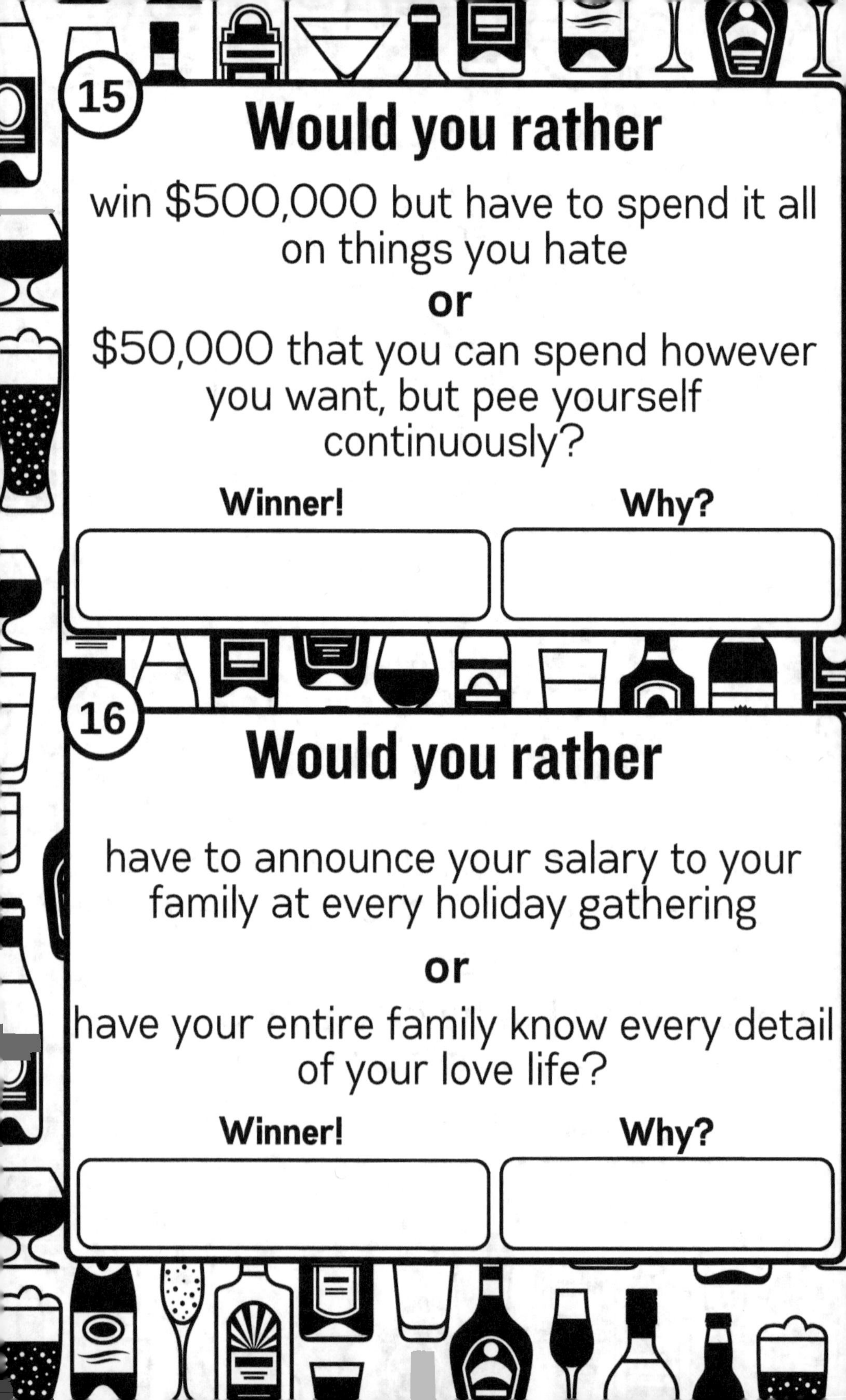

15

Would you rather

win $500,000 but have to spend it all on things you hate

or

$50,000 that you can spend however you want, but pee yourself continuously?

Winner!

Why?

16

Would you rather

have to announce your salary to your family at every holiday gathering

or

have your entire family know every detail of your love life?

Winner!

Why?

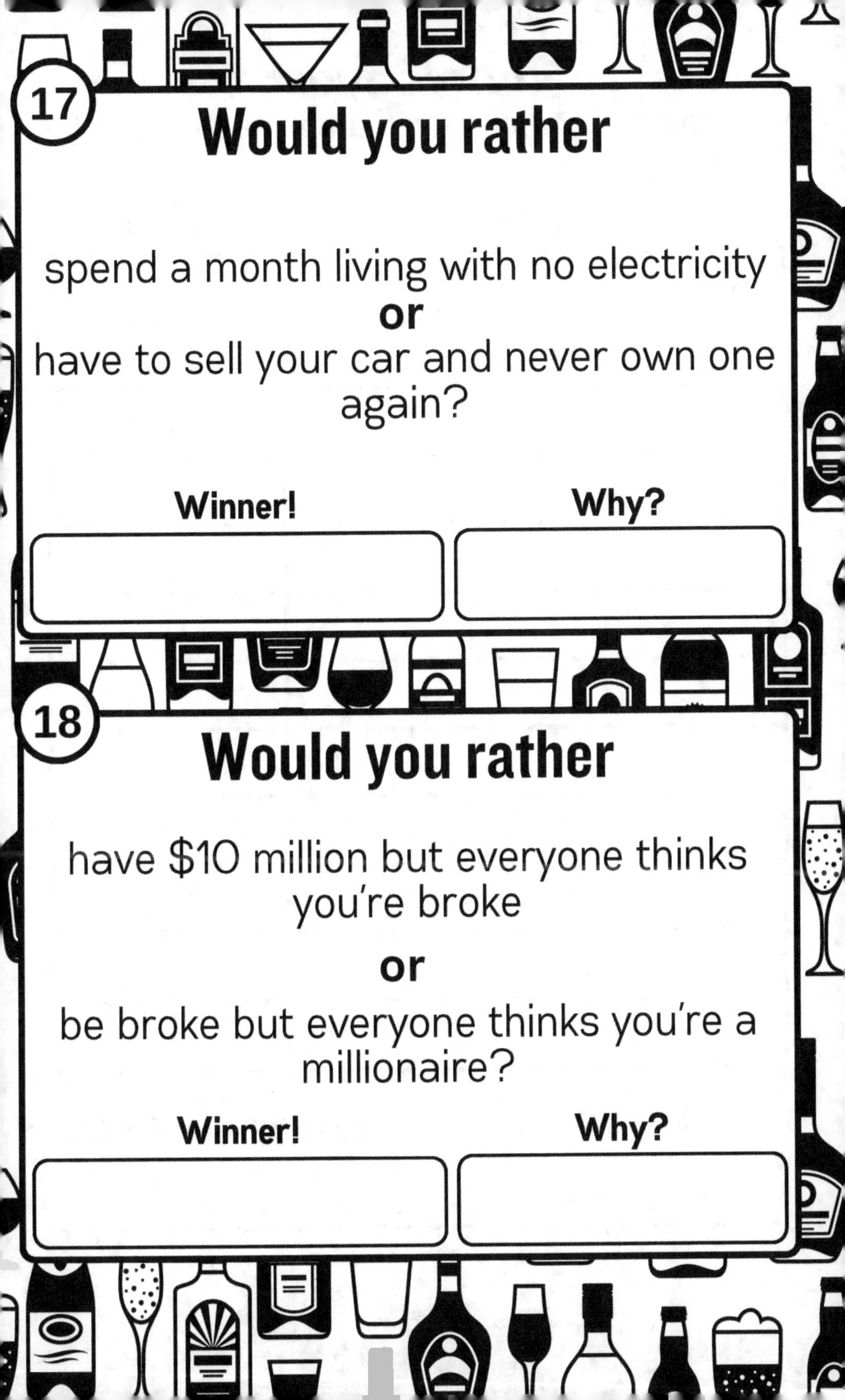

17

Would you rather

spend a month living with no electricity
or
have to sell your car and never own one
again?

Winner!

Why?

18

Would you rather

have $10 million but everyone thinks
you're broke

or

be broke but everyone thinks you're a
millionaire?

Winner!

Why?

Round over!

It's time for the current game-master to add up the scores!

Name	Points

Round Winner	Round Winners Choice

Round 6

Game-Master:

Body Bloopers

1
Would you rather
have uncontrollable farting every time you laugh
or
uncontrollable burping every time you cry?
Winner!
Why?
2
Would you rather
have permanent body odor that no deodorant can fix
or
chronic bad breath that no mint can mask?
Winner!
Why?

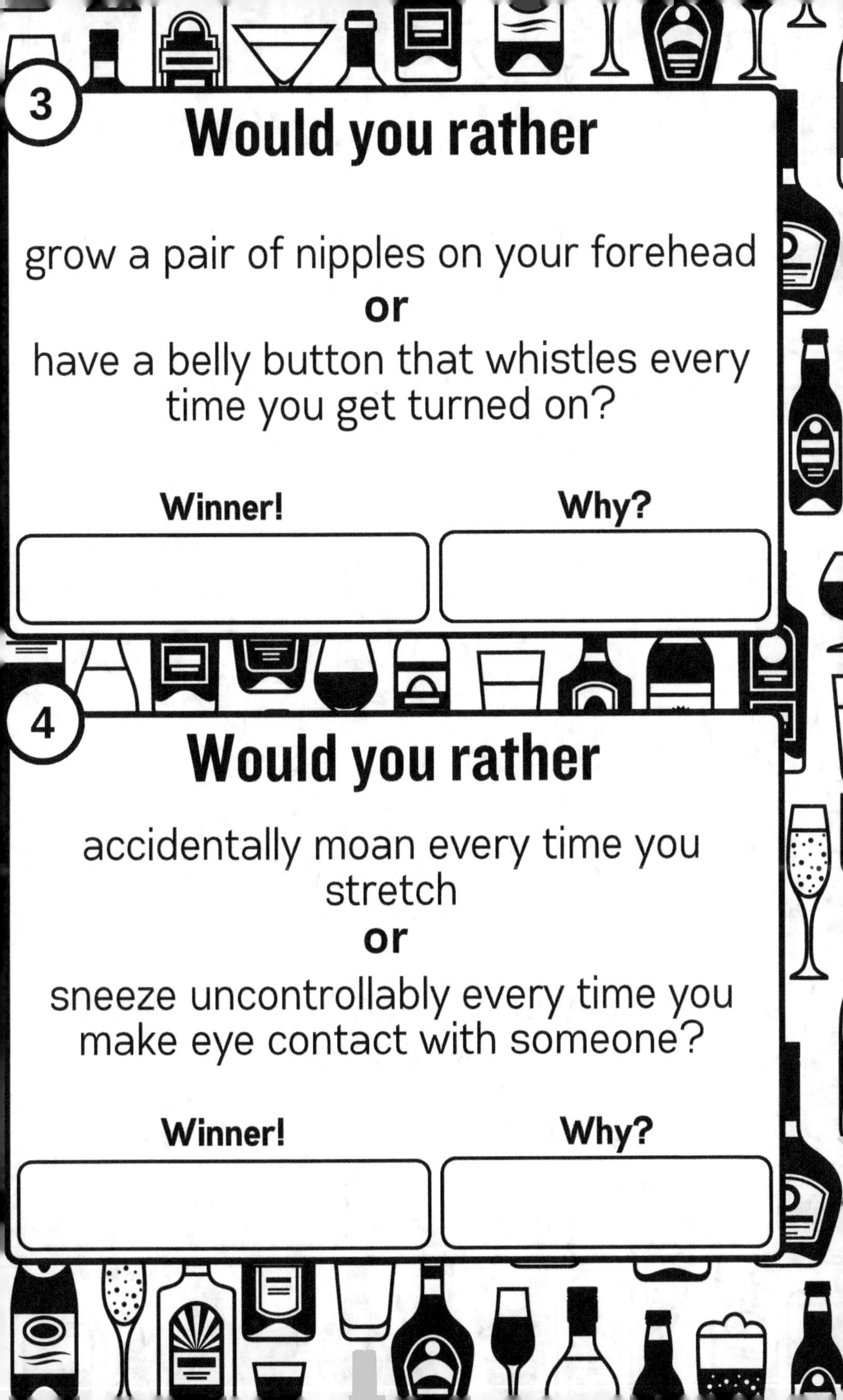

3

Would you rather

grow a pair of nipples on your forehead
or
have a belly button that whistles every
time you get turned on?

Winner!   **Why?**

4

Would you rather

accidentally moan every time you
stretch
or
sneeze uncontrollably every time you
make eye contact with someone?

Winner!   **Why?**

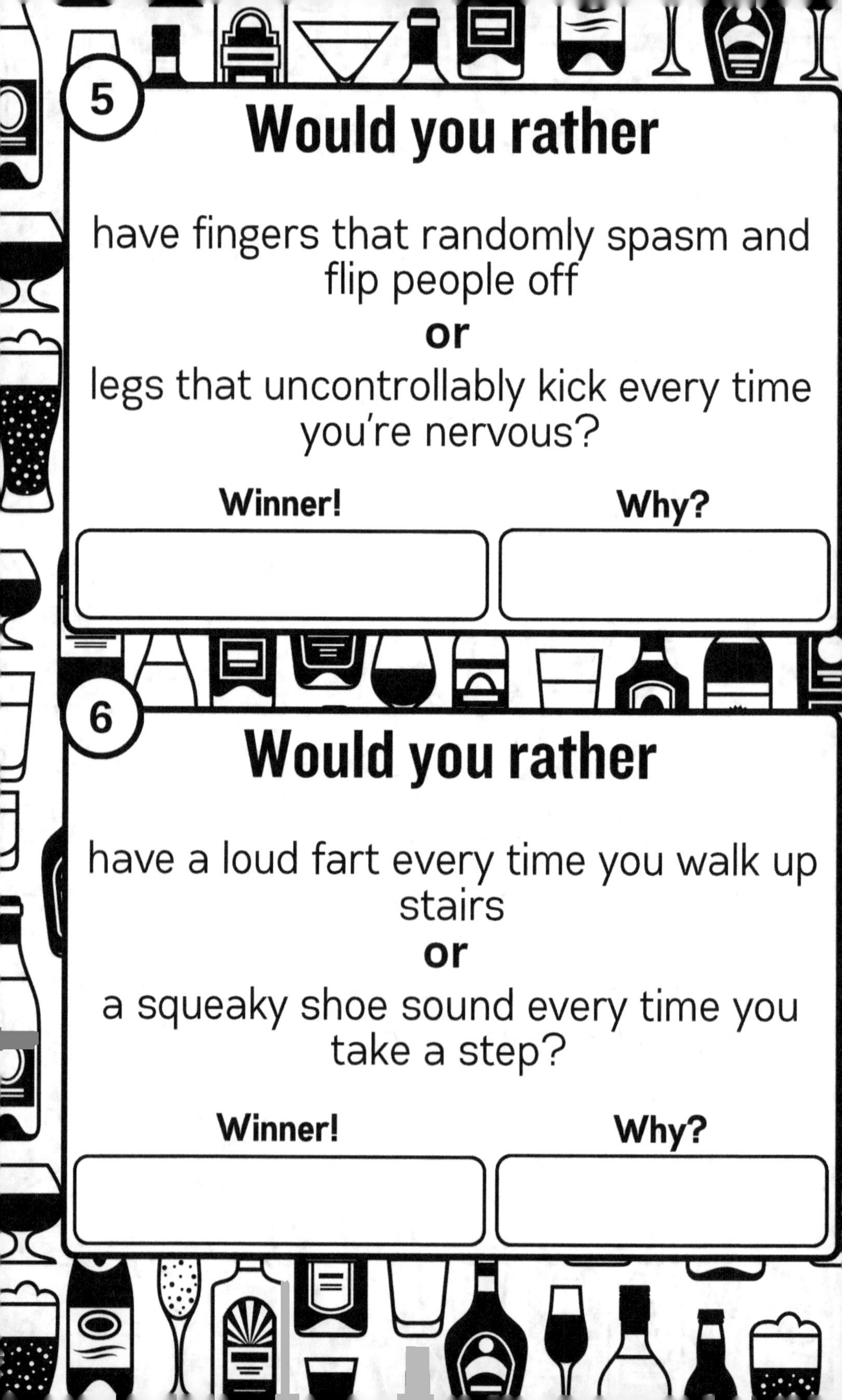

5

Would you rather

have fingers that randomly spasm and flip people off
or
legs that uncontrollably kick every time you're nervous?

Winner!   Why?

6

Would you rather

have a loud fart every time you walk up stairs
or
a squeaky shoe sound every time you take a step?

Winner!   Why?

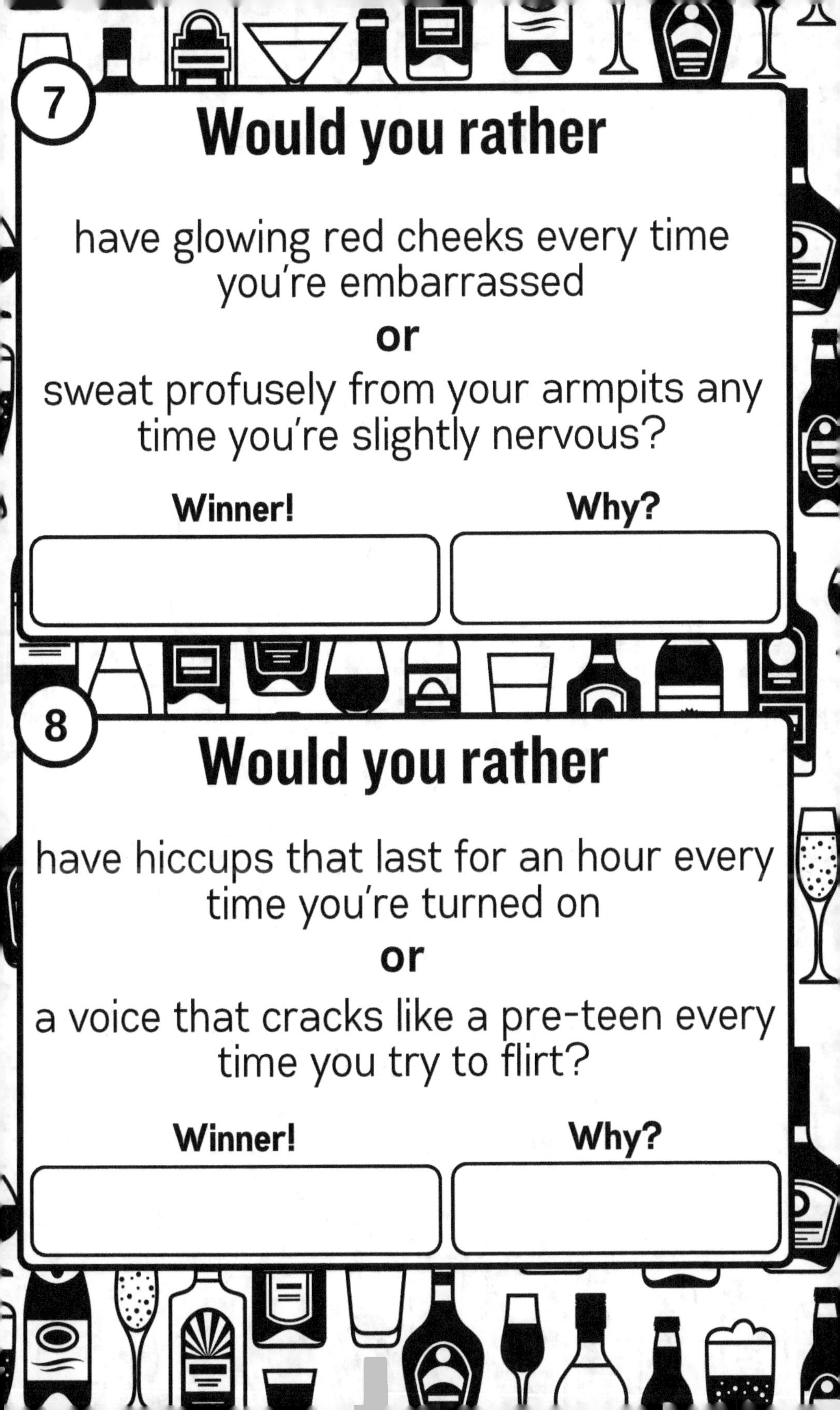
7

Would you rather

have glowing red cheeks every time
you're embarrassed
or
sweat profusely from your armpits any
time you're slightly nervous?

Winner!   **Why?**

8

Would you rather

have hiccups that last for an hour every
time you're turned on
or
a voice that cracks like a pre-teen every
time you try to flirt?

Winner!   **Why?**

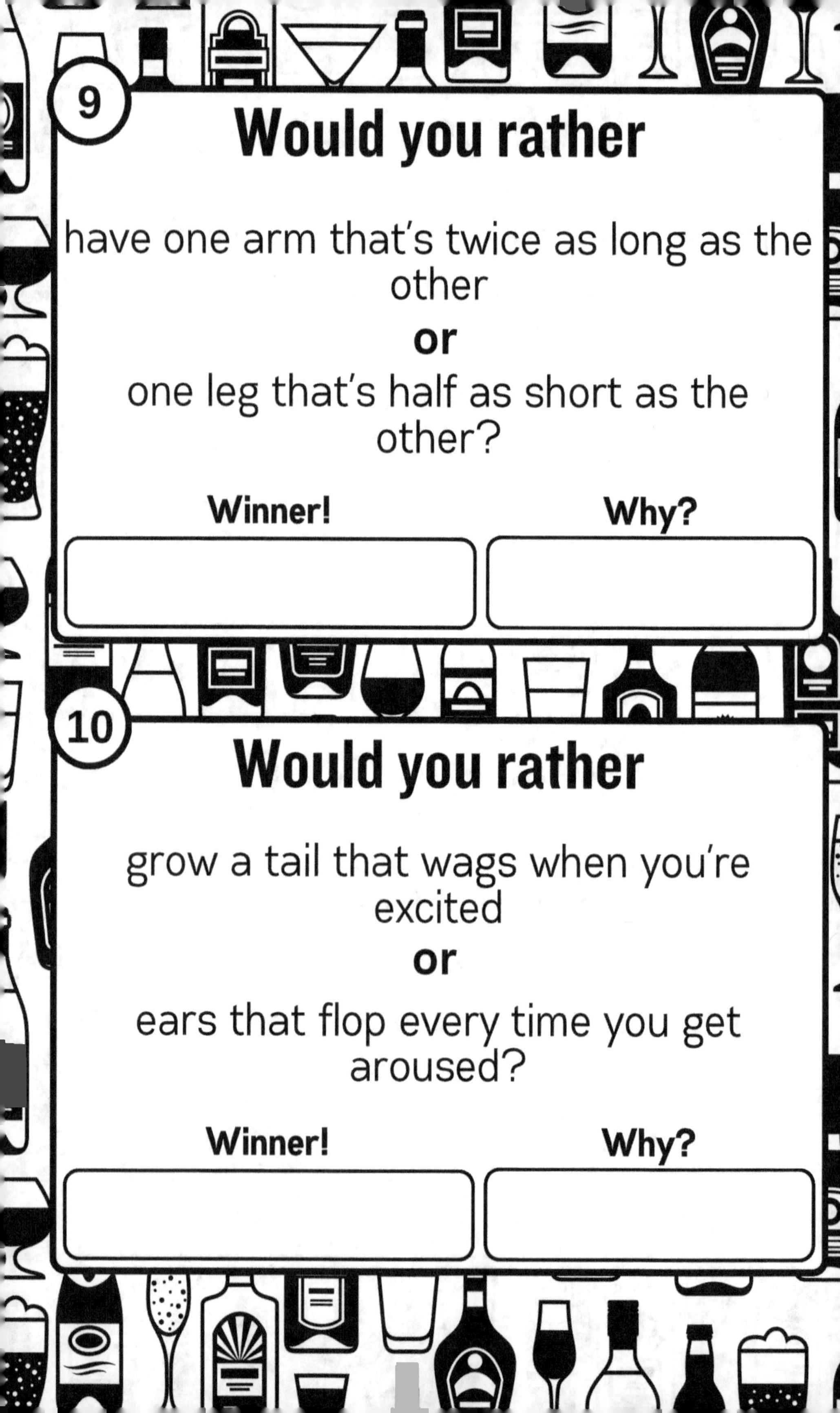

9

Would you rather

have one arm that's twice as long as the other

or

one leg that's half as short as the other?

Winner!

Why?

10

Would you rather

grow a tail that wags when you're excited

or

ears that flop every time you get aroused?

Winner!

Why?

11

Would you rather

have nipples that grow longer every time you lie

or

hair that stands straight up every time you're horny?

Winner!

Why?

12

Would you rather

have to wear a diaper every day for the rest of your life

or

randomly lactate whenever someone touches your chest?

Winner!

Why?

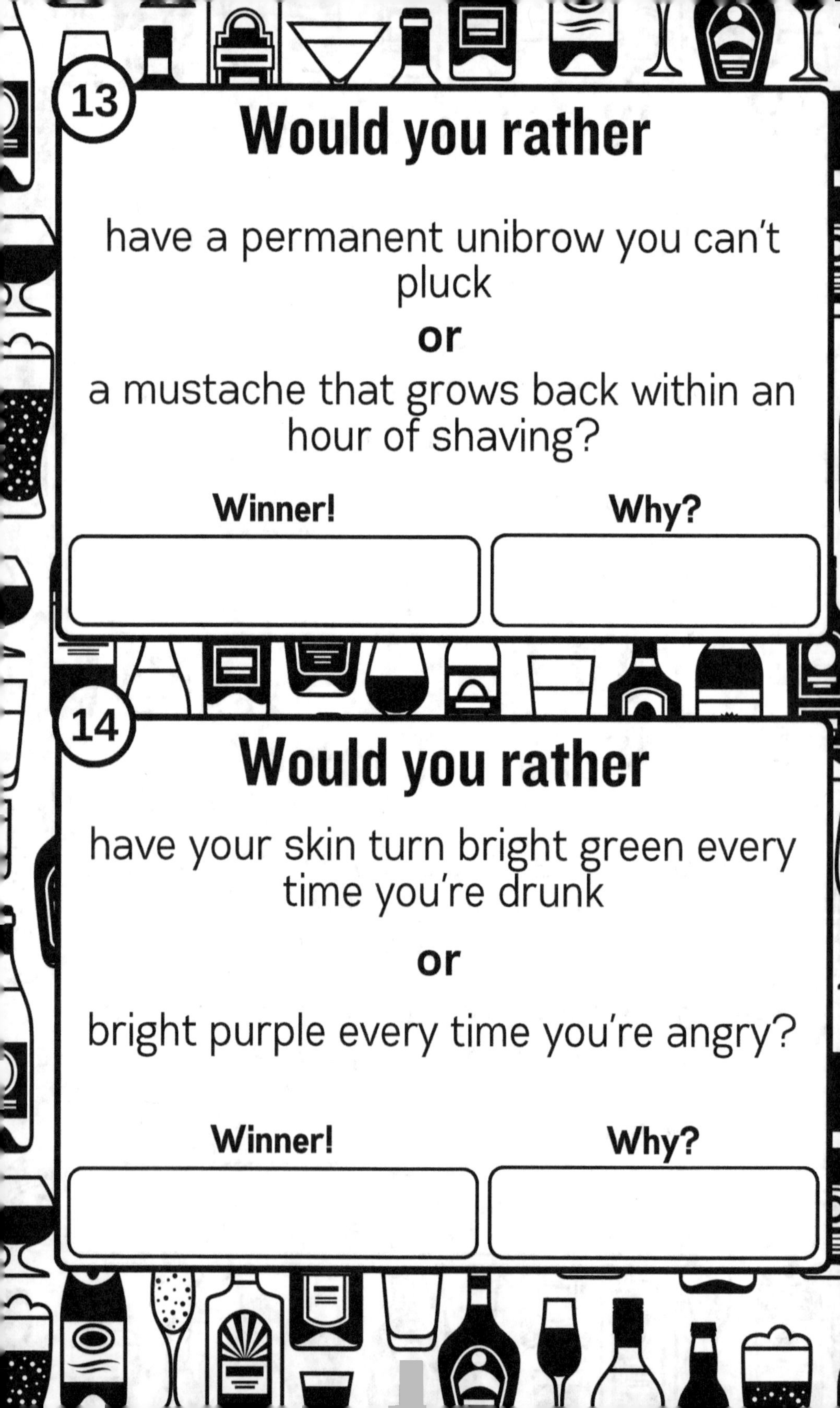

13

Would you rather

have a permanent unibrow you can't pluck

or

a mustache that grows back within an hour of shaving?

Winner!

Why?

14

Would you rather

have your skin turn bright green every time you're drunk

or

bright purple every time you're angry?

Winner!

Why?

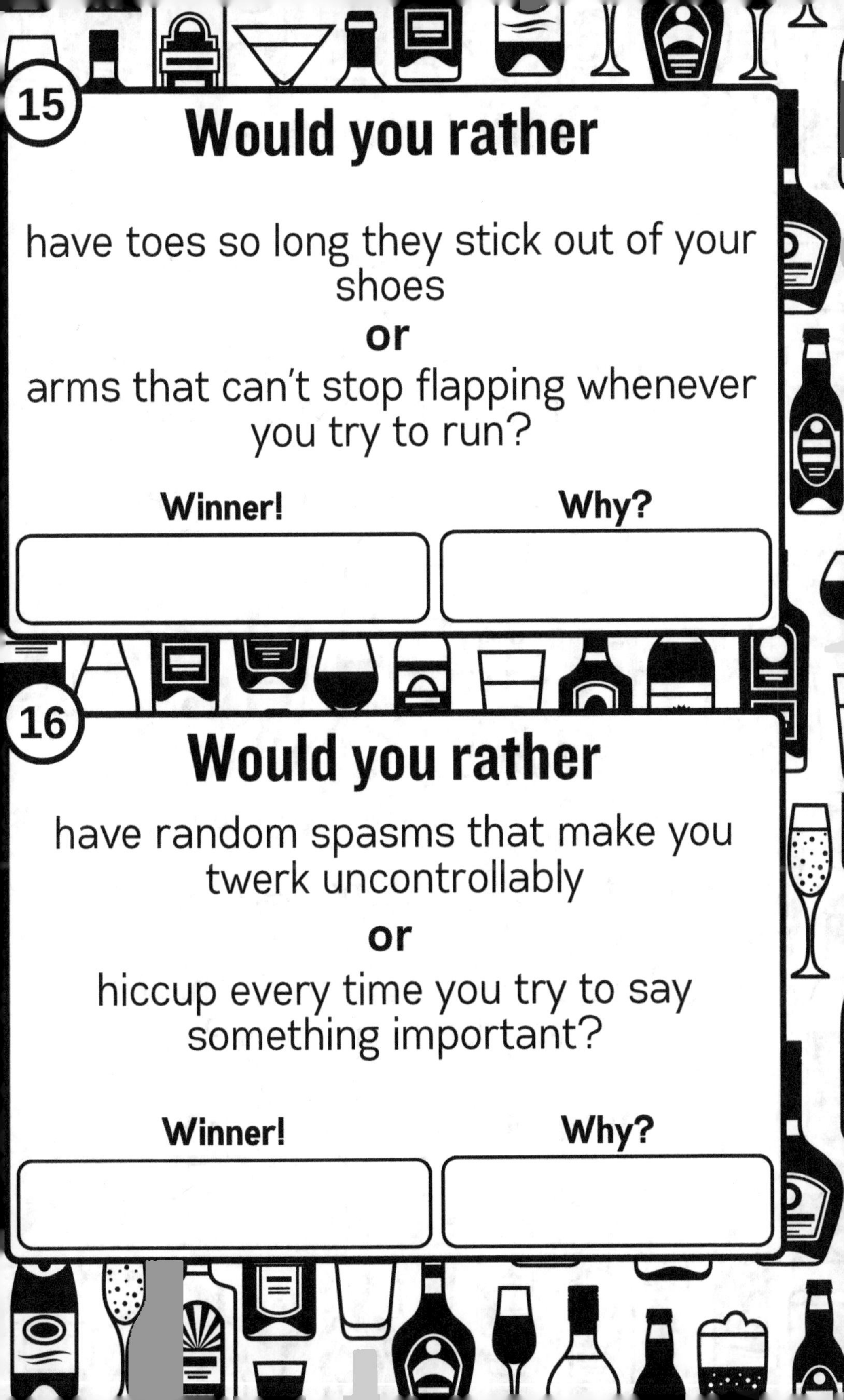
15
Would you rather
have toes so long they stick out of your shoes
or
arms that can't stop flapping whenever you try to run?
Winner!
Why?
16
Would you rather
have random spasms that make you twerk uncontrollably
or
hiccup every time you try to say something important?
Winner!
Why?

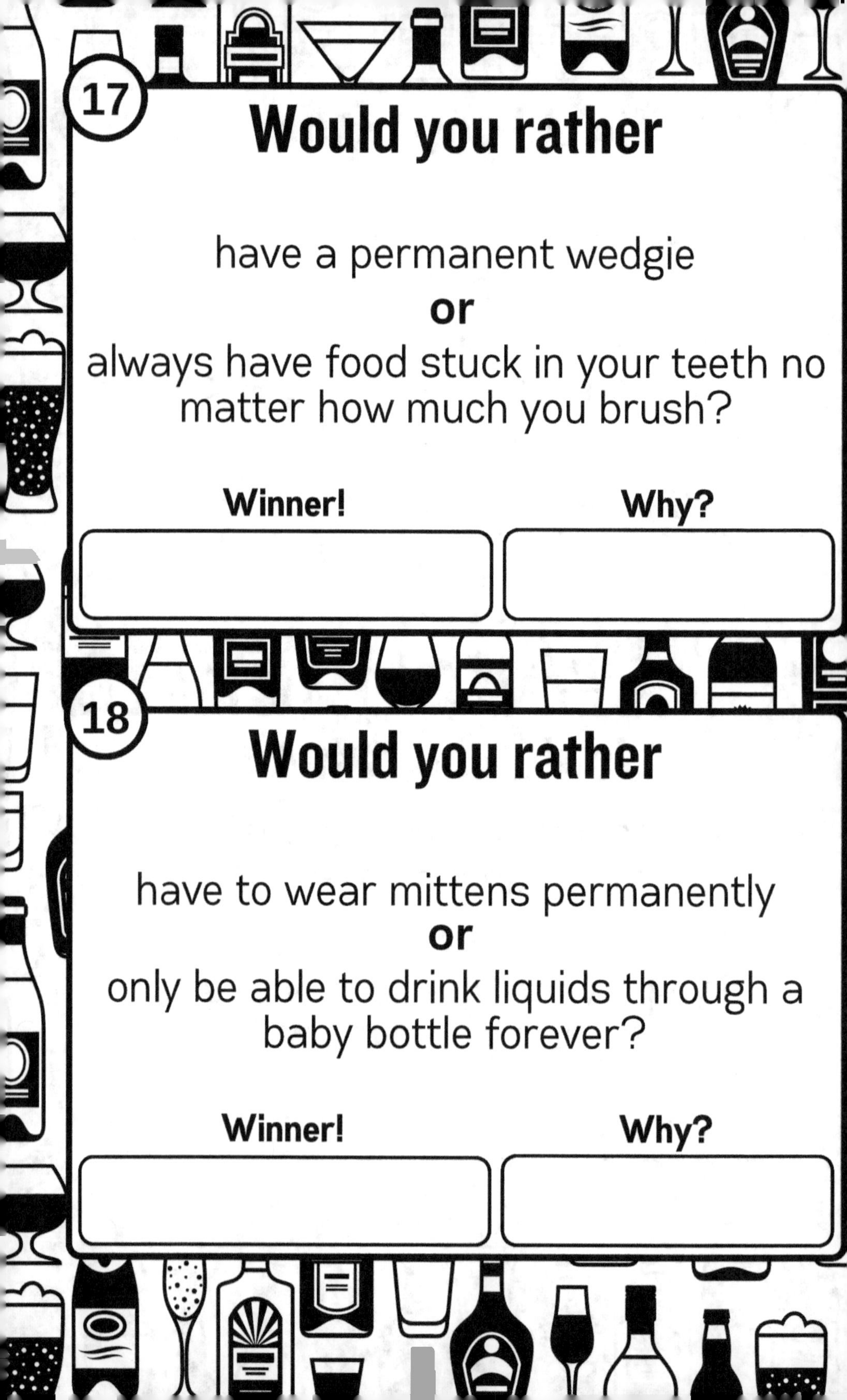

17

Would you rather

have a permanent wedgie
or
always have food stuck in your teeth no matter how much you brush?

Winner!

Why?

18

Would you rather

have to wear mittens permanently
or
only be able to drink liquids through a baby bottle forever?

Winner!

Why?

Round over!

It's time for the current game-master to add up the scores!

Name	Points

Round Winner	Round Winners Choice

Round 7

Game-Master:

Toxic Friendships

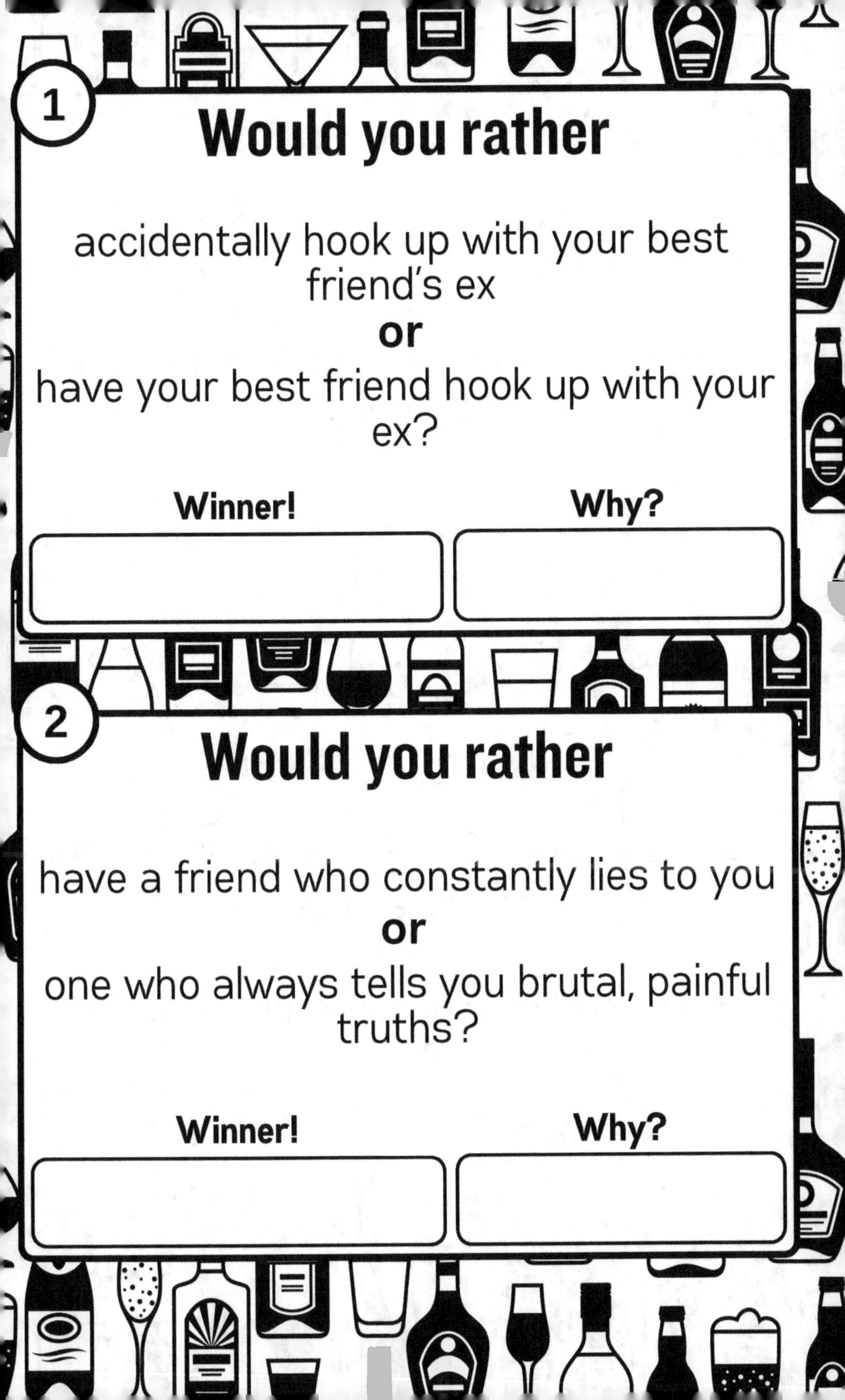

1

Would you rather

accidentally hook up with your best friend's ex

or

have your best friend hook up with your ex?

Winner!

Why?

2

Would you rather

have a friend who constantly lies to you

or

one who always tells you brutal, painful truths?

Winner!

Why?

3

Would you rather

find out your best friend has been secretly bad-mouthing you for years

or

that they've read all your private texts and emails?

Winner!

Why?

4

Would you rather

have a friend who constantly flirts with your partner

or

one who tries to copy everything you do?

Winner!

Why?

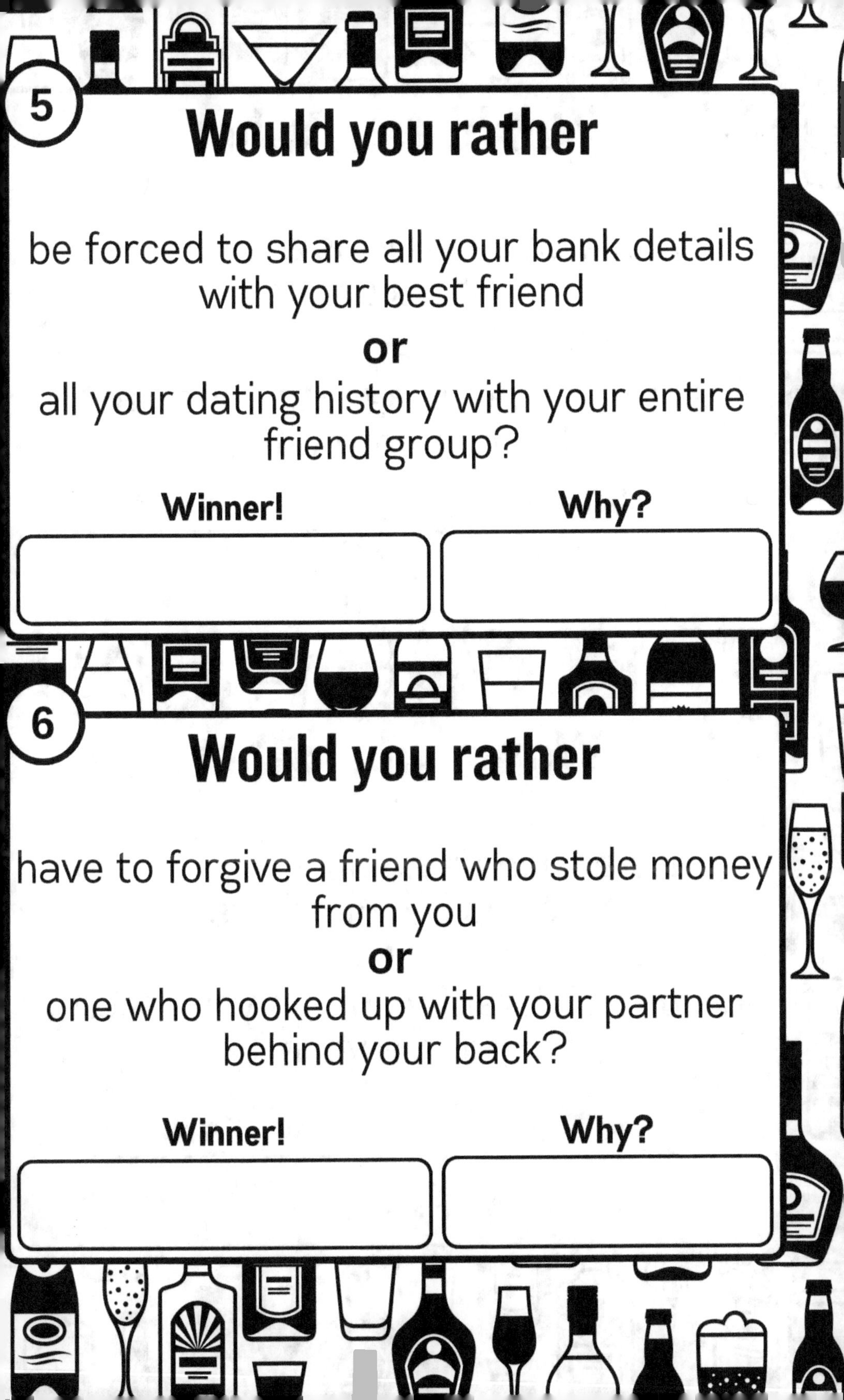

5

Would you rather

be forced to share all your bank details
with your best friend
or
all your dating history with your entire
friend group?

Winner!

Why?

6

Would you rather

have to forgive a friend who stole money
from you
or
one who hooked up with your partner
behind your back?

Winner!

Why?

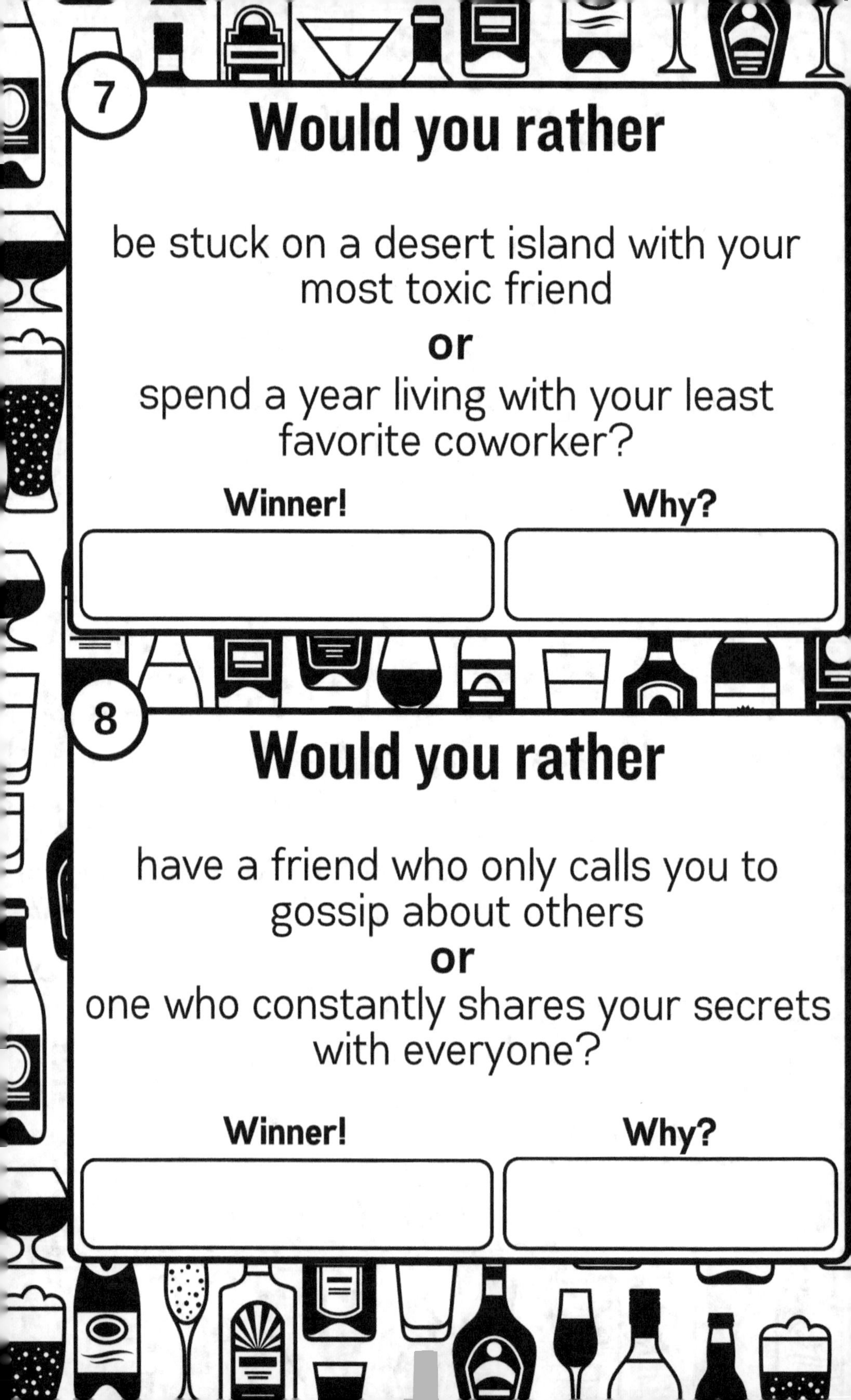

7

Would you rather

be stuck on a desert island with your most toxic friend

or

spend a year living with your least favorite coworker?

Winner!

Why?

8

Would you rather

have a friend who only calls you to gossip about others

or

one who constantly shares your secrets with everyone?

Winner!

Why?

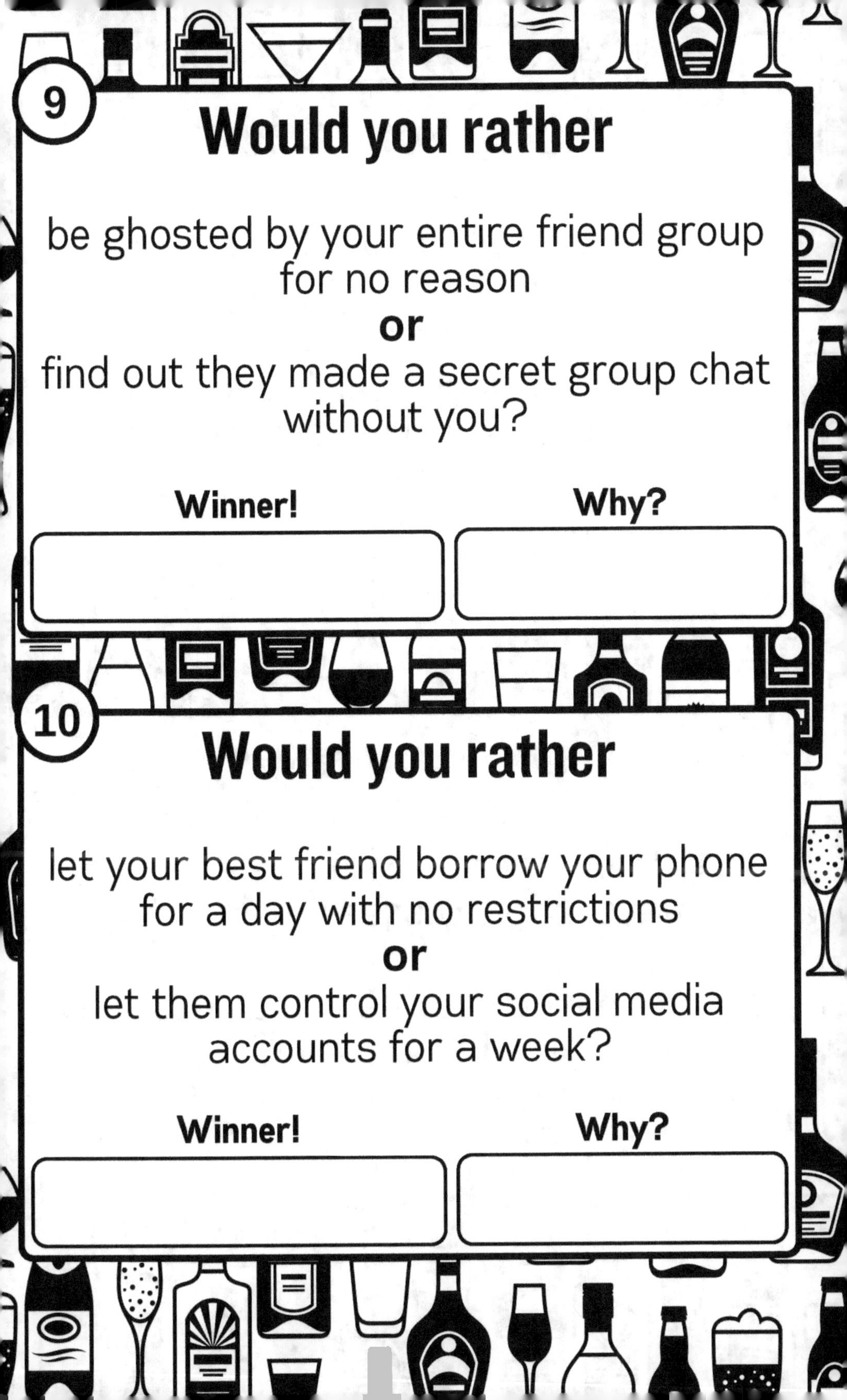
9
Would you rather
be ghosted by your entire friend group
for no reason
or
find out they made a secret group chat
without you?
Winner!
Why?
10
Would you rather
let your best friend borrow your phone
for a day with no restrictions
or
let them control your social media
accounts for a week?
Winner!
Why?

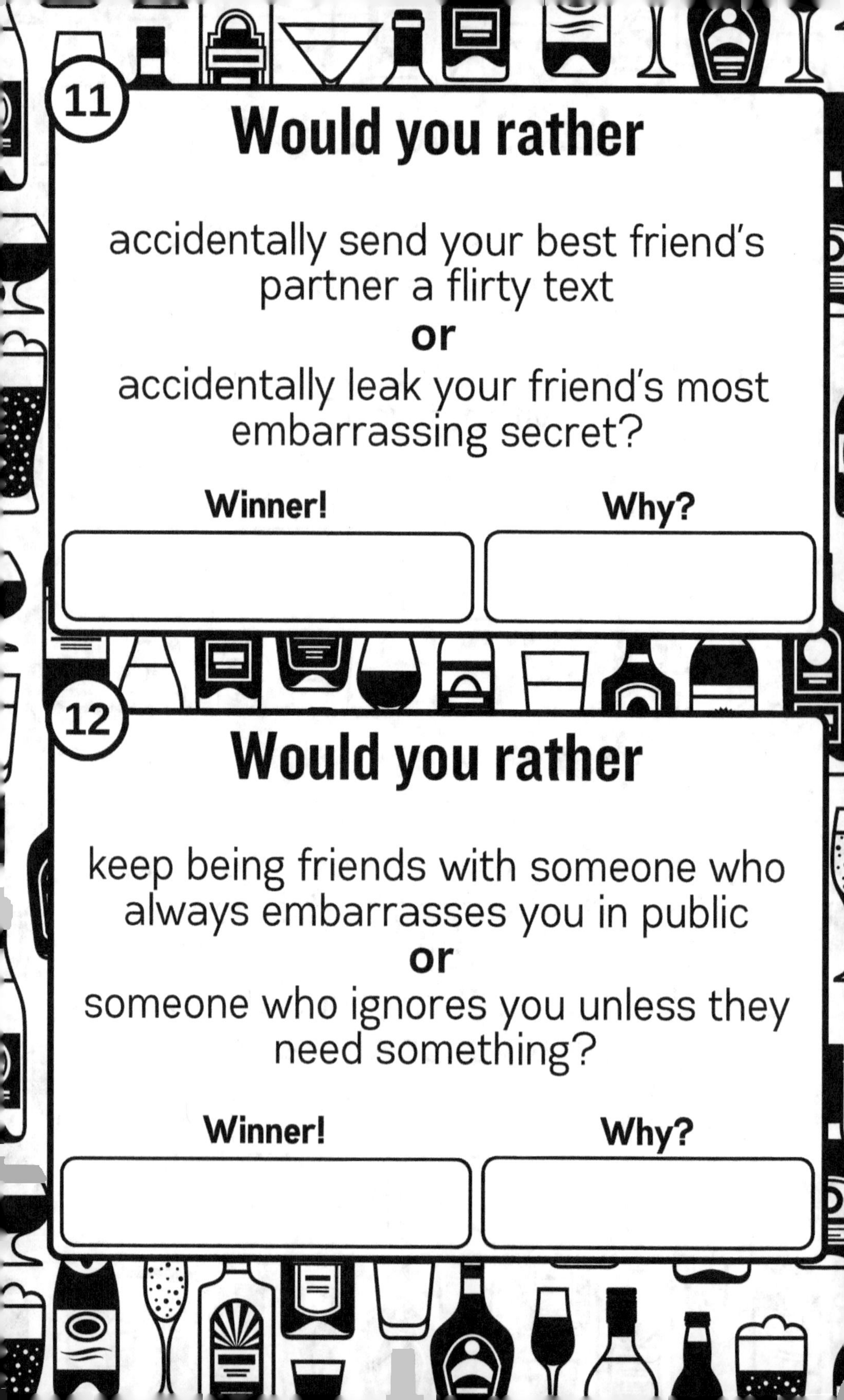

11
Would you rather
accidentally send your best friend's partner a flirty text
or
accidentally leak your friend's most embarrassing secret?
Winner!
Why?
12
Would you rather
keep being friends with someone who always embarrasses you in public
or
someone who ignores you unless they need something?
Winner!
Why?

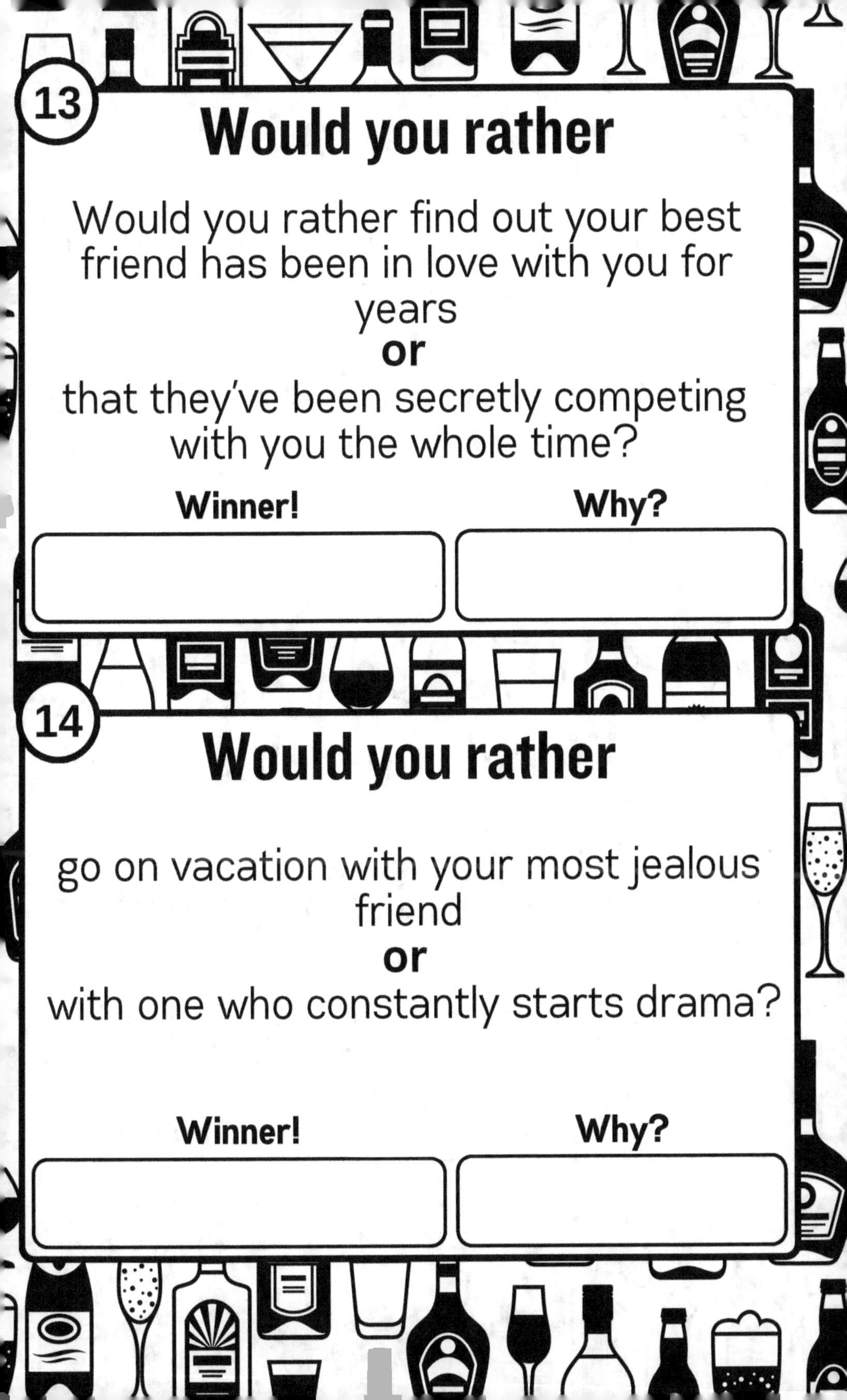

13
Would you rather

Would you rather find out your best friend has been in love with you for years
or
that they've been secretly competing with you the whole time?

Winner!

Why?

14
Would you rather

go on vacation with your most jealous friend
or
with one who constantly starts drama?

Winner!

Why?

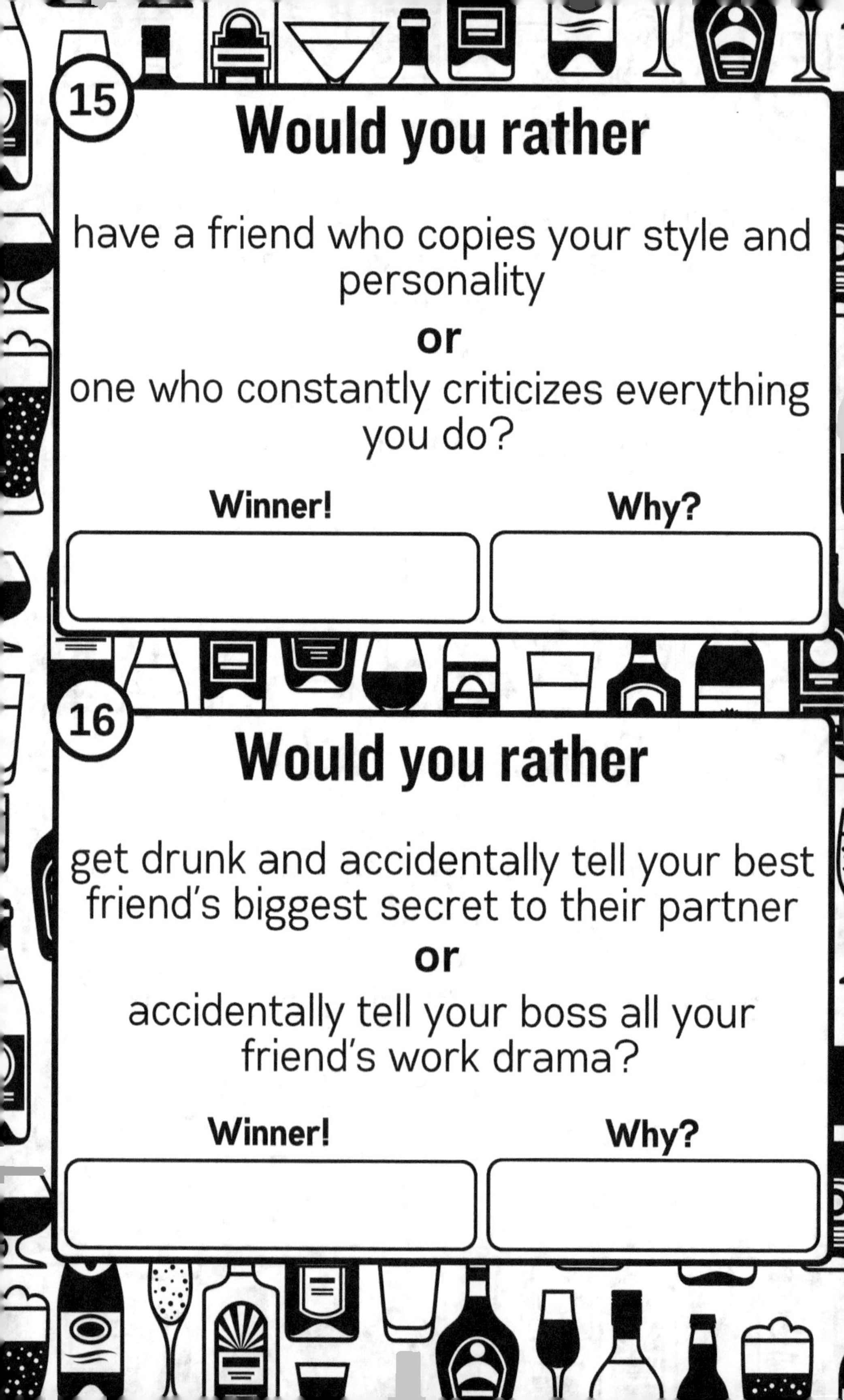

15
Would you rather

have a friend who copies your style and personality

or

one who constantly criticizes everything you do?

Winner!

Why?

16
Would you rather

get drunk and accidentally tell your best friend's biggest secret to their partner

or

accidentally tell your boss all your friend's work drama?

Winner!

Why?

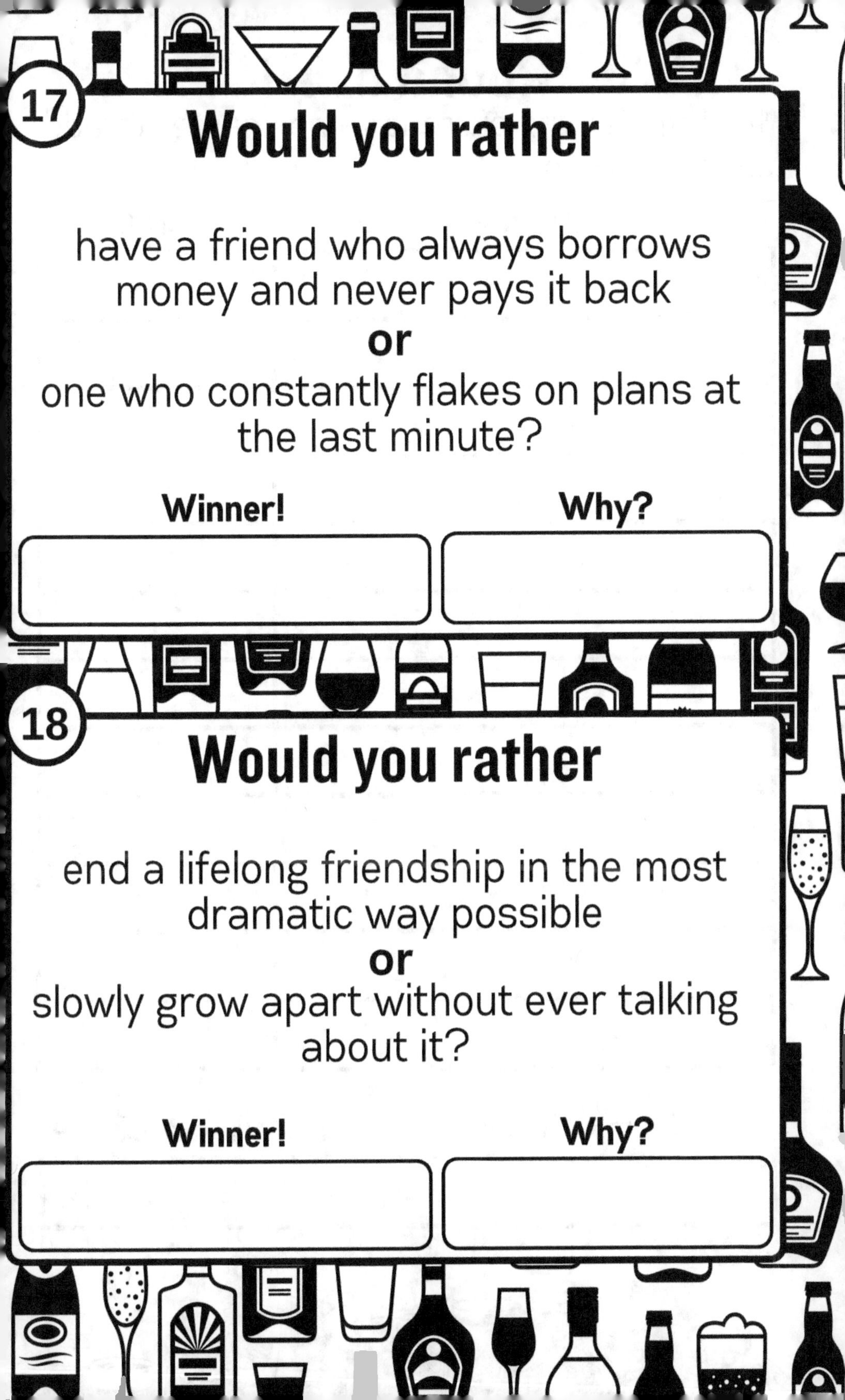

17

Would you rather

have a friend who always borrows
money and never pays it back
or
one who constantly flakes on plans at
the last minute?

Winner!

Why?

18

Would you rather

end a lifelong friendship in the most
dramatic way possible
or
slowly grow apart without ever talking
about it?

Winner!

Why?

Round over!

It's time for the current game-master to add up the scores!

Name	Points

Round Winner	Round Winners Choice

Round 8

Game-Master:

Risky Rewards

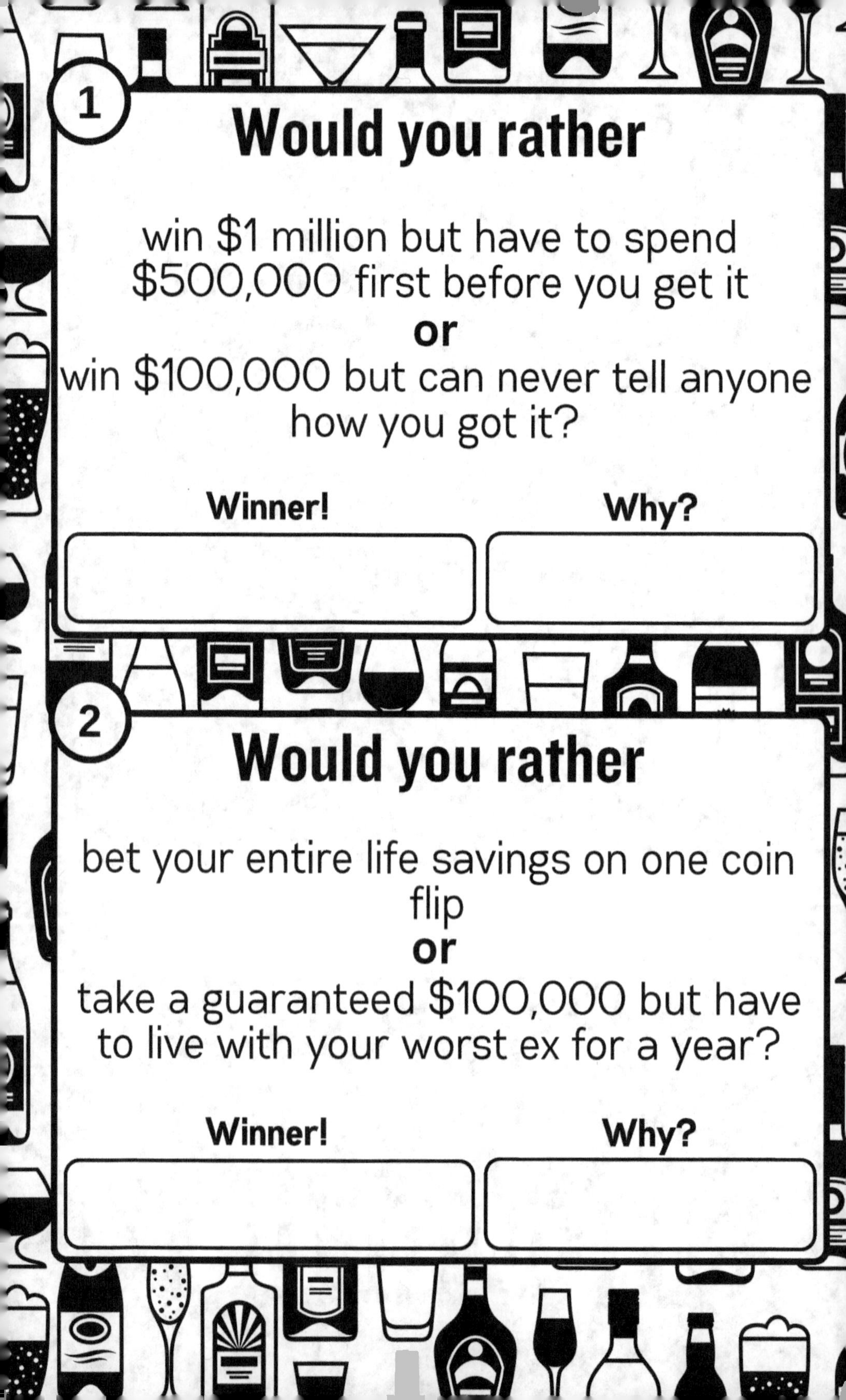

1

Would you rather

win $1 million but have to spend $500,000 first before you get it
or
win $100,000 but can never tell anyone how you got it?

Winner!

Why?

2

Would you rather

bet your entire life savings on one coin flip
or
take a guaranteed $100,000 but have to live with your worst ex for a year?

Winner!

Why?

3
Would you rather
win $500,000 but never be able to have sex again
or
win $100,000 but have to announce every time you orgasm for the rest of your life?
Winner!
Why?
4
Would you rather
have a 50% chance of winning $10 million, or a random ailment for the rest of your life
or
a 100% chance of winning $1 million—but you can't touch it for 20 years?
Winner!
Why?

5

Would you rather

accept $1 million but you can never drink alcohol again
or
take $100,000 but have to drink every single day for a year?

Winner!

Why?

6

Would you rather

have to spend 24 hours in a haunted house for $100,000
or
spend a night in the same bed as your ex for $1,000?

Winner!

Why?

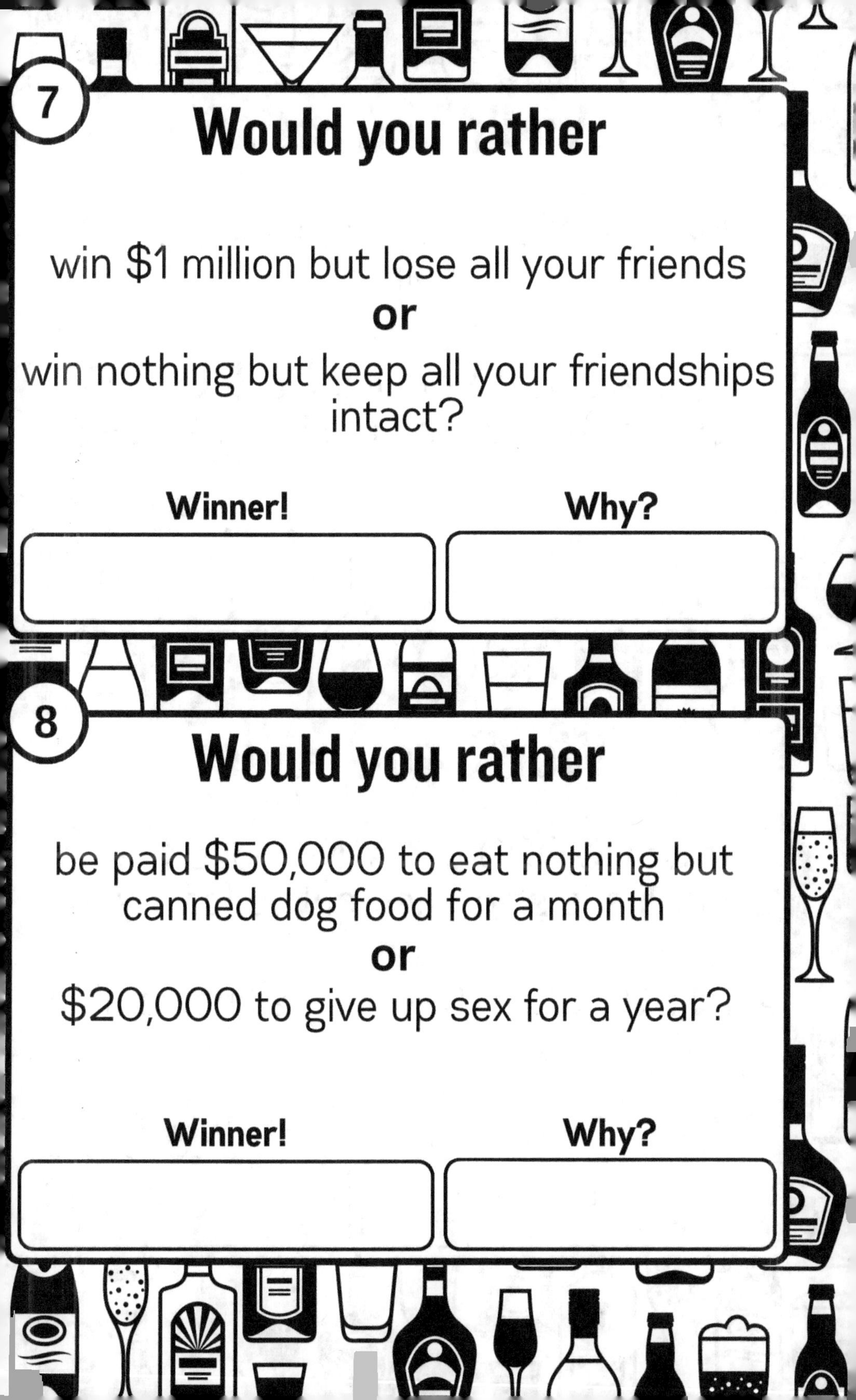

7

Would you rather

win $1 million but lose all your friends
or
win nothing but keep all your friendships intact?

Winner!

Why?

8

Would you rather

be paid $50,000 to eat nothing but canned dog food for a month
or
$20,000 to give up sex for a year?

Winner!

Why?

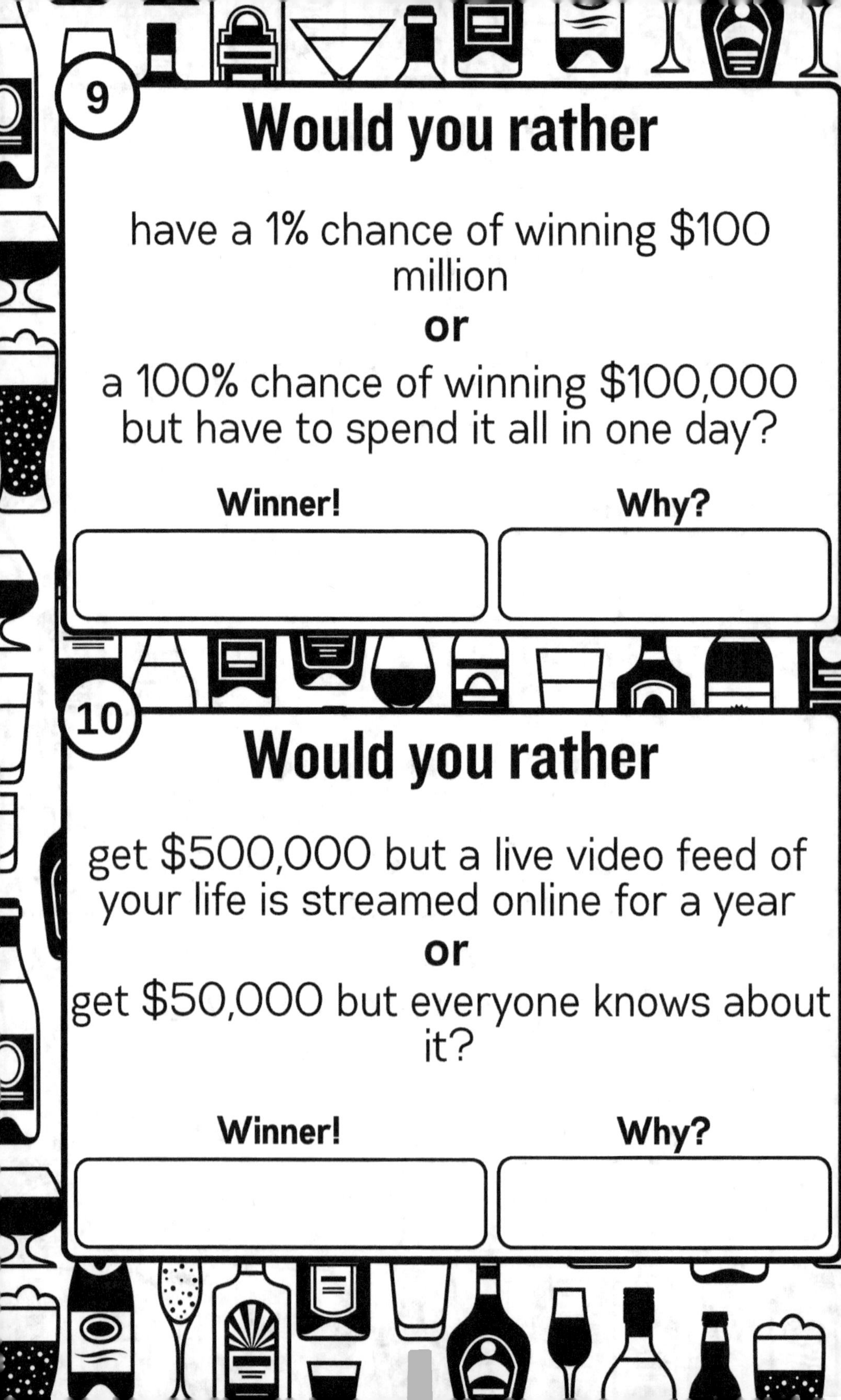
9

Would you rather

have a 1% chance of winning $100 million
or
a 100% chance of winning $100,000 but have to spend it all in one day?

Winner!

Why?

10

Would you rather

get $500,000 but a live video feed of your life is streamed online for a year
or
get $50,000 but everyone knows about it?

Winner!

Why?

11
Would you rather
win $10,000 every time you publicly embarrass yourself
or
win $1,000 every time you get into a fight with someone?
Winner!
Why?
12
Would you rather
win $200,000 but have to post your entire search history online
or
get $50,000 and let your boss read your last 20 text messages?
Winner!
Why?

13
Would you rather
take $10,000 but you can never masturbate again
or
take $1,000 and have to give a detailed speech about your sex life to your family?
Winner!
Why?
14
Would you rather
win $100,000 but have to tattoo your ex's name somewhere visible
or
win $10,000 and have to shave your head completely?
Winner!
Why?

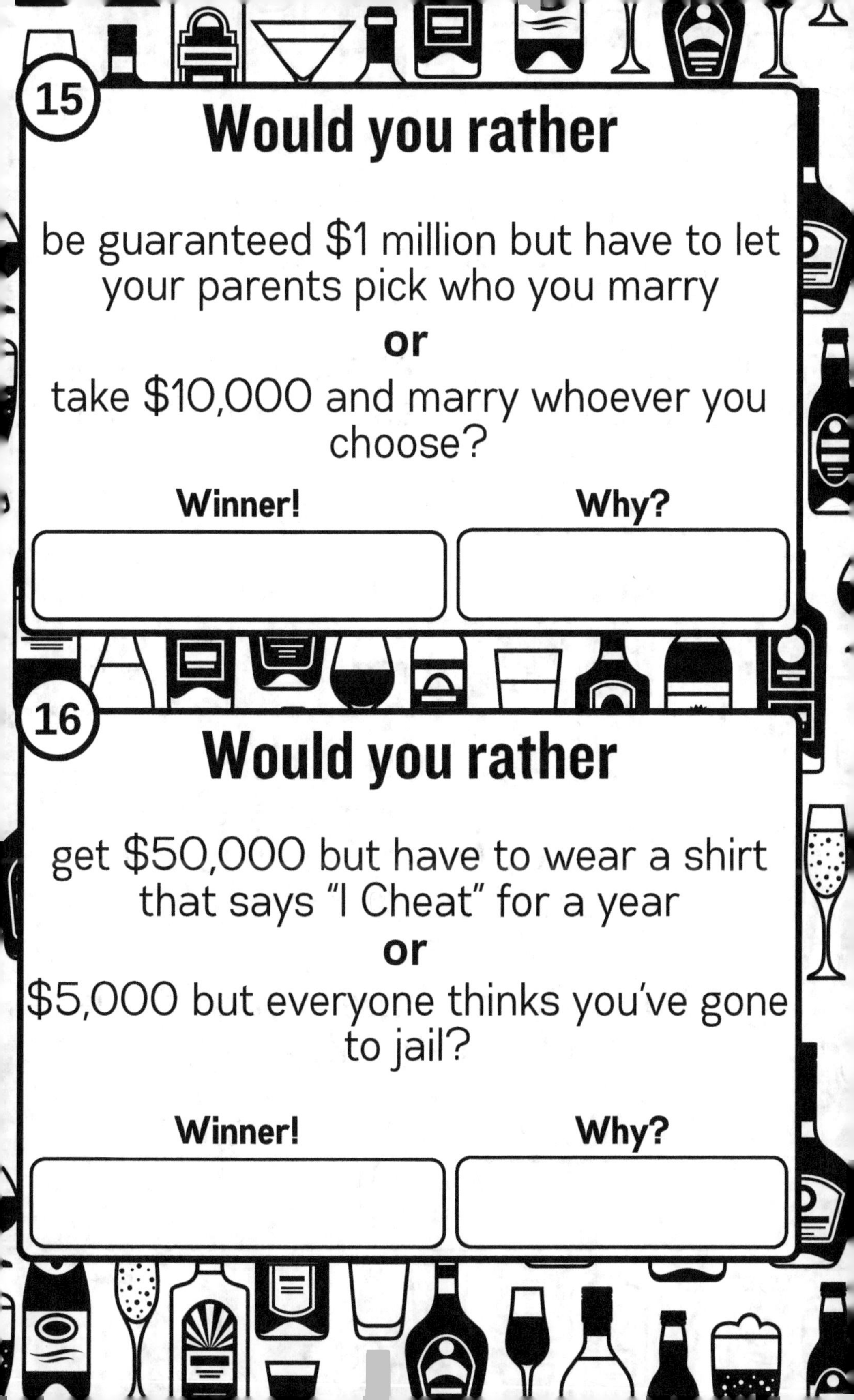

15
Would you rather

be guaranteed $1 million but have to let your parents pick who you marry
or
take $10,000 and marry whoever you choose?

Winner!
Why?

16
Would you rather

get $50,000 but have to wear a shirt that says "I Cheat" for a year
or
$5,000 but everyone thinks you've gone to jail?

Winner!
Why?

17
Would you rather
take $1 million but have to publicly share your biggest secret
or
take $10,000 and let someone else tell a fake but embarrassing story about you?
Winner!
Why?
18
Would you rather
win $500,000 but be banned from social media forever
or
get $50,000 but have to post a video of you streaking?
Winner!
Why?

Round over!

It's time for the current game-master to add up the scores!

Name	Points

Round Winner	Round Winners Choice

Round 9

Game-Master:

Vacation Disasters

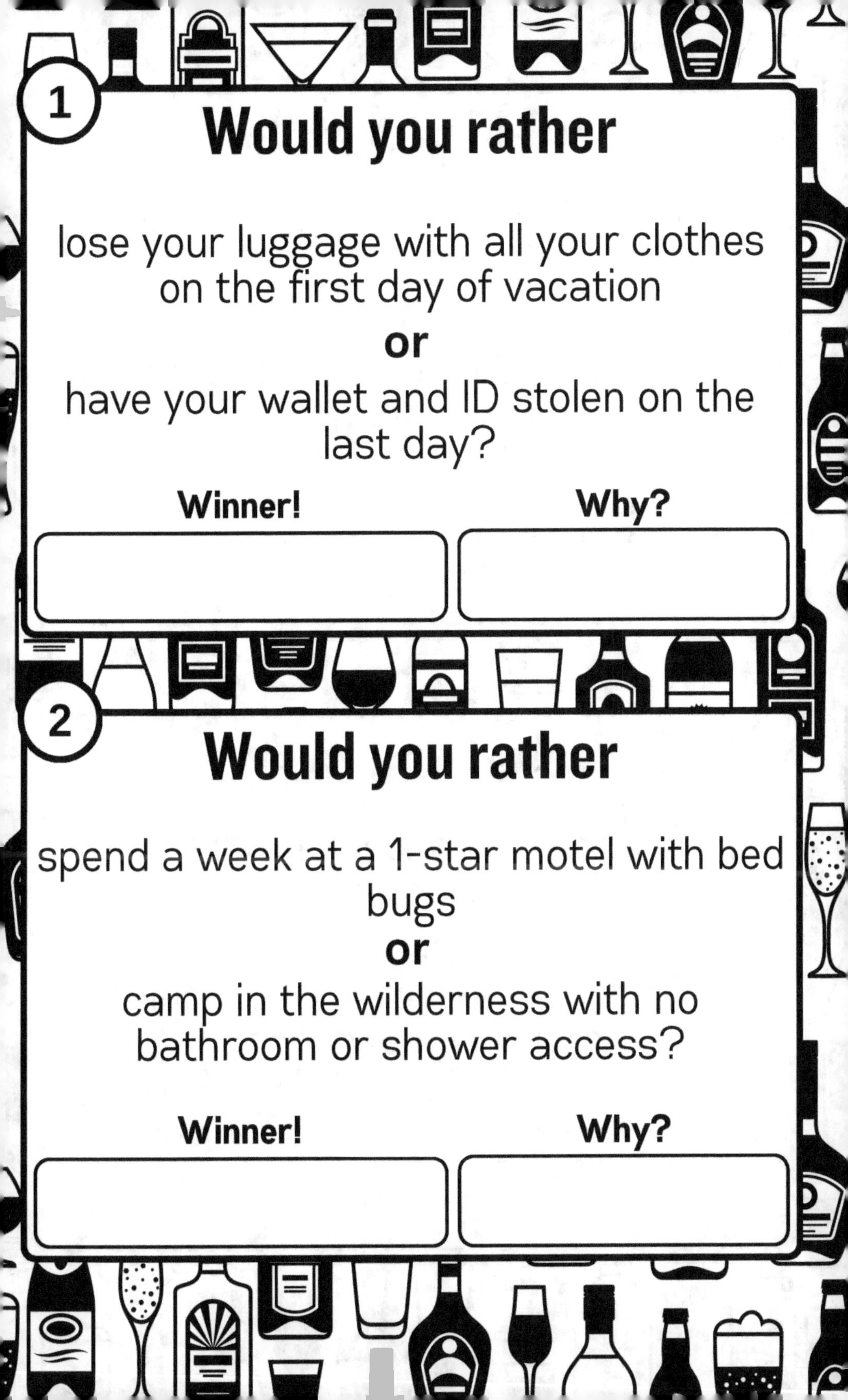

1
Would you rather

lose your luggage with all your clothes on the first day of vacation
or
have your wallet and ID stolen on the last day?

Winner!

Why?

2
Would you rather

spend a week at a 1-star motel with bed bugs
or
camp in the wilderness with no bathroom or shower access?

Winner!

Why?

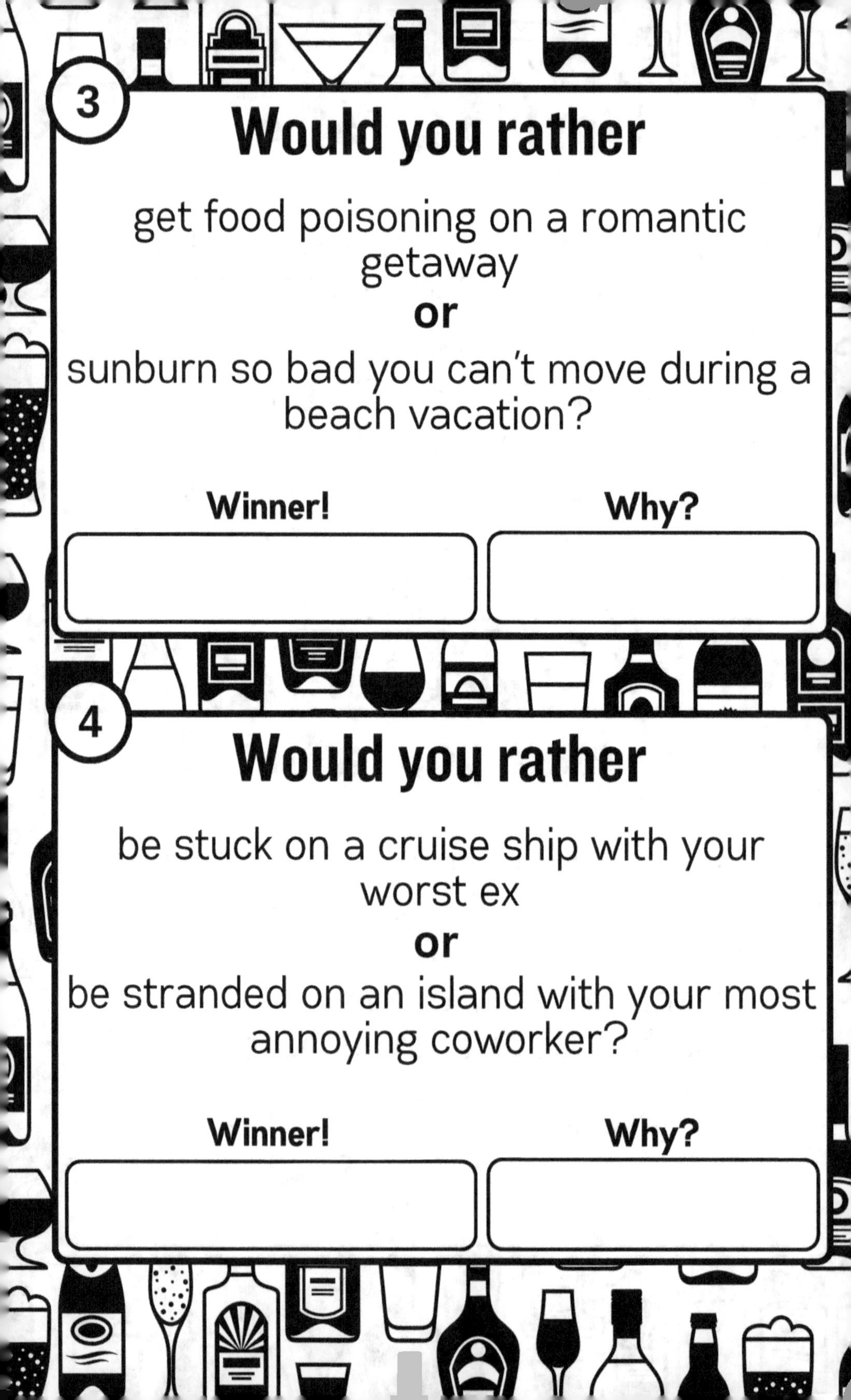

3

Would you rather

get food poisoning on a romantic getaway

or

sunburn so bad you can't move during a beach vacation?

Winner!

Why?

4

Would you rather

be stuck on a cruise ship with your worst ex

or

be stranded on an island with your most annoying coworker?

Winner!

Why?

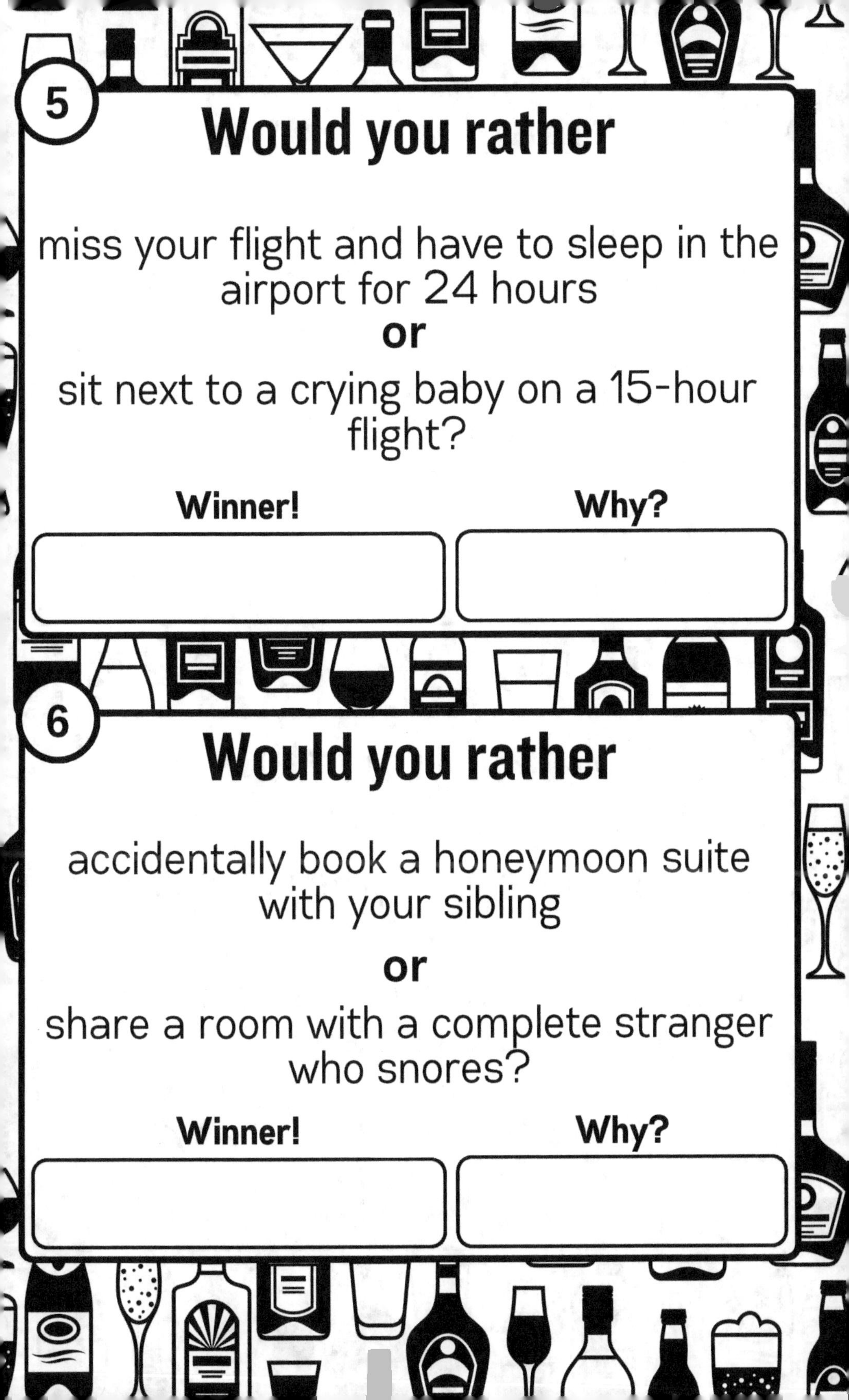
5

Would you rather

miss your flight and have to sleep in the airport for 24 hours
or
sit next to a crying baby on a 15-hour flight?

Winner!

Why?

6

Would you rather

accidentally book a honeymoon suite with your sibling

or

share a room with a complete stranger who snores?

Winner!

Why?

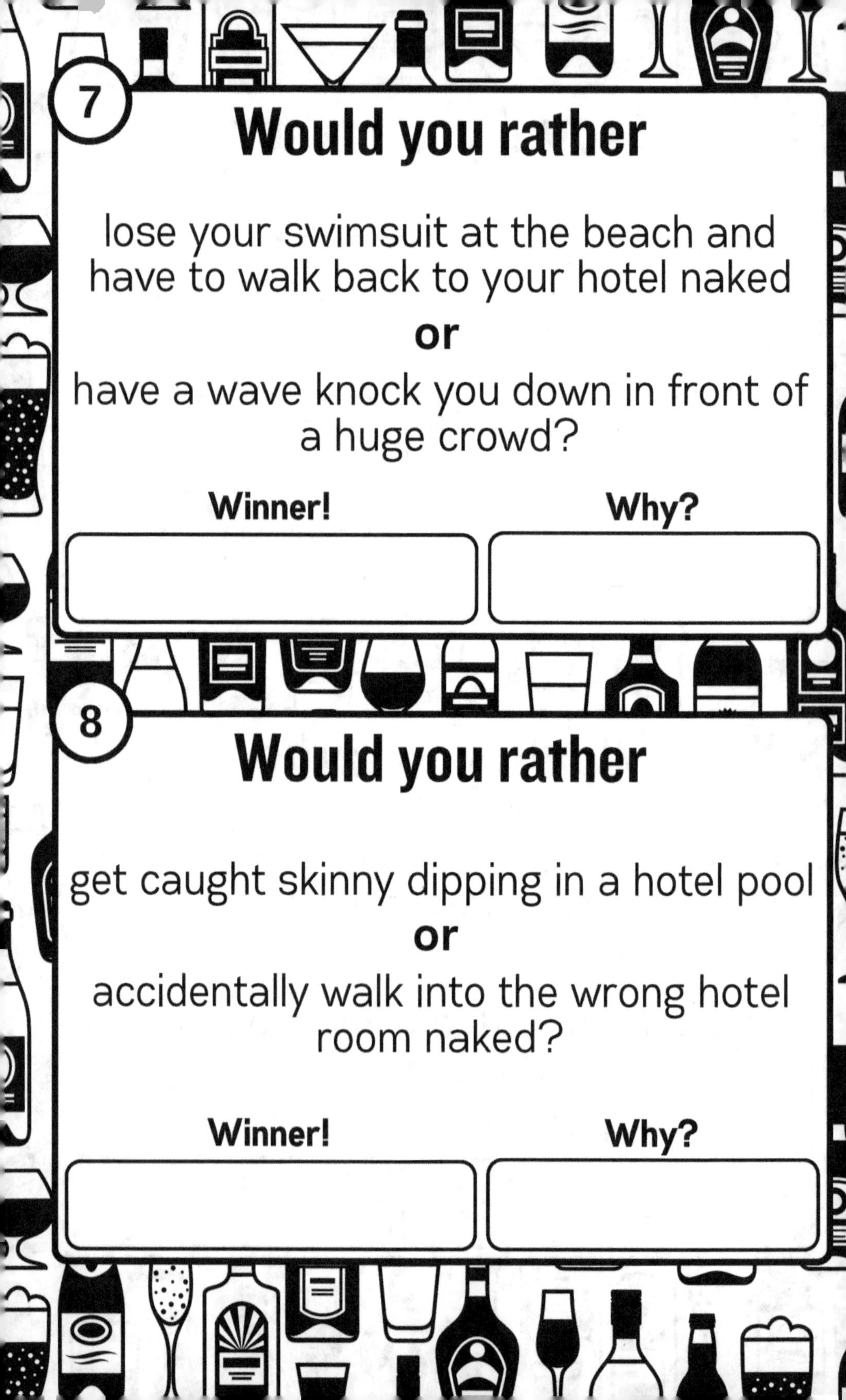
7

Would you rather

lose your swimsuit at the beach and have to walk back to your hotel naked

or

have a wave knock you down in front of a huge crowd?

Winner!   Why?

8

Would you rather

get caught skinny dipping in a hotel pool

or

accidentally walk into the wrong hotel room naked?

Winner!   Why?

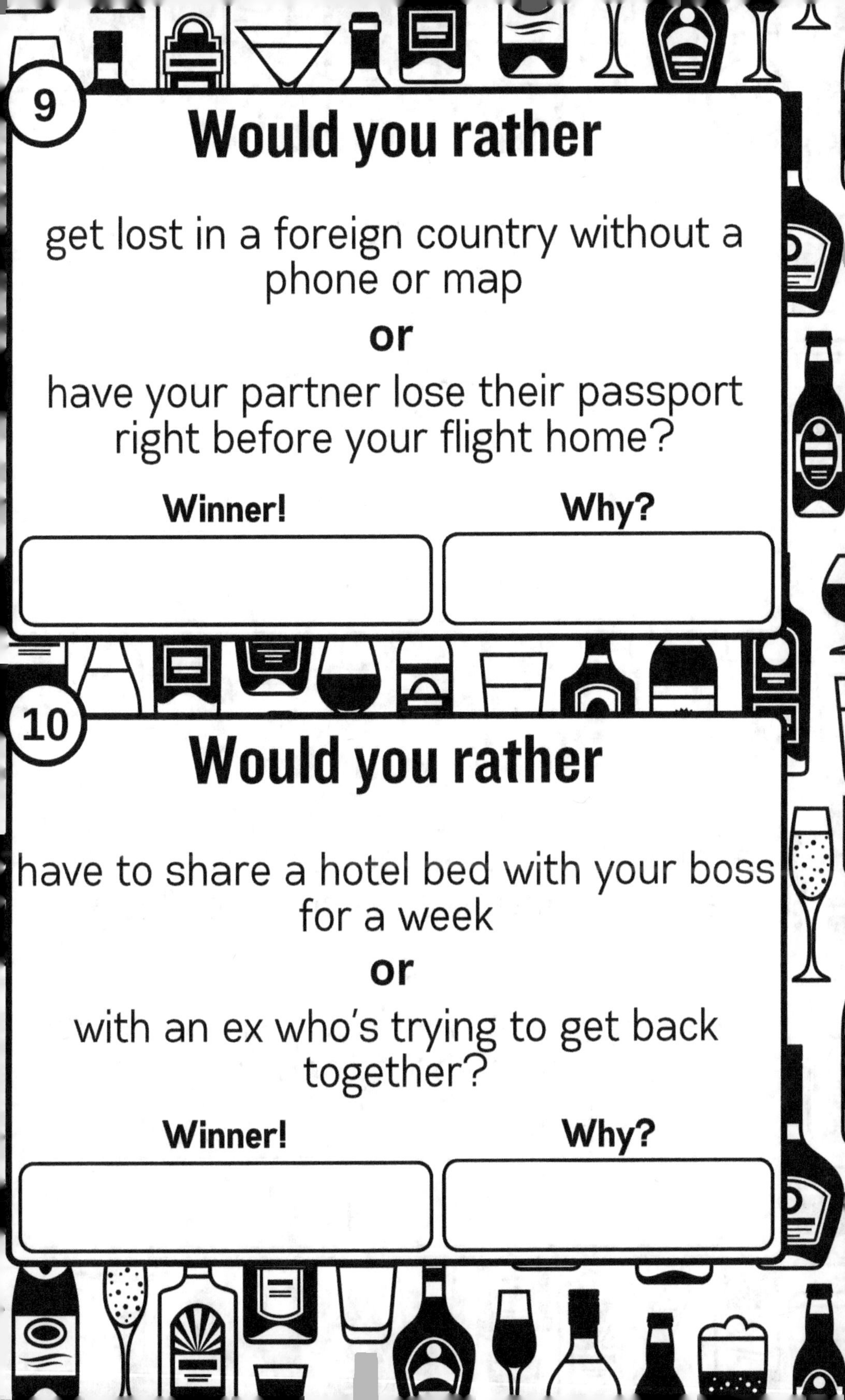

9

Would you rather

get lost in a foreign country without a phone or map

or

have your partner lose their passport right before your flight home?

Winner!

Why?

10

Would you rather

have to share a hotel bed with your boss for a week

or

with an ex who's trying to get back together?

Winner!

Why?

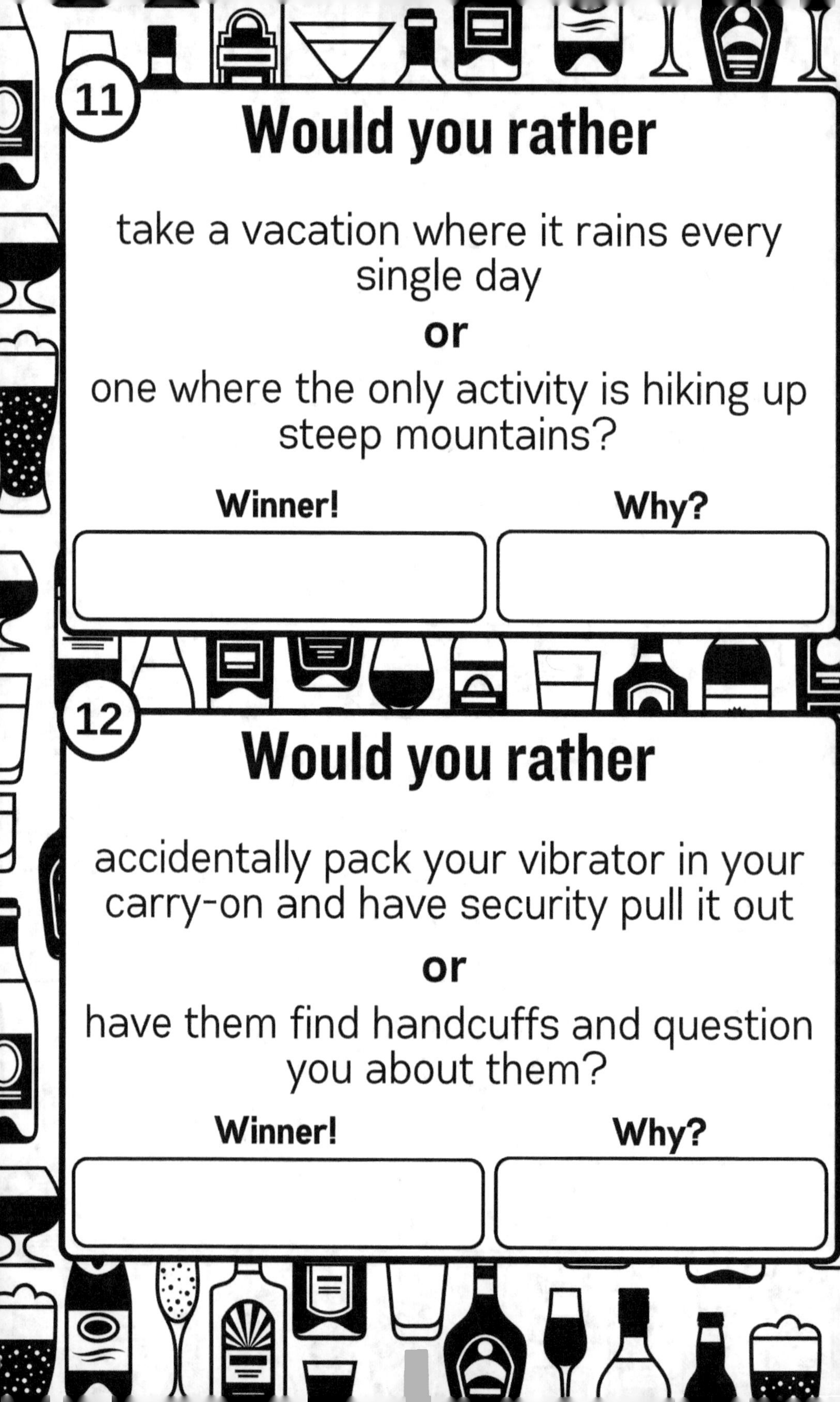

11

Would you rather

take a vacation where it rains every single day

or

one where the only activity is hiking up steep mountains?

Winner!   **Why?**

12

Would you rather

accidentally pack your vibrator in your carry-on and have security pull it out

or

have them find handcuffs and question you about them?

Winner!   **Why?**

13

Would you rather

have your swimsuit fall off while diving into a pool

or

have a seagull poop on your head during a crowded beach party?

Winner!

Why?

14

Would you rather

be stuck at a nudist resort with your family

or

at a swingers resort with your boss?

Winner!

Why?

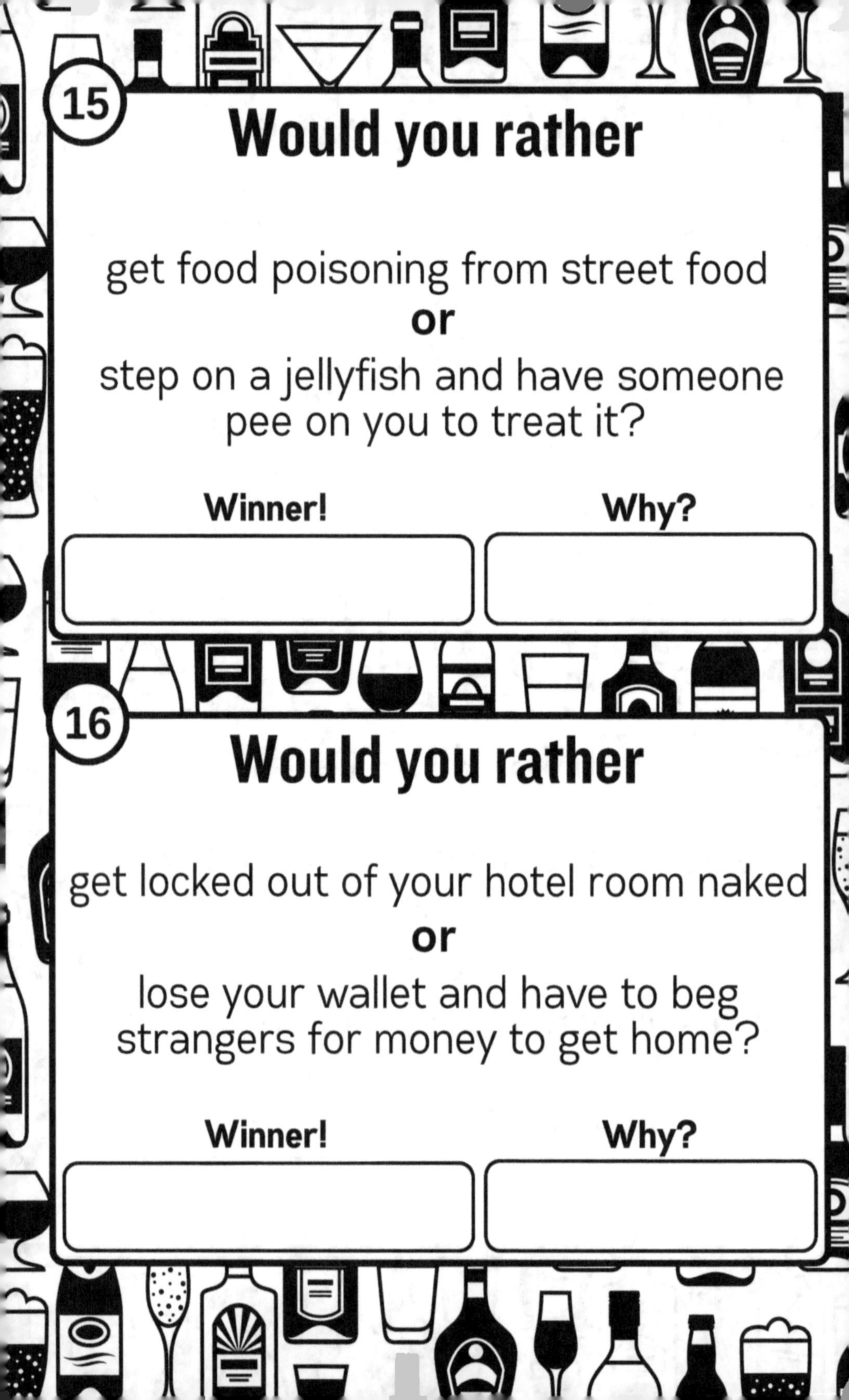

15
Would you rather
get food poisoning from street food
or
step on a jellyfish and have someone
pee on you to treat it?
Winner!
Why?
16
Would you rather
get locked out of your hotel room naked
or
lose your wallet and have to beg
strangers for money to get home?
Winner!
Why?

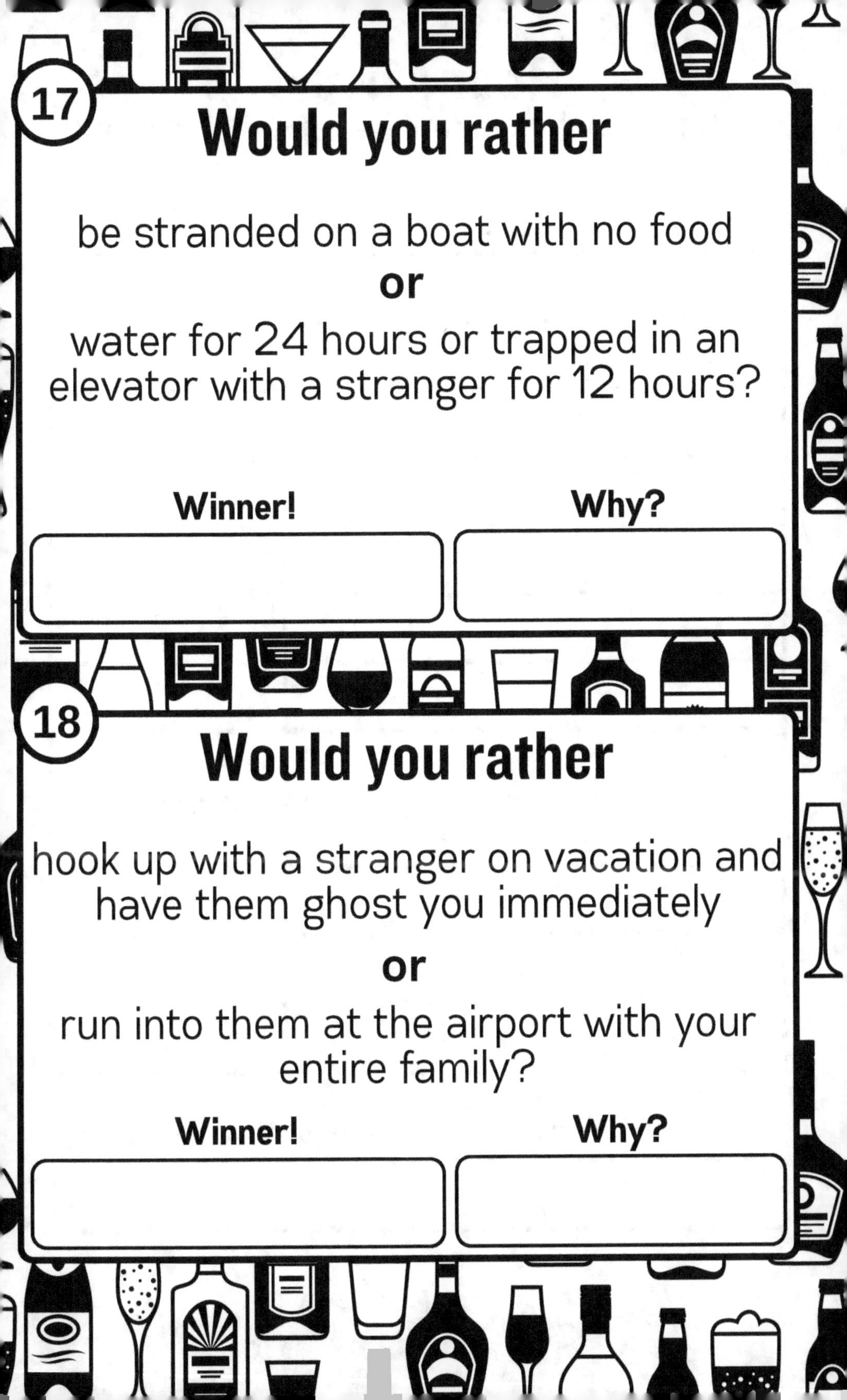

17

Would you rather

be stranded on a boat with no food
or
water for 24 hours or trapped in an
elevator with a stranger for 12 hours?

Winner!

Why?

18

Would you rather

hook up with a stranger on vacation and
have them ghost you immediately

or

run into them at the airport with your
entire family?

Winner!

Why?

Round over!

It's time for the current game-master to add up the scores!

Name	Points

Round Winner	Round Winners Choice

Round 10

Game-Master:

Nostalgia Mayhem

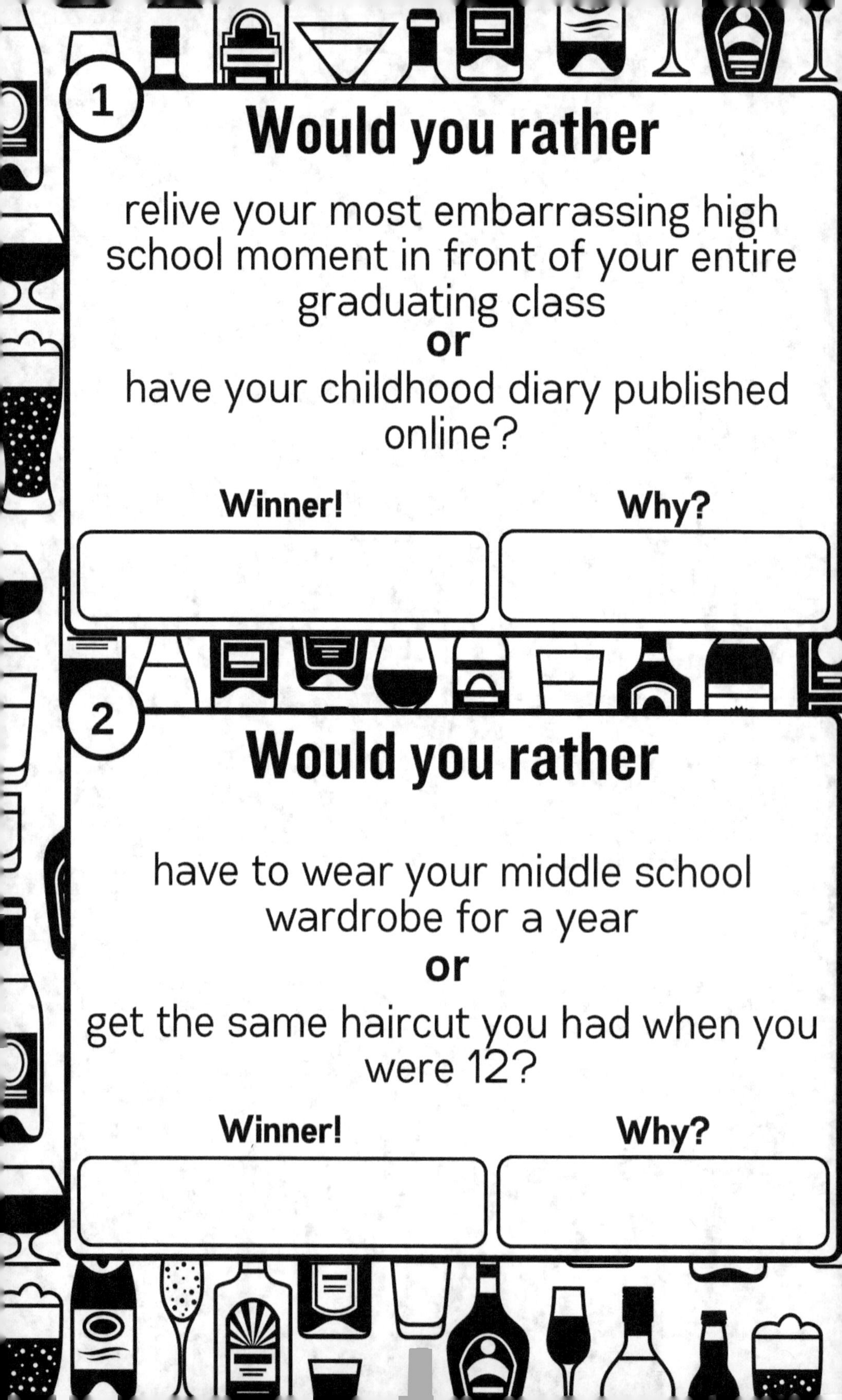

1
Would you rather
relive your most embarrassing high school moment in front of your entire graduating class
or
have your childhood diary published online?
Winner!
Why?
2
Would you rather
have to wear your middle school wardrobe for a year
or
get the same haircut you had when you were 12?
Winner!
Why?

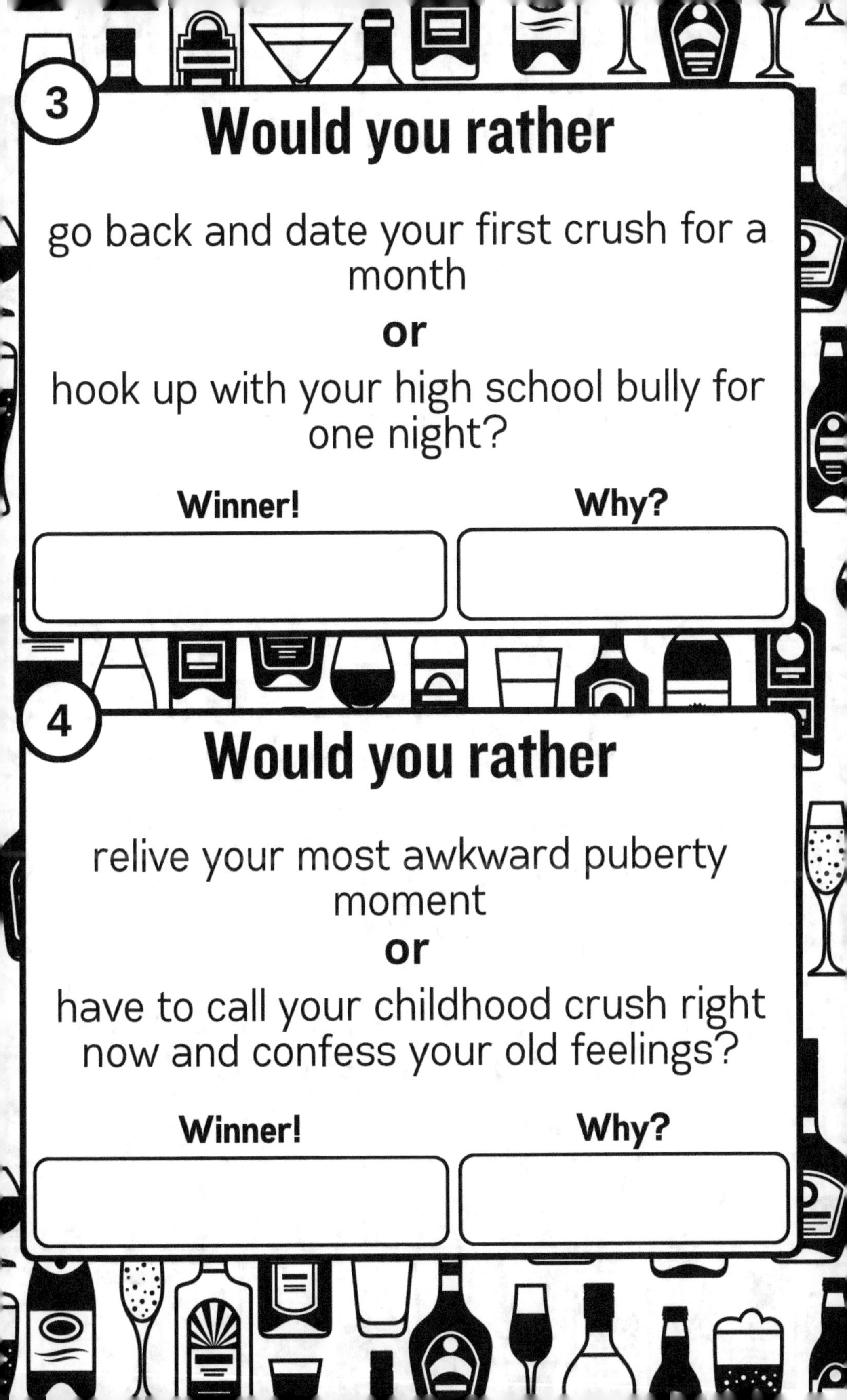

3

Would you rather

go back and date your first crush for a month

or

hook up with your high school bully for one night?

Winner!

Why?

4

Would you rather

relive your most awkward puberty moment

or

have to call your childhood crush right now and confess your old feelings?

Winner!

Why?

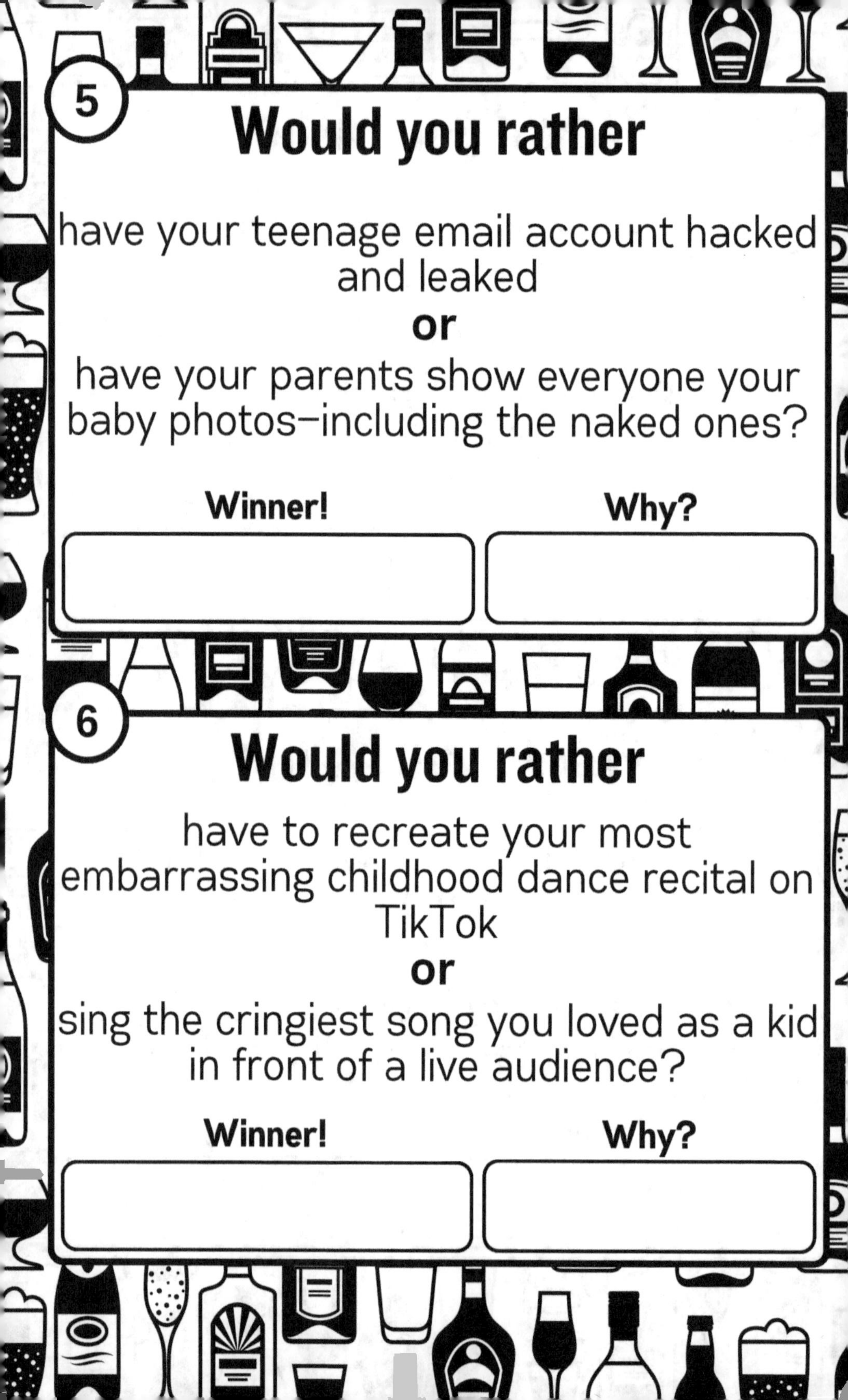

5

Would you rather

have your teenage email account hacked and leaked

or

have your parents show everyone your baby photos—including the naked ones?

Winner!

Why?

6

Would you rather

have to recreate your most embarrassing childhood dance recital on TikTok

or

sing the cringiest song you loved as a kid in front of a live audience?

Winner!

Why?

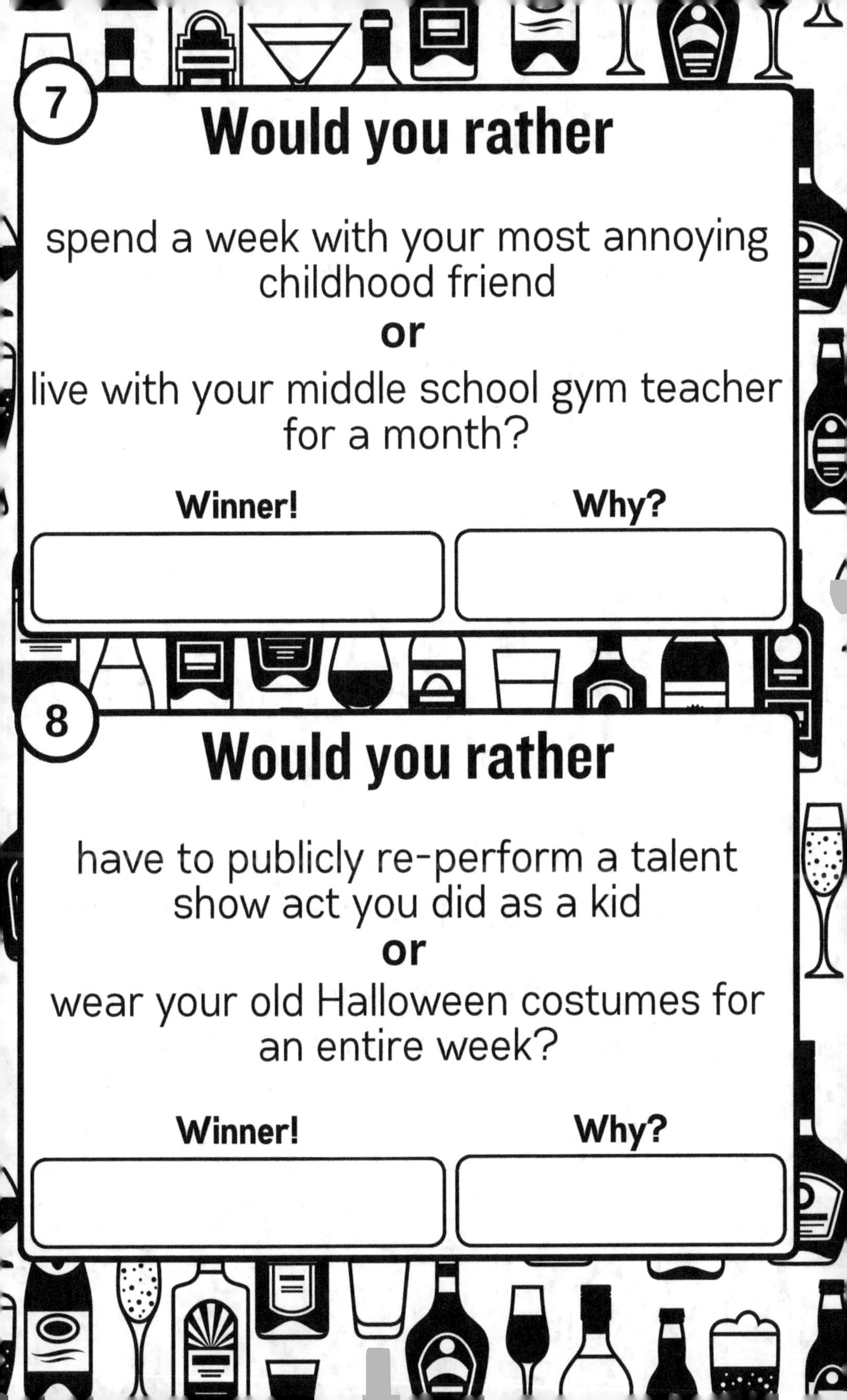

7

Would you rather

spend a week with your most annoying childhood friend
or
live with your middle school gym teacher for a month?

Winner!

Why?

8

Would you rather

have to publicly re-perform a talent show act you did as a kid
or
wear your old Halloween costumes for an entire week?

Winner!

Why?

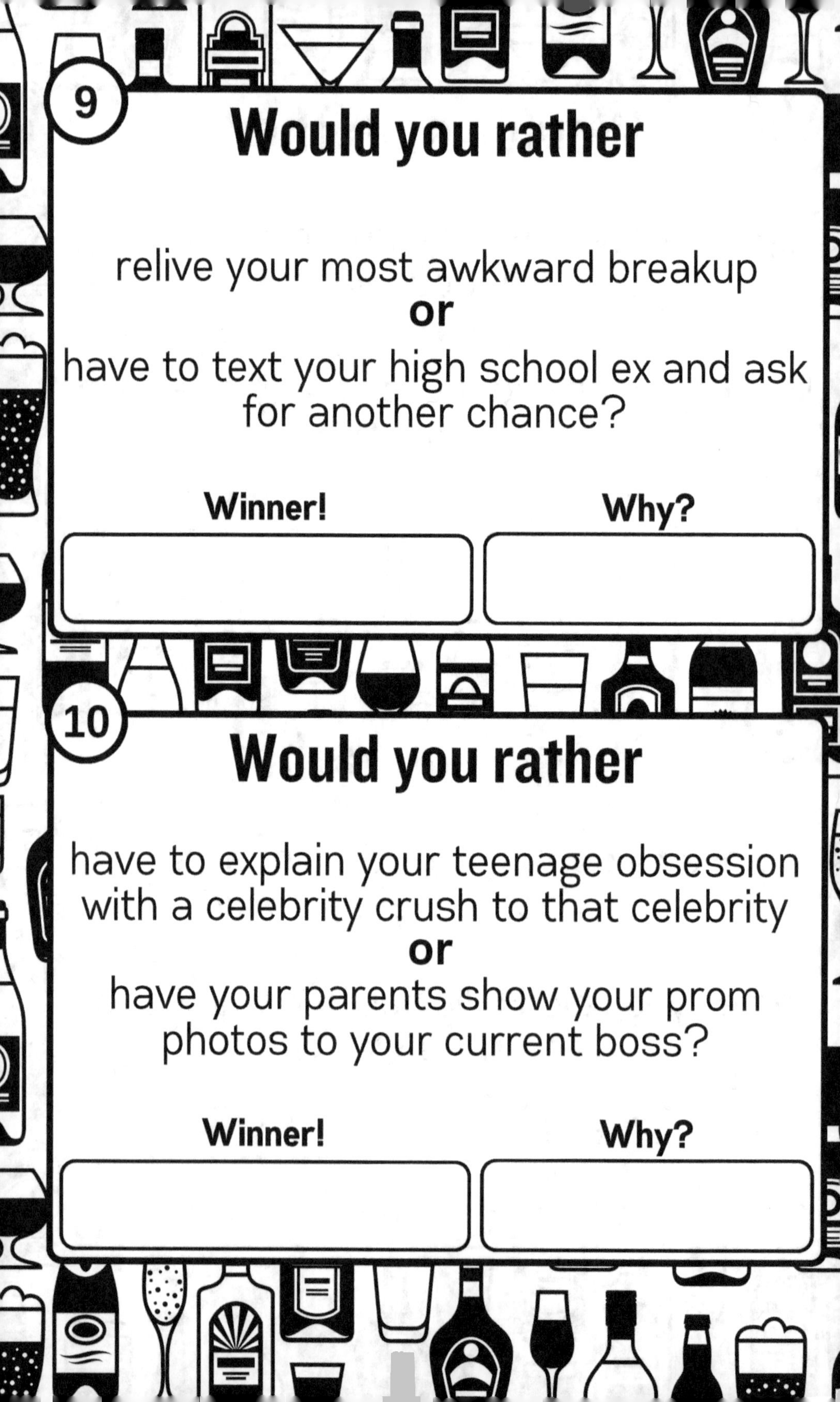

9

Would you rather

relive your most awkward breakup
or
have to text your high school ex and ask for another chance?

Winner!

Why?

10

Would you rather

have to explain your teenage obsession with a celebrity crush to that celebrity
or
have your parents show your prom photos to your current boss?

Winner!

Why?

11

Would you rather

be stuck in the worst family road trip
from your childhood

or

have to go back to middle school for an
entire month?

Winner!

Why?

12

Would you rather

have your most embarrassing AIM/MSN
Messenger chat logs read aloud

or

have your old MySpace profile revived
and made public?

Winner!

Why?

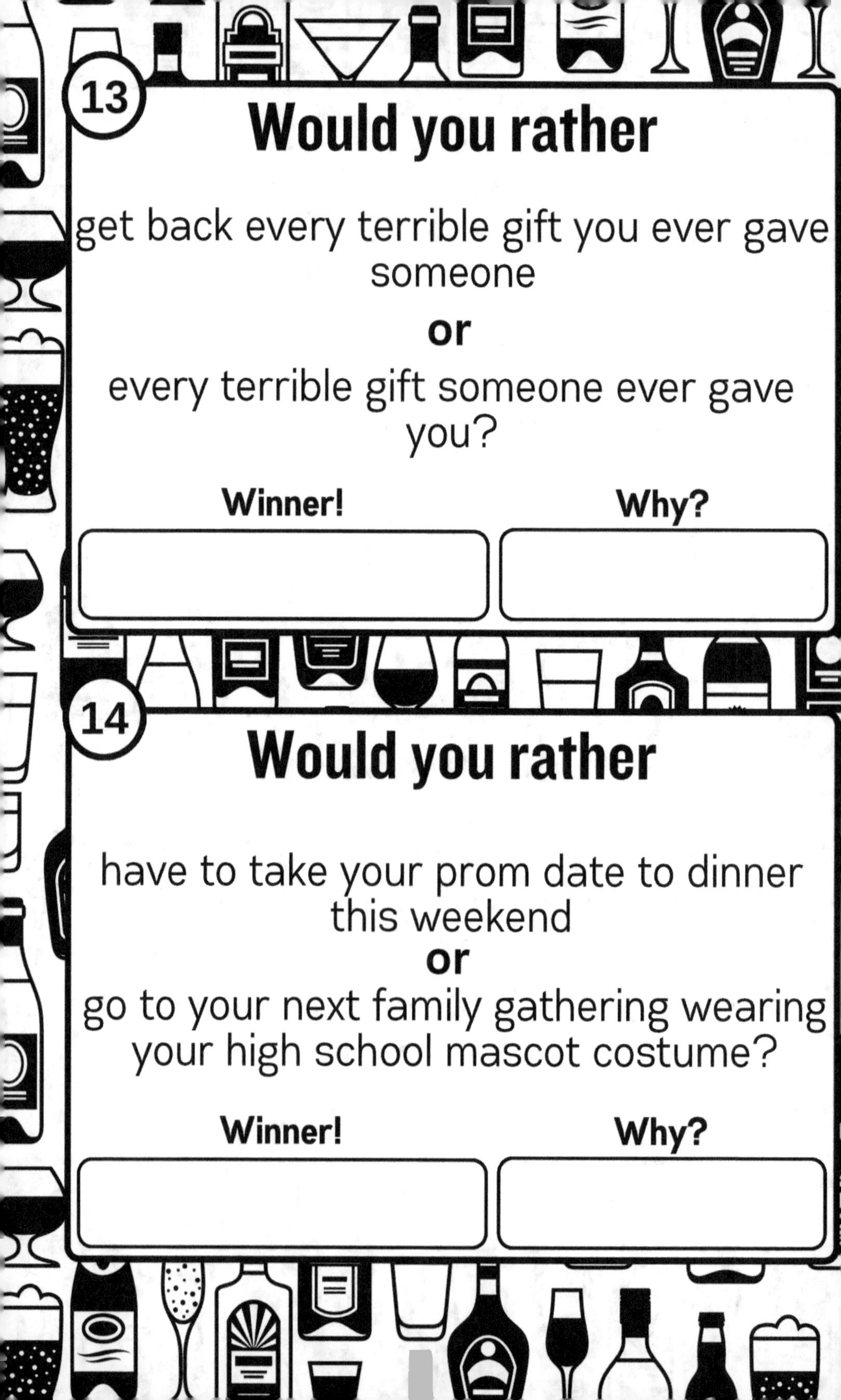

13
Would you rather

get back every terrible gift you ever gave someone

or

every terrible gift someone ever gave you?

Winner!

Why?

14
Would you rather

have to take your prom date to dinner this weekend

or

go to your next family gathering wearing your high school mascot costume?

Winner!

Why?

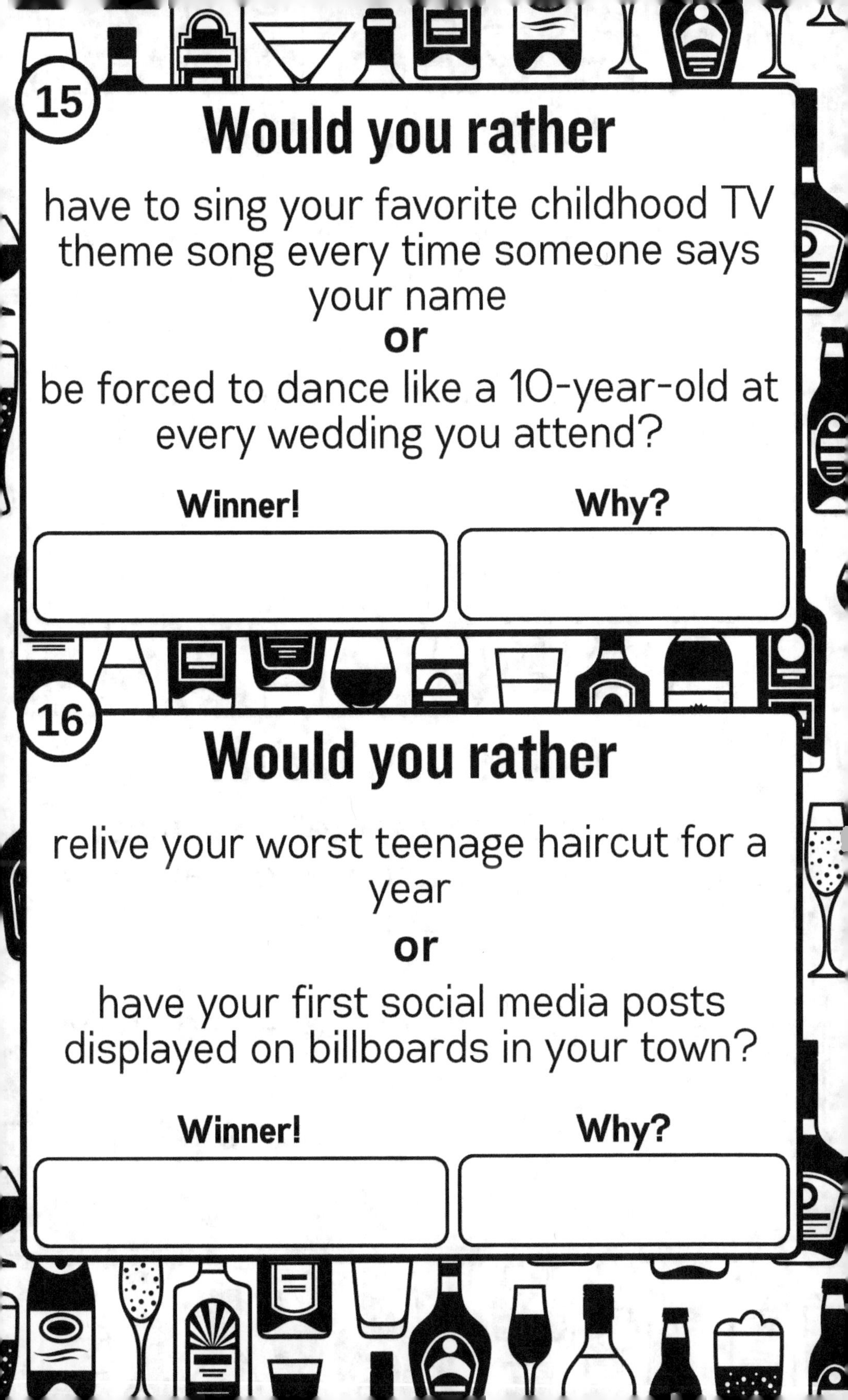

15

Would you rather

have to sing your favorite childhood TV theme song every time someone says your name

or

be forced to dance like a 10-year-old at every wedding you attend?

Winner!

Why?

16

Would you rather

relive your worst teenage haircut for a year

or

have your first social media posts displayed on billboards in your town?

Winner!

Why?

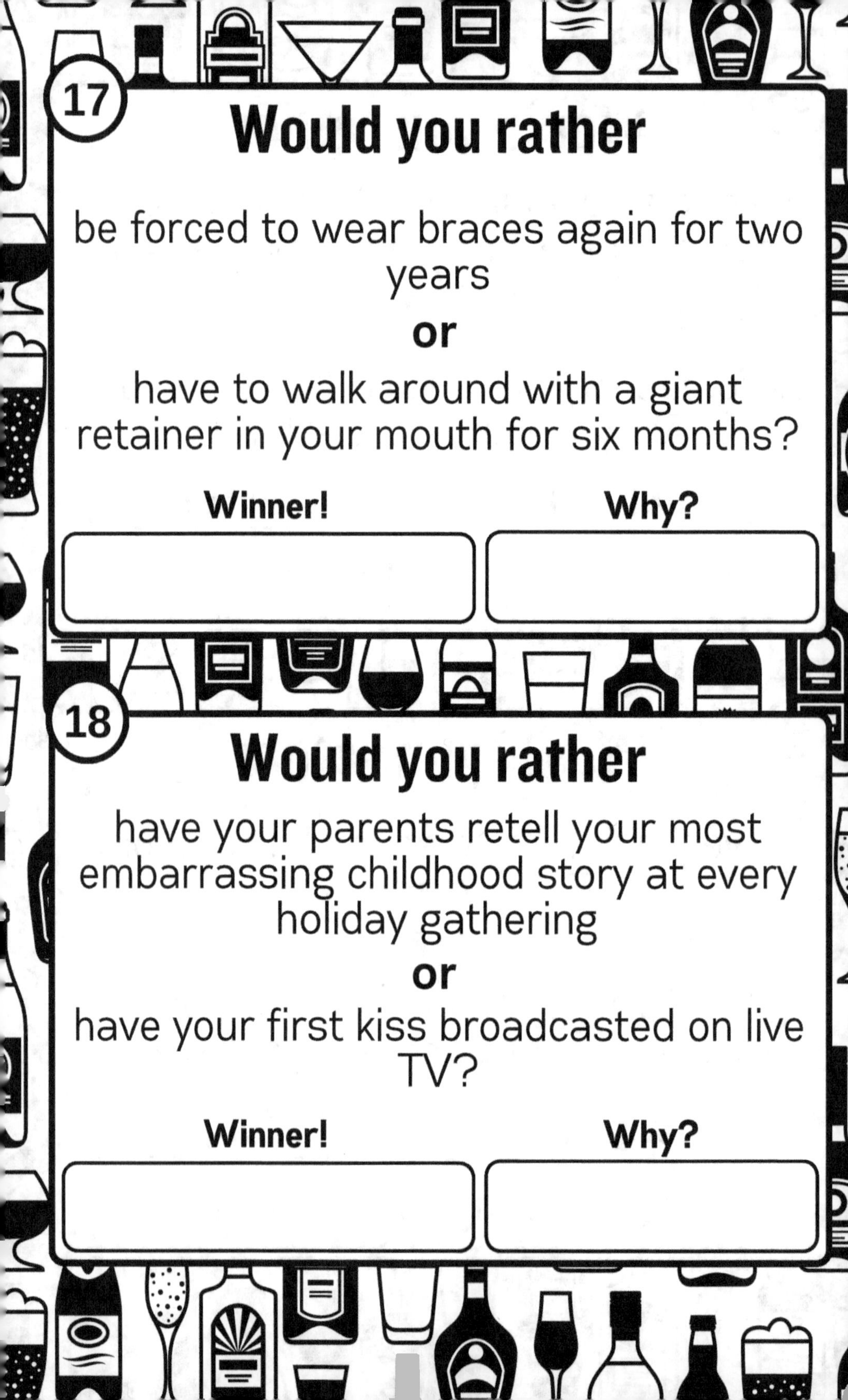

17
Would you rather
be forced to wear braces again for two years
or
have to walk around with a giant retainer in your mouth for six months?
Winner!
Why?
18
Would you rather
have your parents retell your most embarrassing childhood story at every holiday gathering
or
have your first kiss broadcasted on live TV?
Winner!
Why?

Round over!

It's time for the current game-master to add up the scores!

Name	Points

Round Winner	Round Winners Choice

Round II

Game-Master:

Drunken Debacles

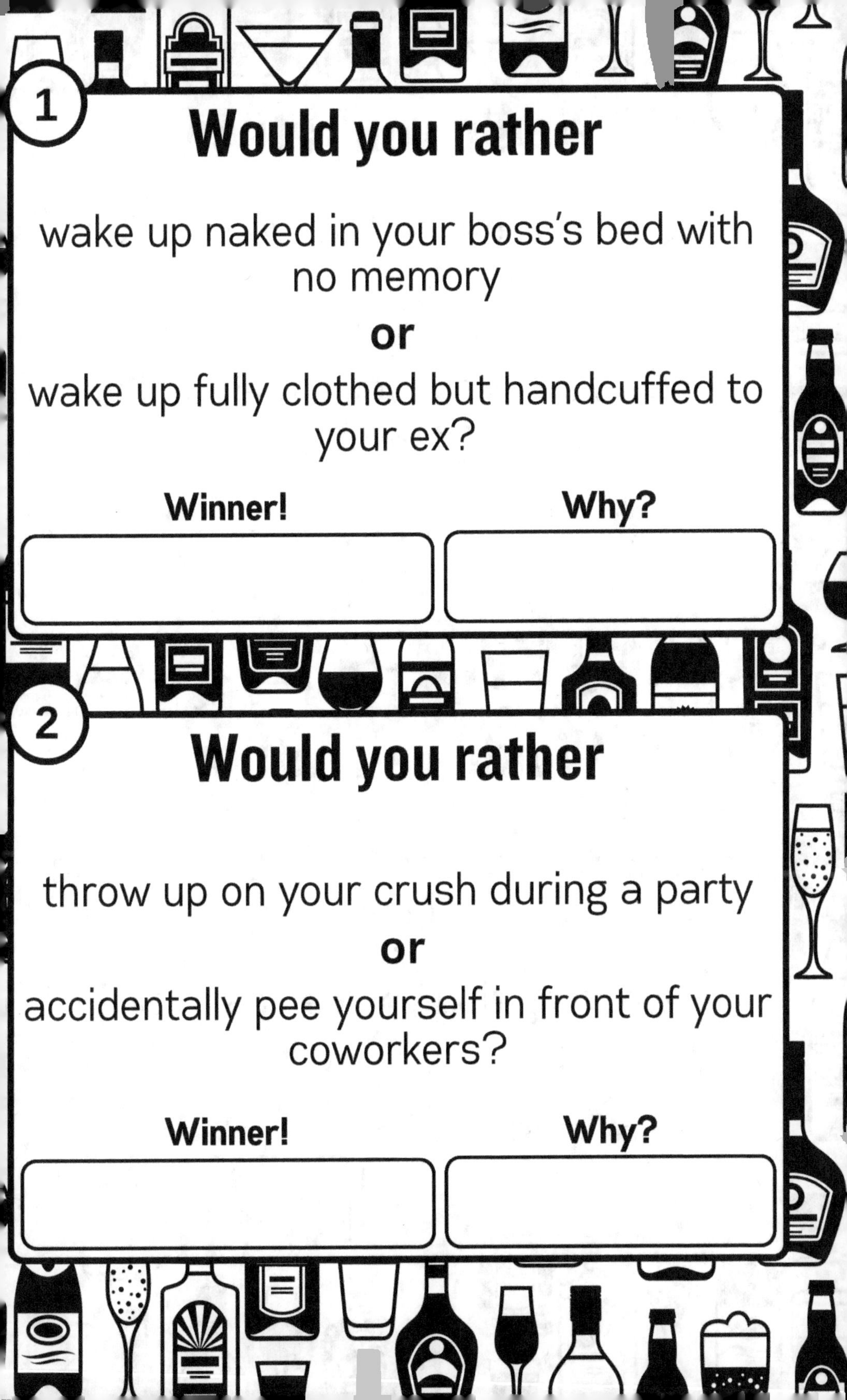
1
Would you rather
wake up naked in your boss's bed with no memory
or
wake up fully clothed but handcuffed to your ex?
Winner!
Why?
2
Would you rather
throw up on your crush during a party
or
accidentally pee yourself in front of your coworkers?
Winner!
Why?

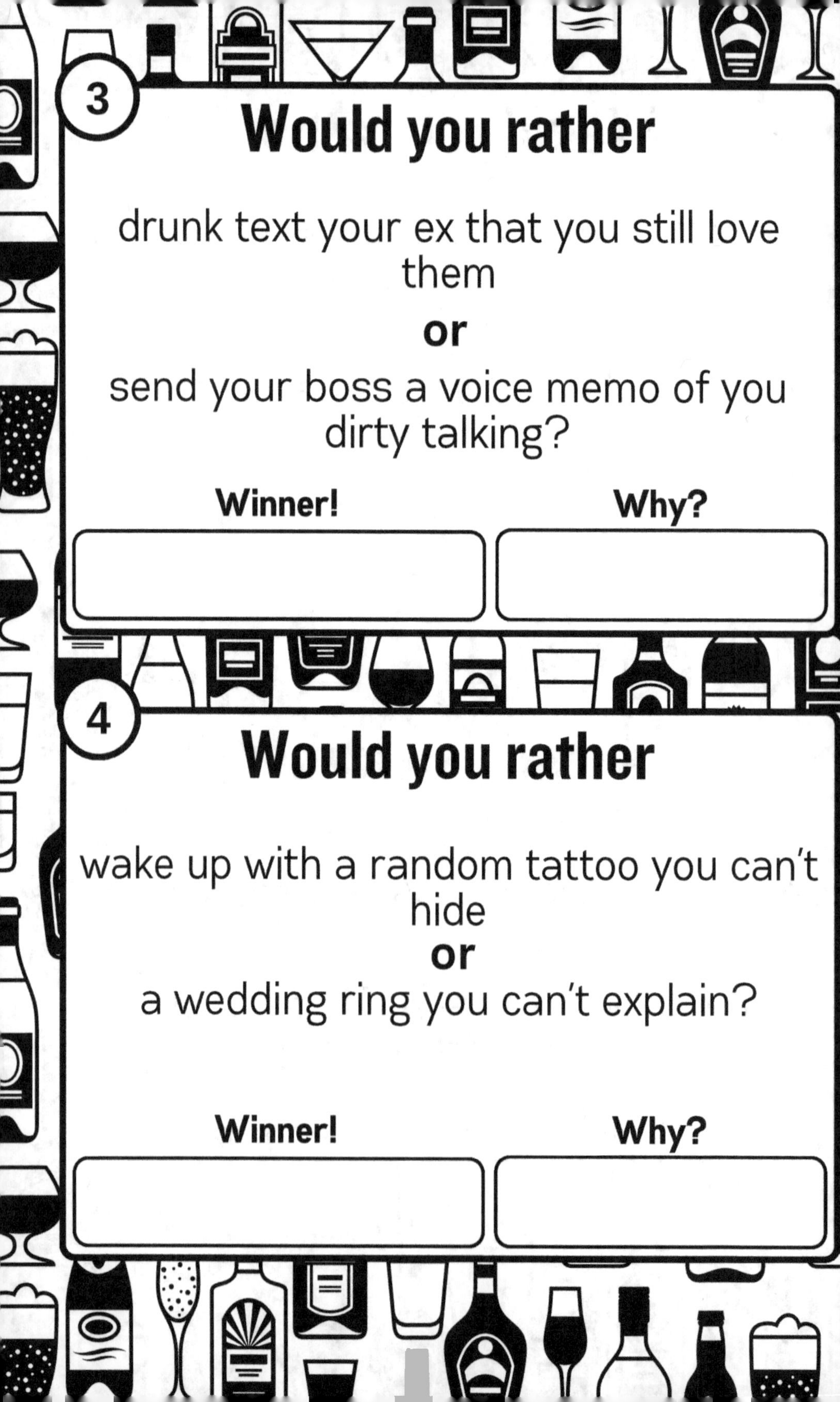

3
Would you rather
drunk text your ex that you still love them
or
send your boss a voice memo of you dirty talking?
Winner!
Why?
4
Would you rather
wake up with a random tattoo you can't hide
or
a wedding ring you can't explain?
Winner!
Why?

5

Would you rather

get caught having drunk sex in public
or
passed out in a bathroom stall, naked?

Winner!

Why?

6

Would you rather

wake up with a black eye and no memory
or
wake up next to someone you don't recognize?

Winner!

Why?

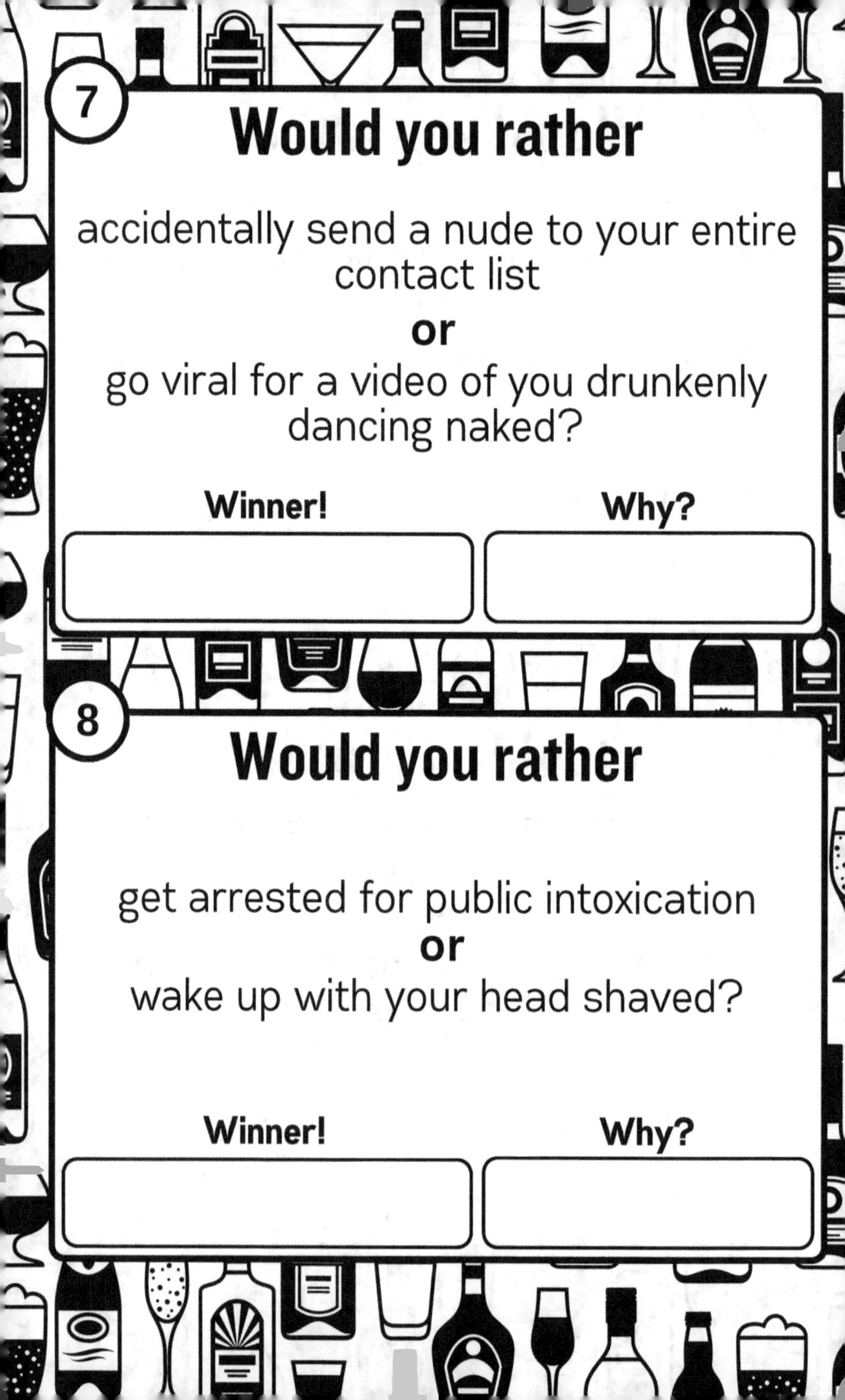

7

Would you rather

accidentally send a nude to your entire contact list

or

go viral for a video of you drunkenly dancing naked?

Winner!

Why?

8

Would you rather

get arrested for public intoxication
or
wake up with your head shaved?

Winner!

Why?

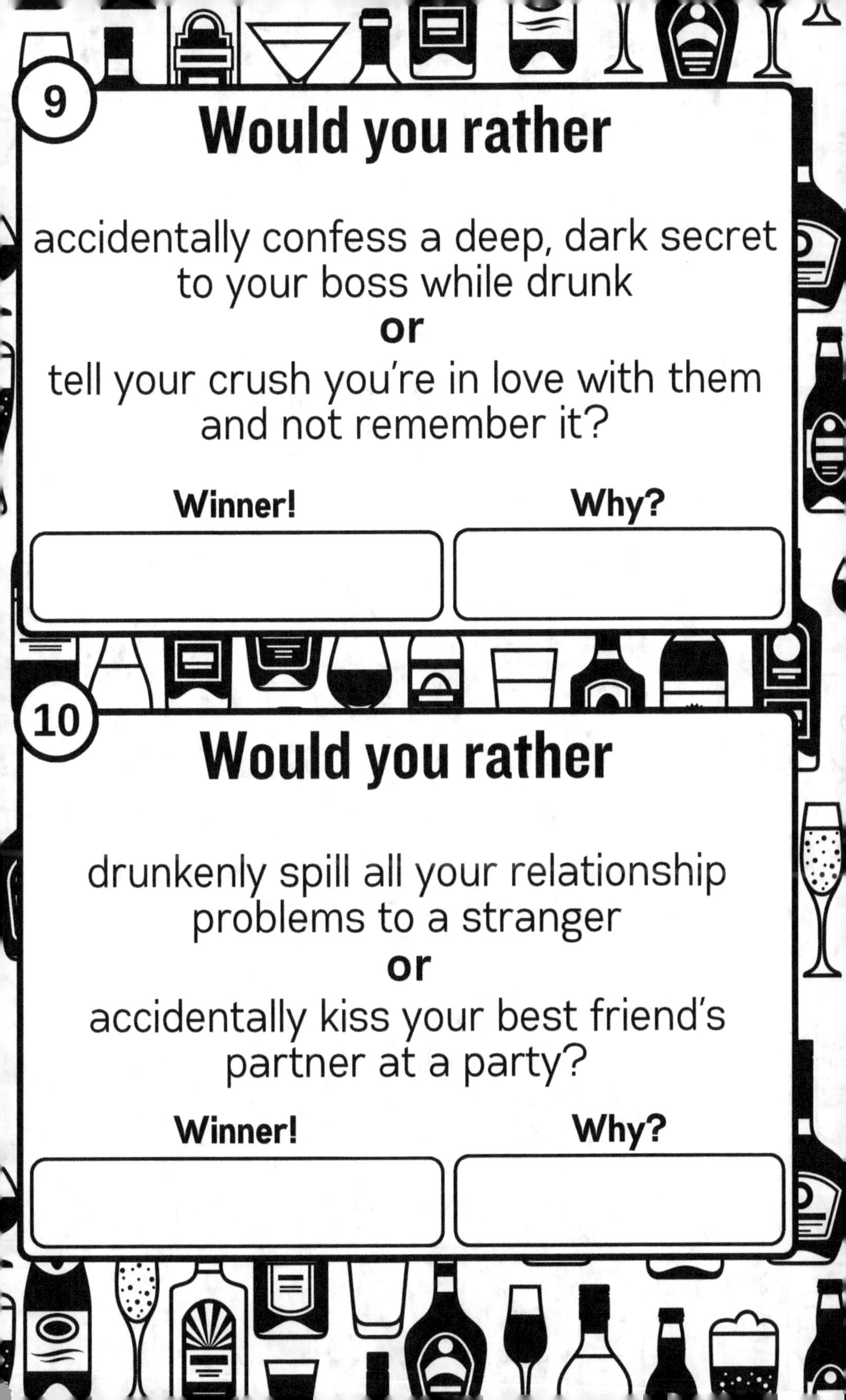

9

Would you rather

accidentally confess a deep, dark secret
to your boss while drunk
or
tell your crush you're in love with them
and not remember it?

Winner!   **Why?**

10

Would you rather

drunkenly spill all your relationship
problems to a stranger
or
accidentally kiss your best friend's
partner at a party?

Winner!   **Why?**

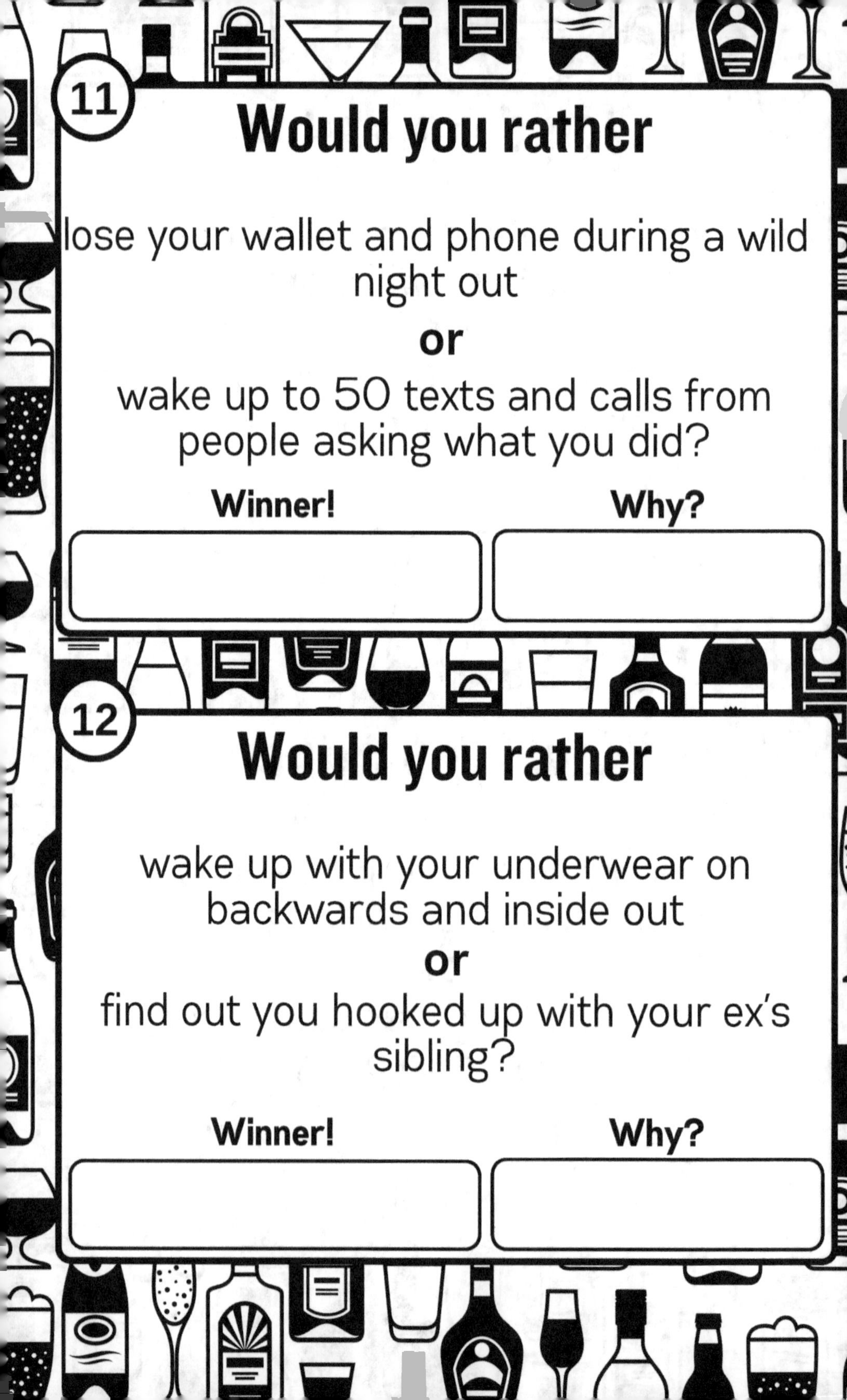

11

Would you rather

lose your wallet and phone during a wild night out

or

wake up to 50 texts and calls from people asking what you did?

Winner!

Why?

12

Would you rather

wake up with your underwear on backwards and inside out

or

find out you hooked up with your ex's sibling?

Winner!

Why?

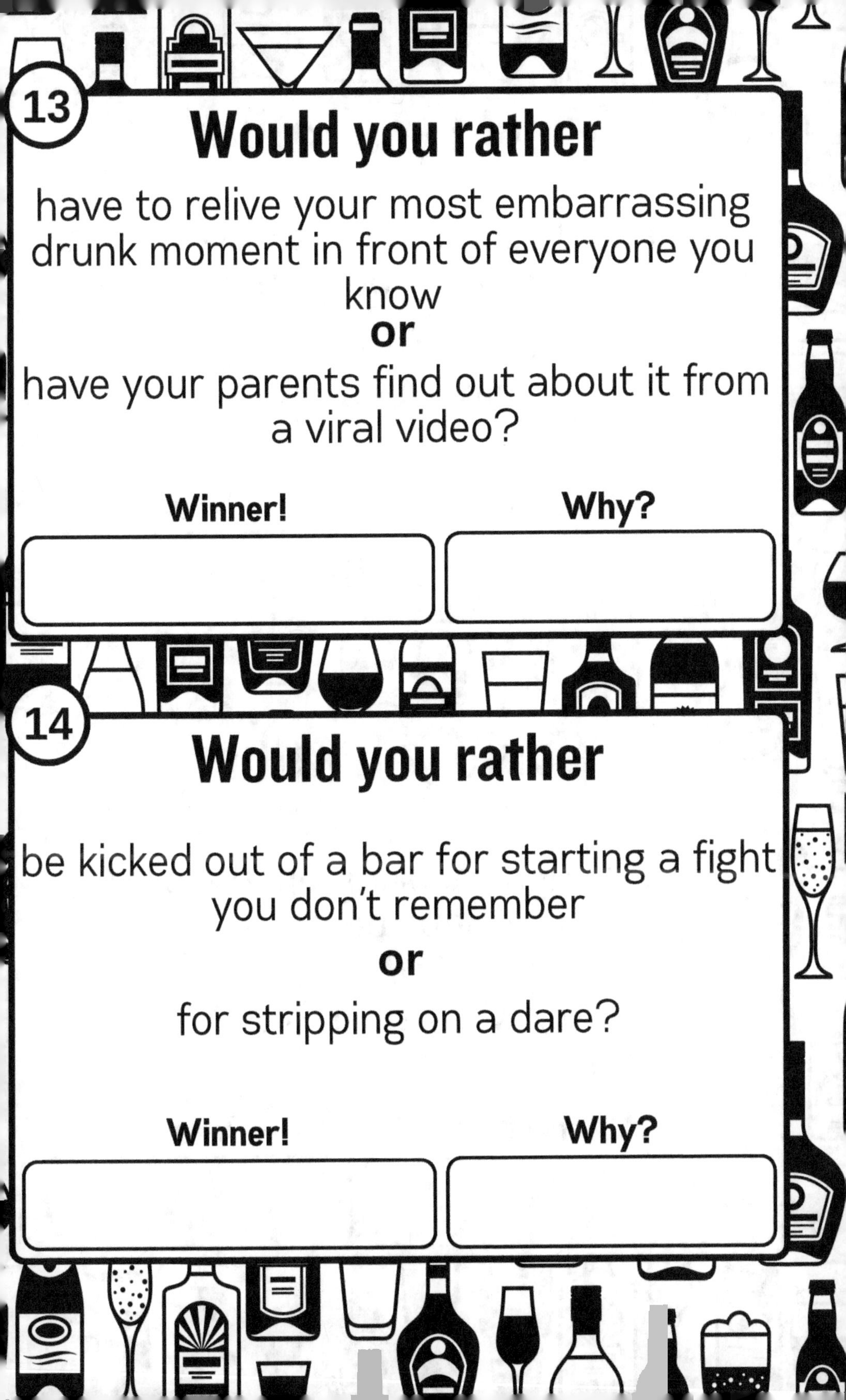

13

Would you rather

have to relive your most embarrassing drunk moment in front of everyone you know
or
have your parents find out about it from a viral video?

Winner!

Why?

14

Would you rather

be kicked out of a bar for starting a fight you don't remember
or
for stripping on a dare?

Winner!

Why?

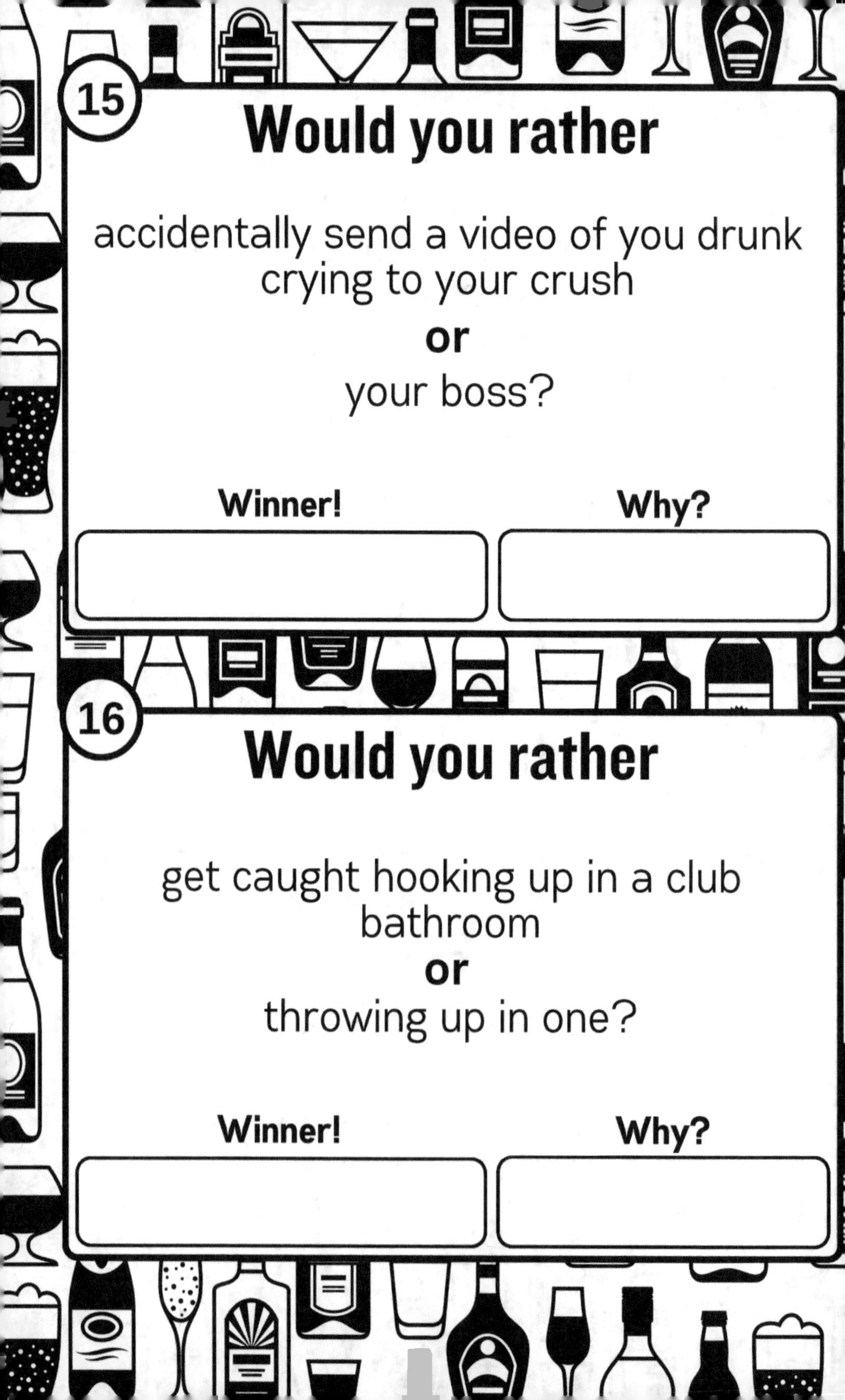

15
Would you rather
accidentally send a video of you drunk crying to your crush
or
your boss?
Winner!
Why?
16
Would you rather
get caught hooking up in a club bathroom
or
throwing up in one?
Winner!
Why?

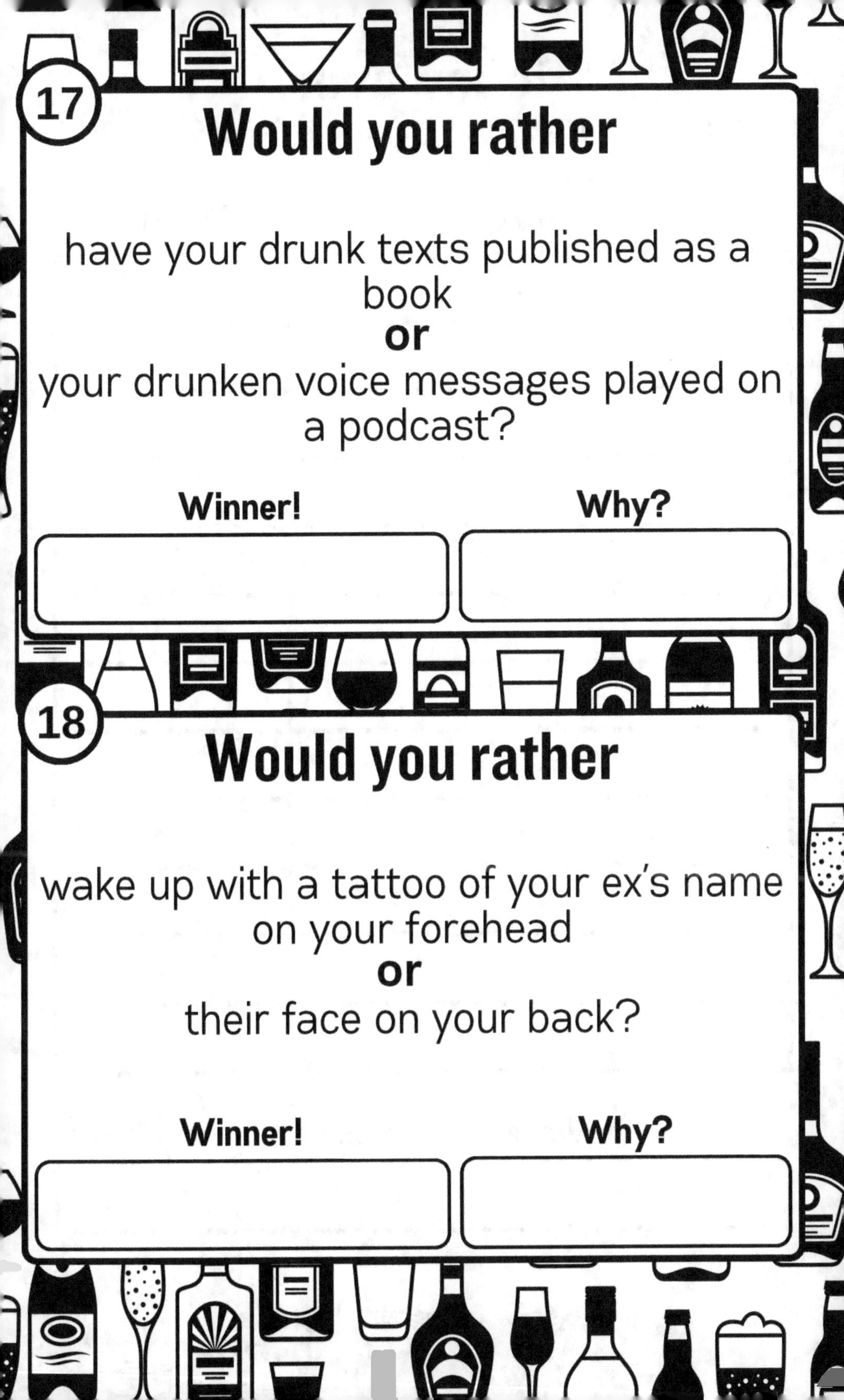

17
Would you rather
have your drunk texts published as a book
or
your drunken voice messages played on a podcast?
Winner!
Why?
18
Would you rather
wake up with a tattoo of your ex's name on your forehead
or
their face on your back?
Winner!
Why?

Round over!

It's time for the current game-master to add up the scores!

Name	Points

Round Winner	Round Winners Choice

Round 12

Game-Master:

Cringe Confessions

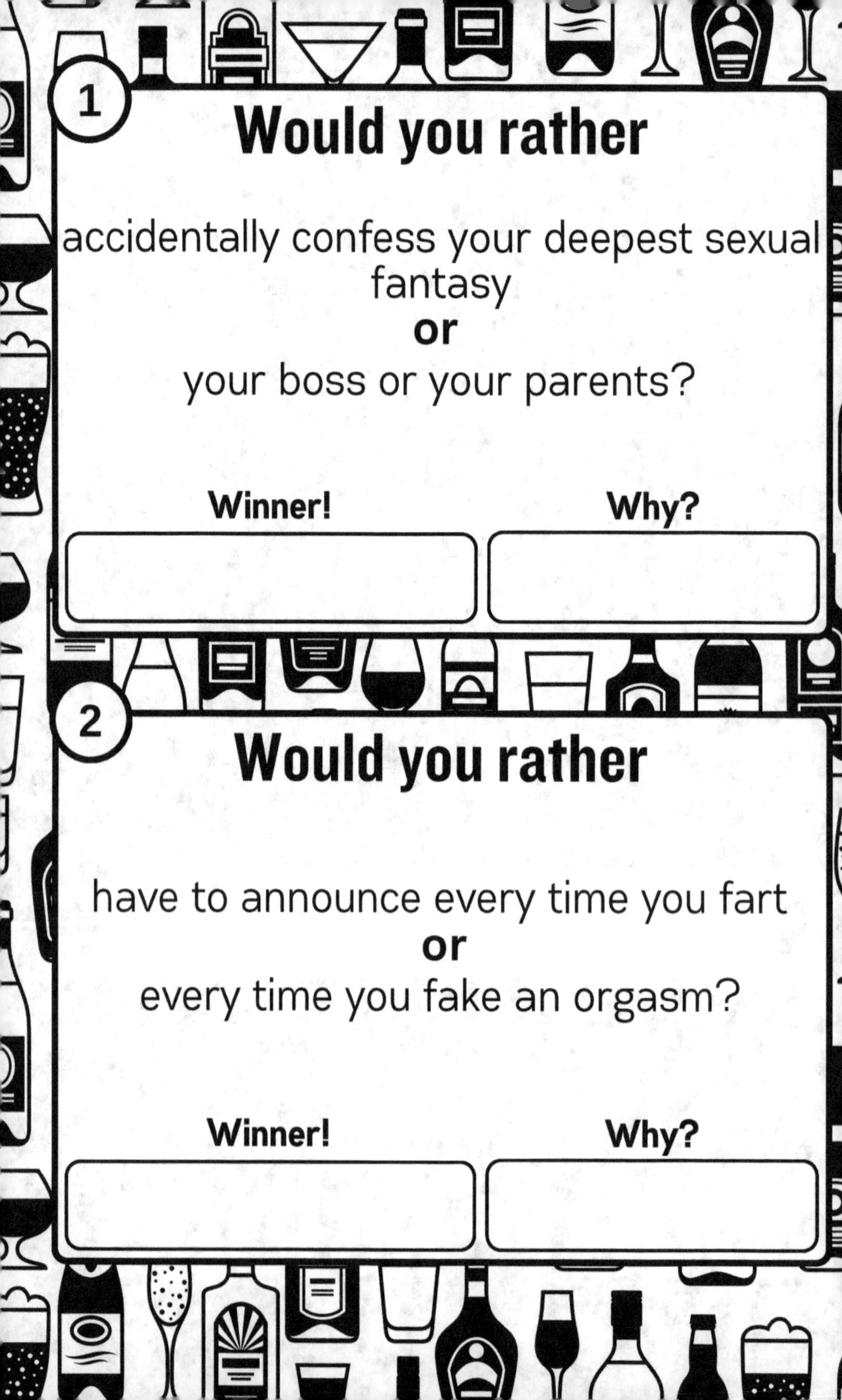

1
Would you rather

accidentally confess your deepest sexual fantasy
or
your boss or your parents?

Winner!

Why?

2
Would you rather

have to announce every time you fart
or
every time you fake an orgasm?

Winner!

Why?

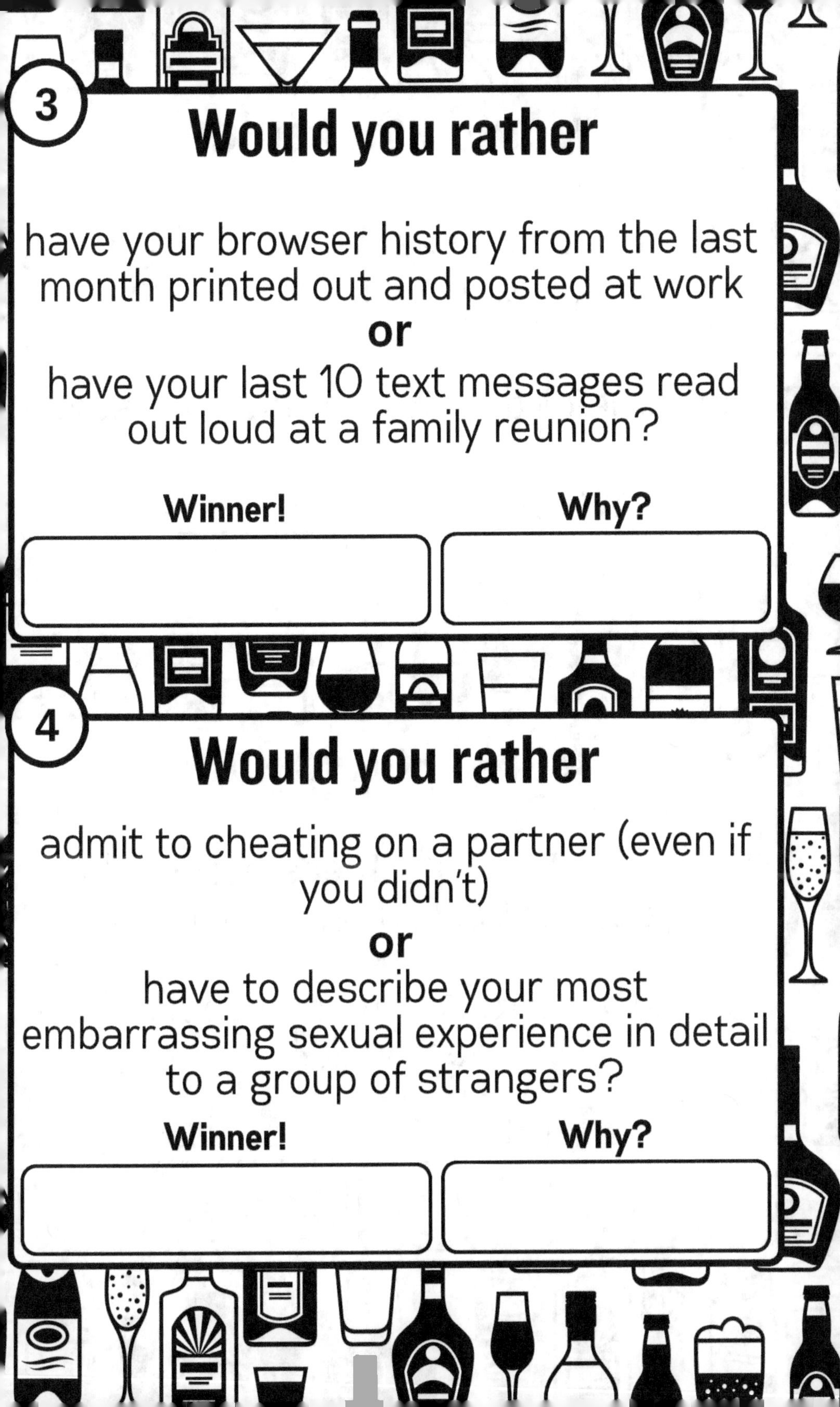

3

Would you rather

have your browser history from the last month printed out and posted at work
or
have your last 10 text messages read out loud at a family reunion?

Winner!

Why?

4

Would you rather

admit to cheating on a partner (even if you didn't)
or
have to describe your most embarrassing sexual experience in detail to a group of strangers?

Winner!

Why?

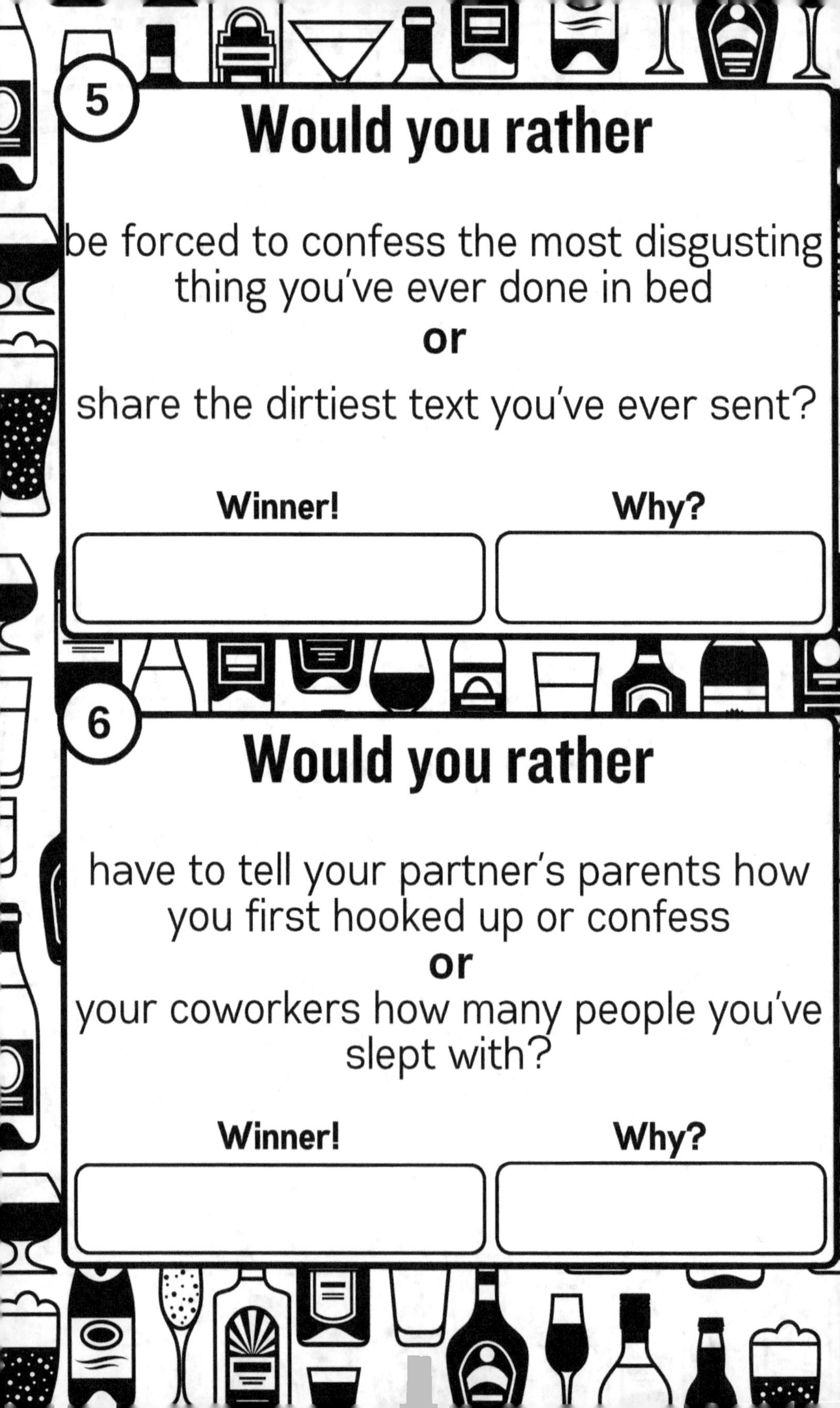

5

Would you rather

be forced to confess the most disgusting thing you've ever done in bed
or
share the dirtiest text you've ever sent?

Winner!   Why?

6

Would you rather

have to tell your partner's parents how you first hooked up or confess
or
your coworkers how many people you've slept with?

Winner!   Why?

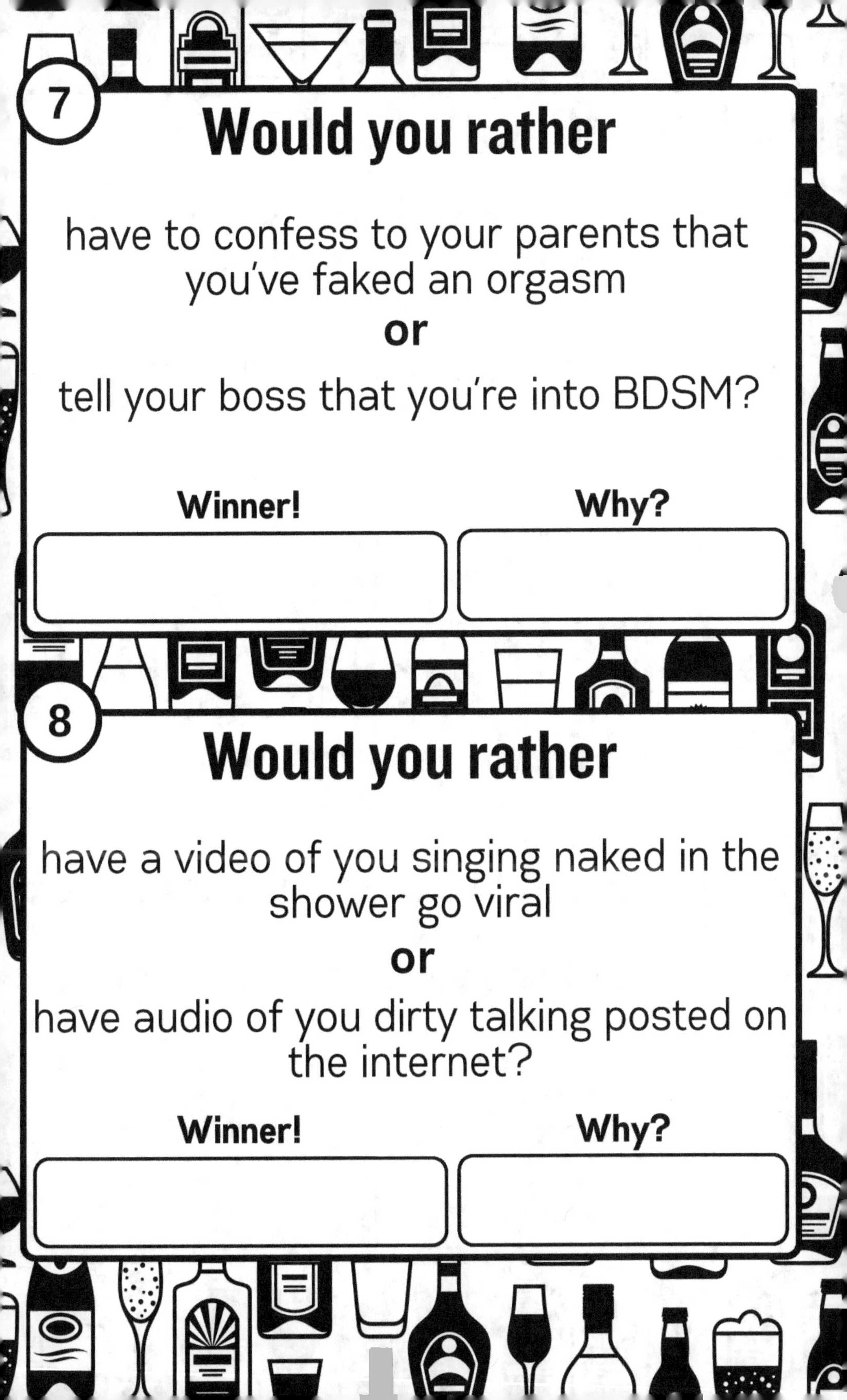

7

Would you rather

have to confess to your parents that you've faked an orgasm

or

tell your boss that you're into BDSM?

Winner!

Why?

8

Would you rather

have a video of you singing naked in the shower go viral

or

have audio of you dirty talking posted on the internet?

Winner!

Why?

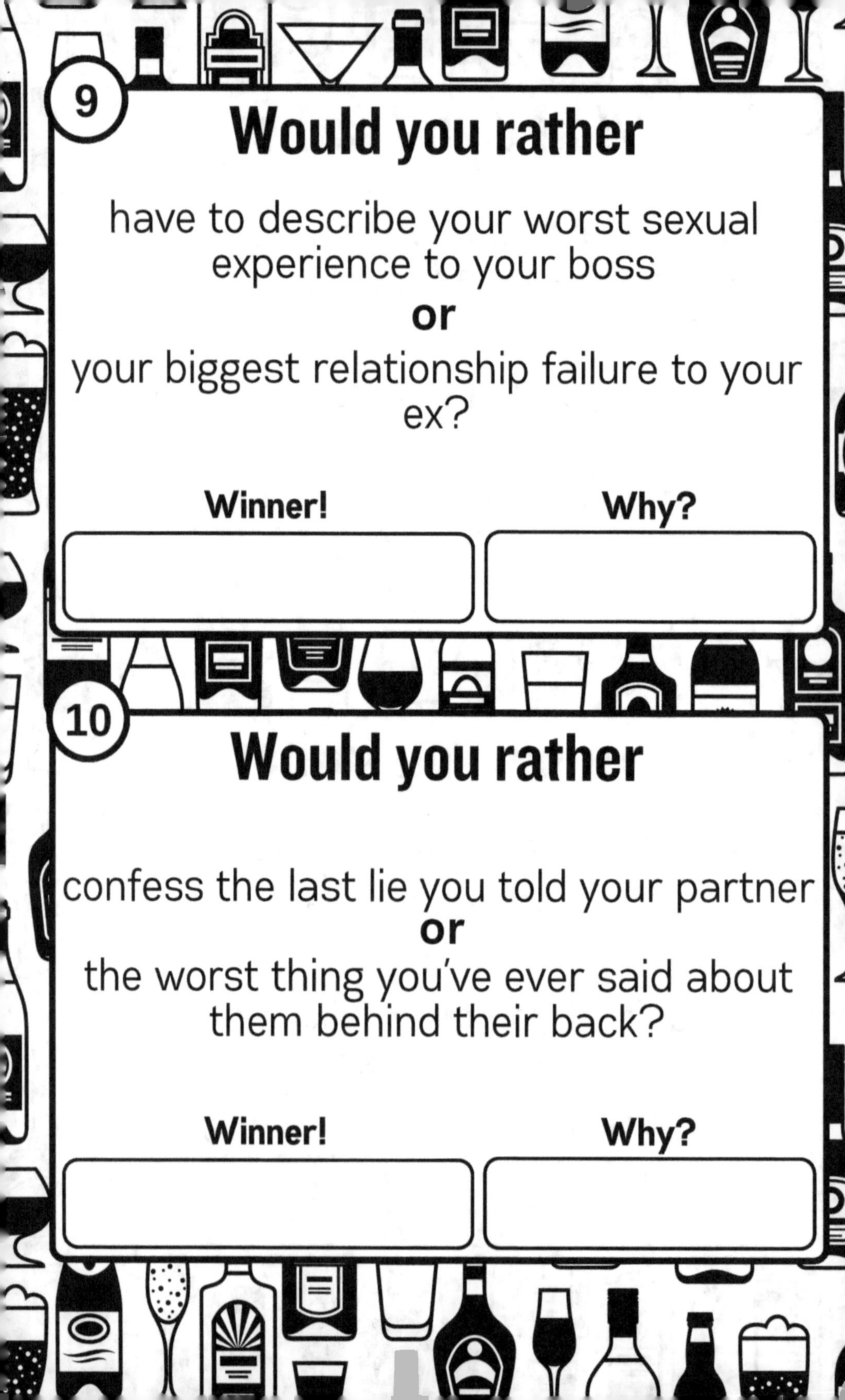

9
Would you rather
have to describe your worst sexual experience to your boss
or
your biggest relationship failure to your ex?
Winner!
Why?
10
Would you rather
confess the last lie you told your partner
or
the worst thing you've ever said about them behind their back?
Winner!
Why?

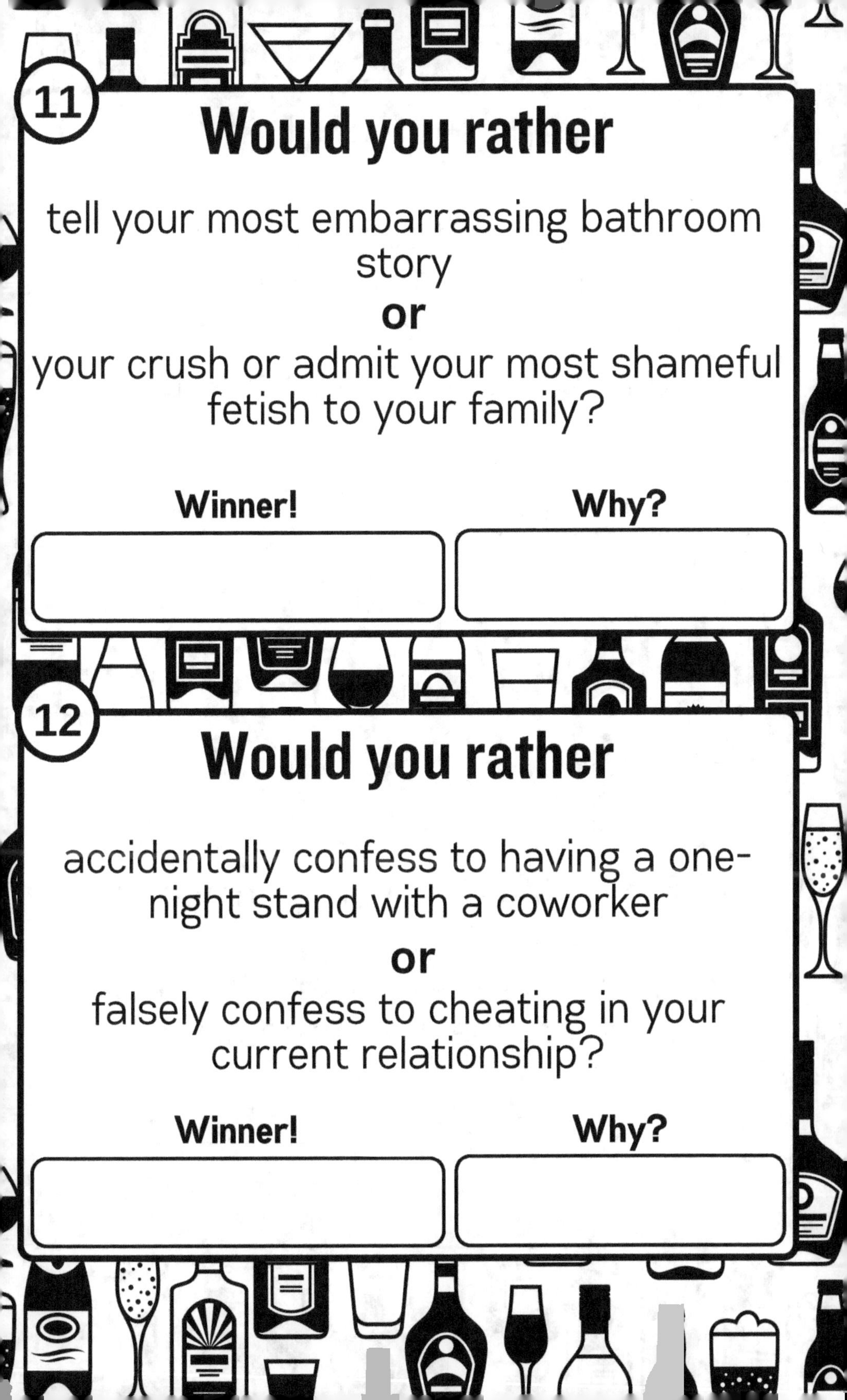

11

Would you rather

tell your most embarrassing bathroom story

or

your crush or admit your most shameful fetish to your family?

Winner!

Why?

12

Would you rather

accidentally confess to having a one-night stand with a coworker

or

falsely confess to cheating in your current relationship?

Winner!

Why?

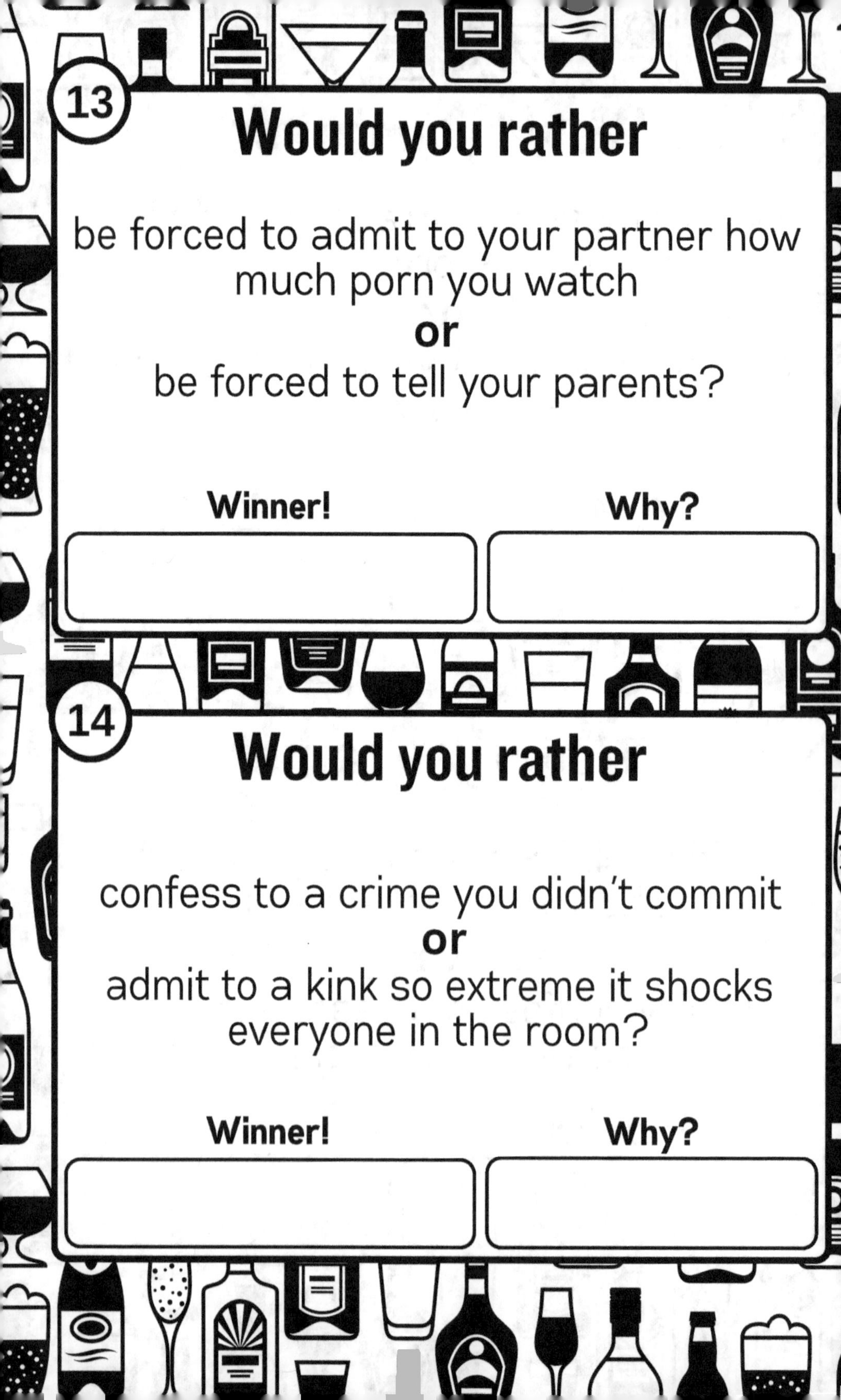

13
Would you rather
be forced to admit to your partner how much porn you watch
or
be forced to tell your parents?
Winner!
Why?
14
Would you rather
confess to a crime you didn't commit
or
admit to a kink so extreme it shocks everyone in the room?
Winner!
Why?

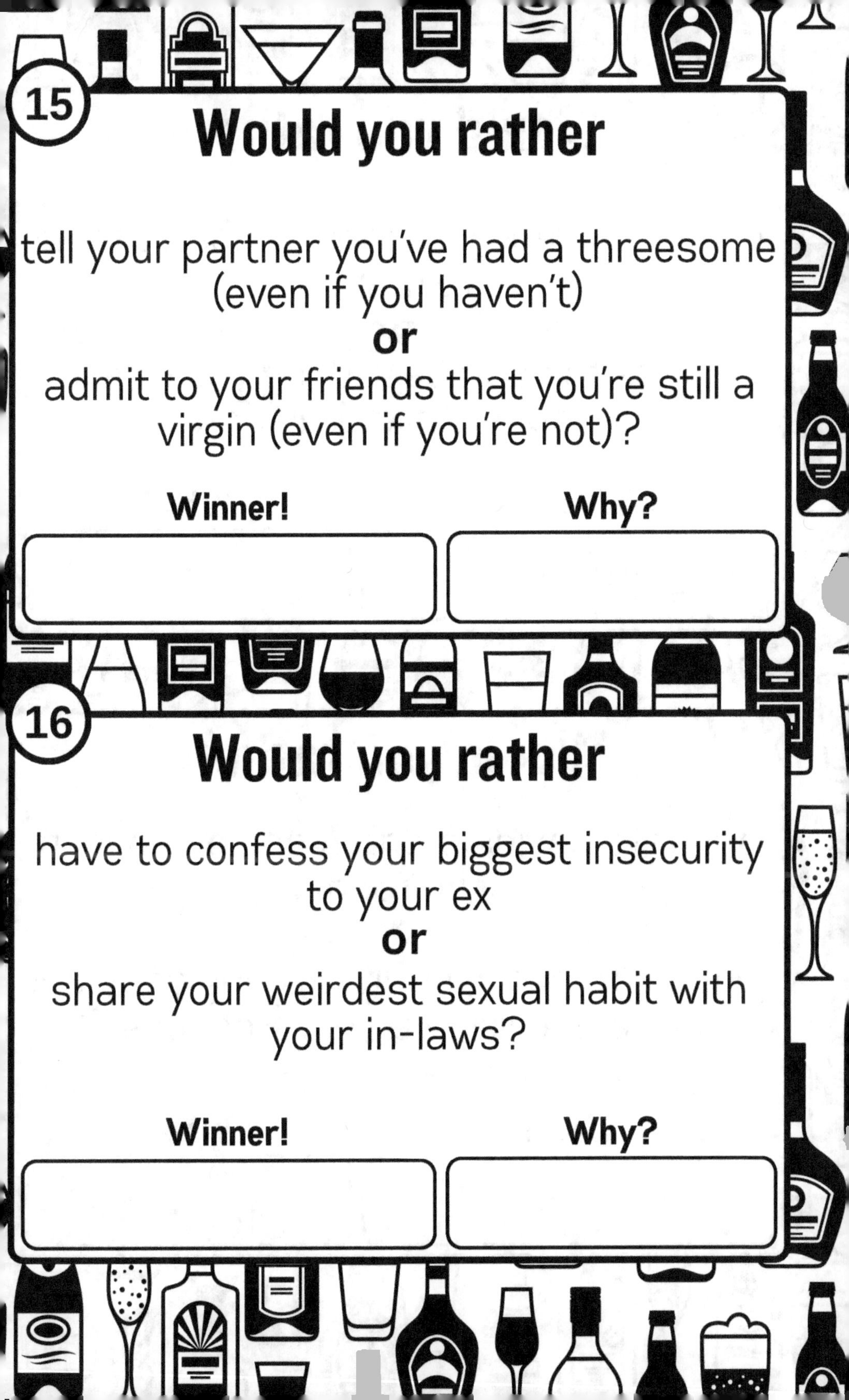

15

Would you rather

tell your partner you've had a threesome
(even if you haven't)
or
admit to your friends that you're still a
virgin (even if you're not)?

Winner!   **Why?**

16

Would you rather

have to confess your biggest insecurity
to your ex
or
share your weirdest sexual habit with
your in-laws?

Winner!   **Why?**

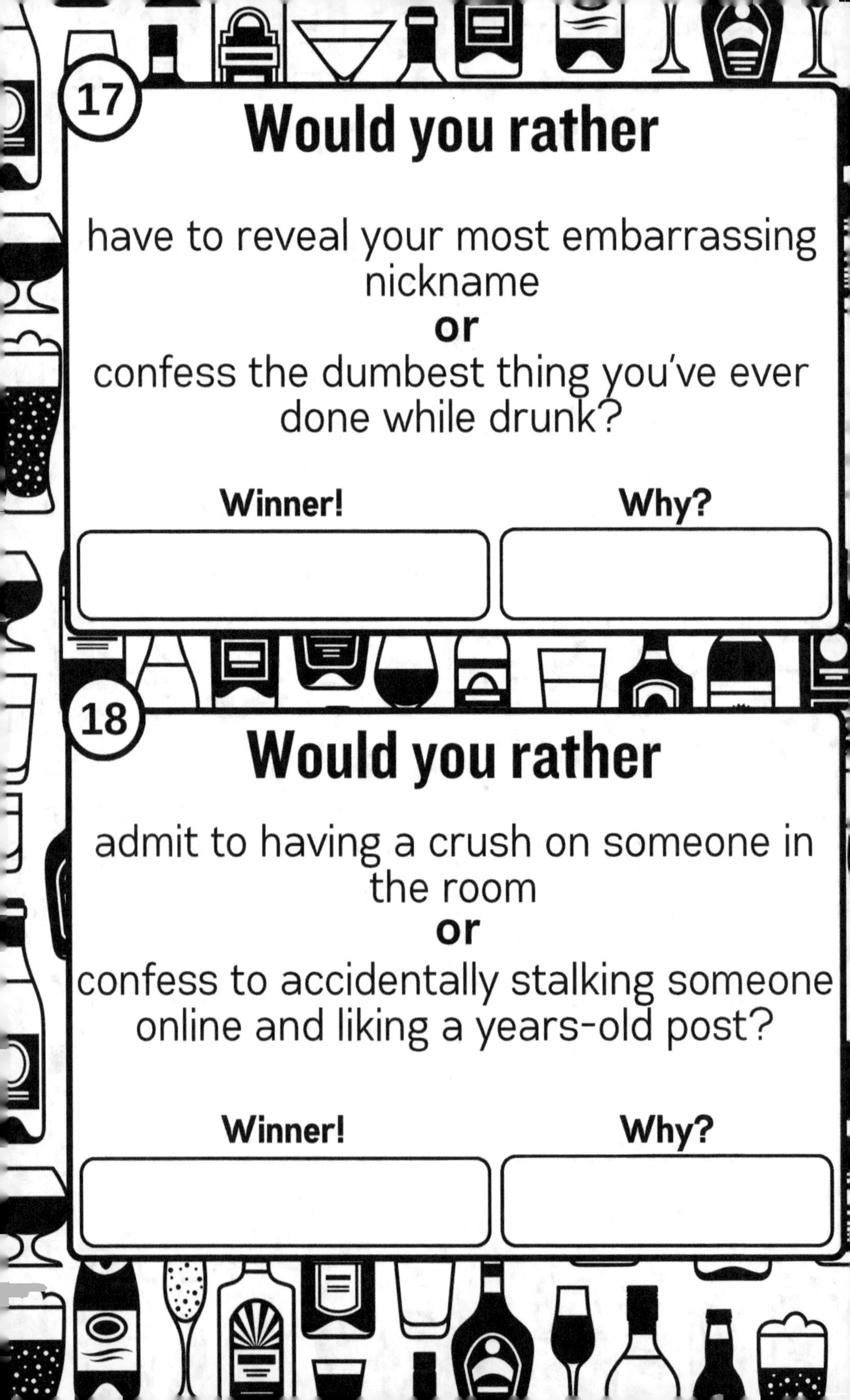

17
Would you rather
have to reveal your most embarrassing nickname
or
confess the dumbest thing you've ever done while drunk?
Winner!
Why?
18
Would you rather
admit to having a crush on someone in the room
or
confess to accidentally stalking someone online and liking a years-old post?
Winner!
Why?

Round over!

It's time for the current game-master to add up the scores!

Name	Points

Round Winner	Round Winners Choice

Round 13

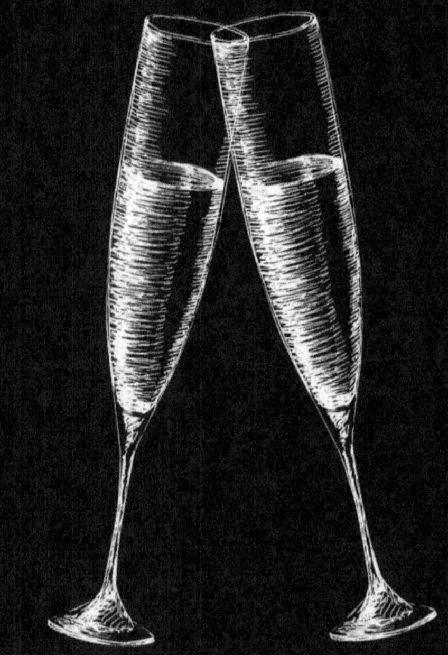

Game-Master:

Your Creative Twist

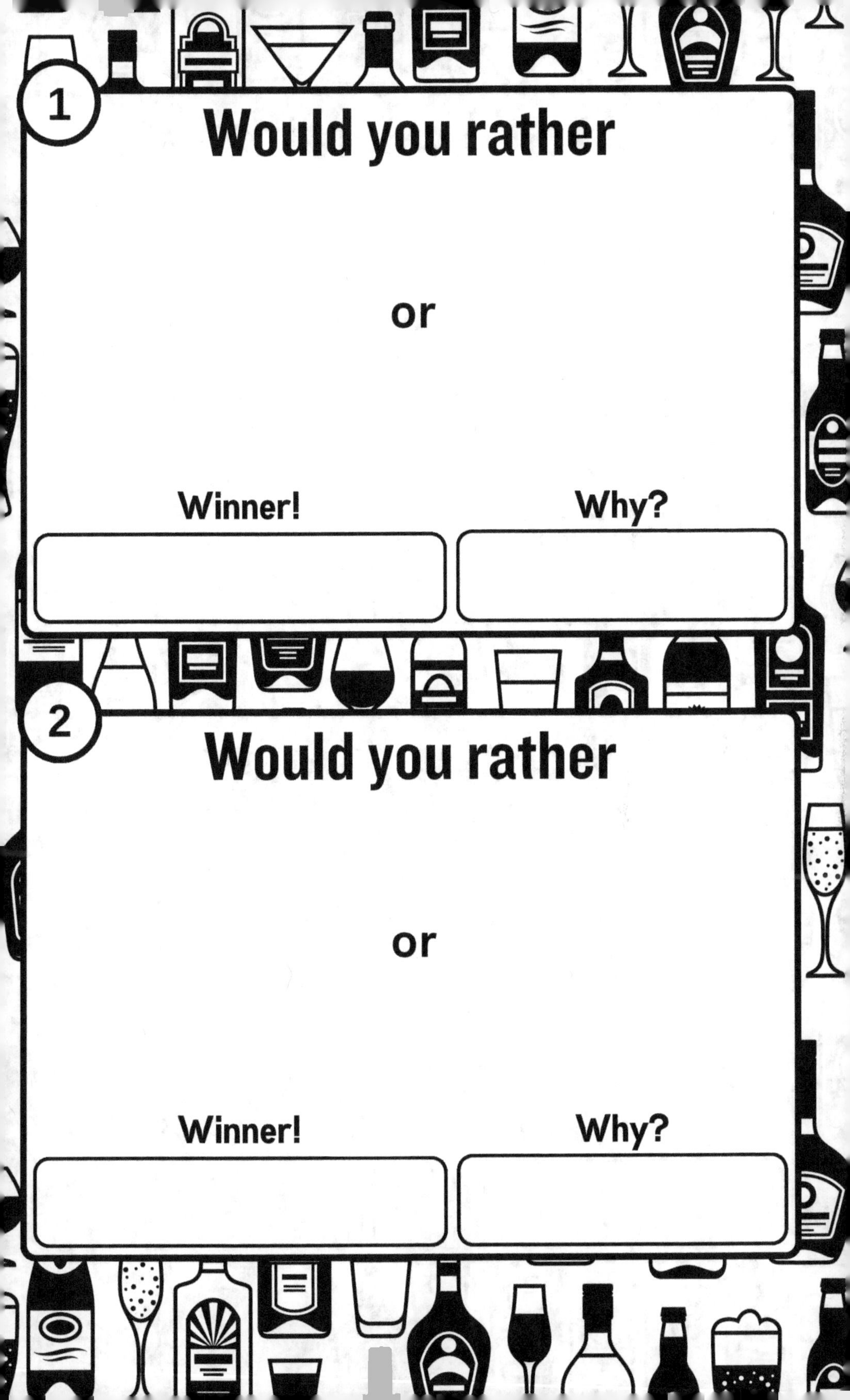

1
Would you rather
or
Winner!
Why?
2
Would you rather
or
Winner!
Why?

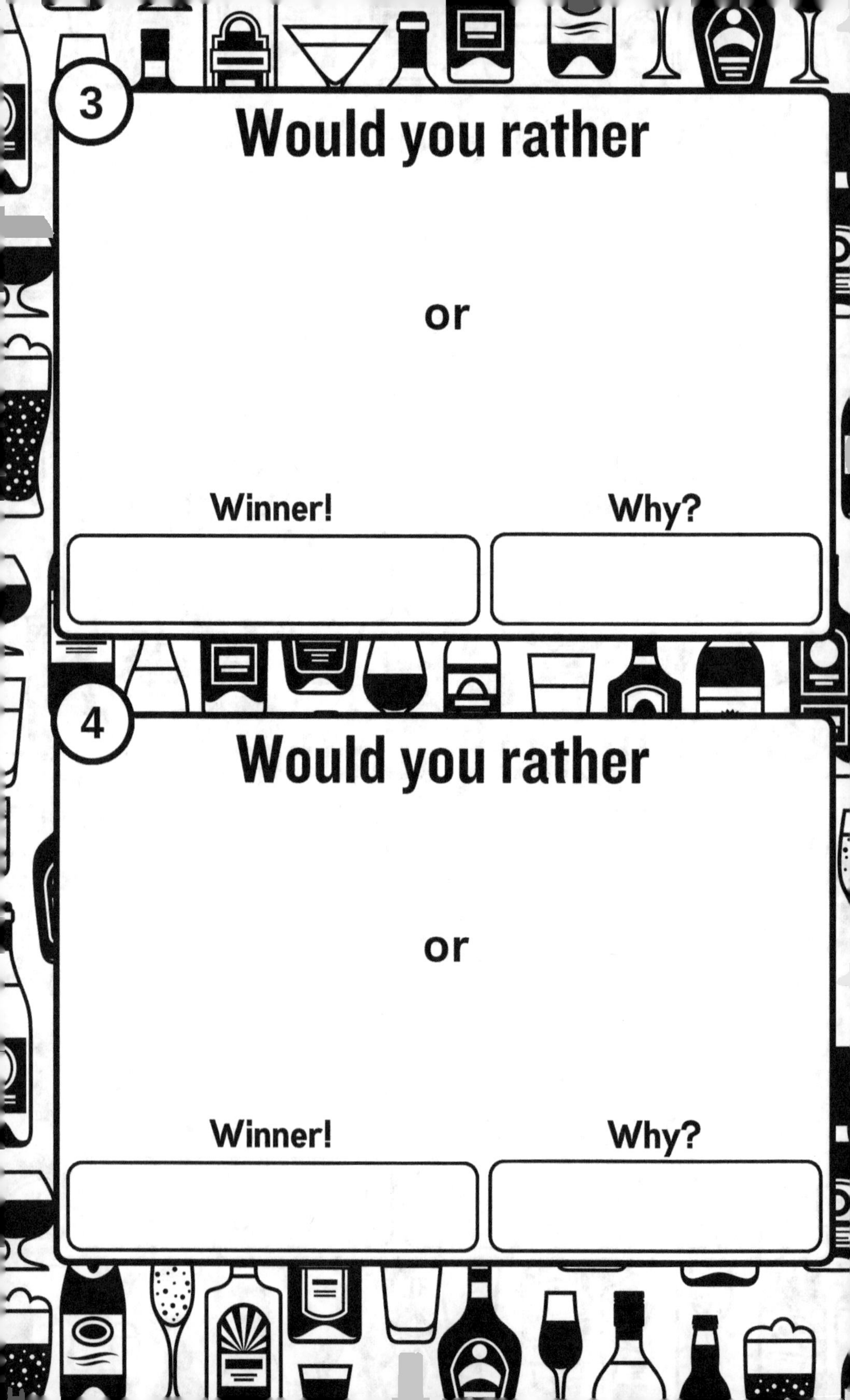

3
Would you rather
or
Winner!
Why?
4
Would you rather
or
Winner!
Why?

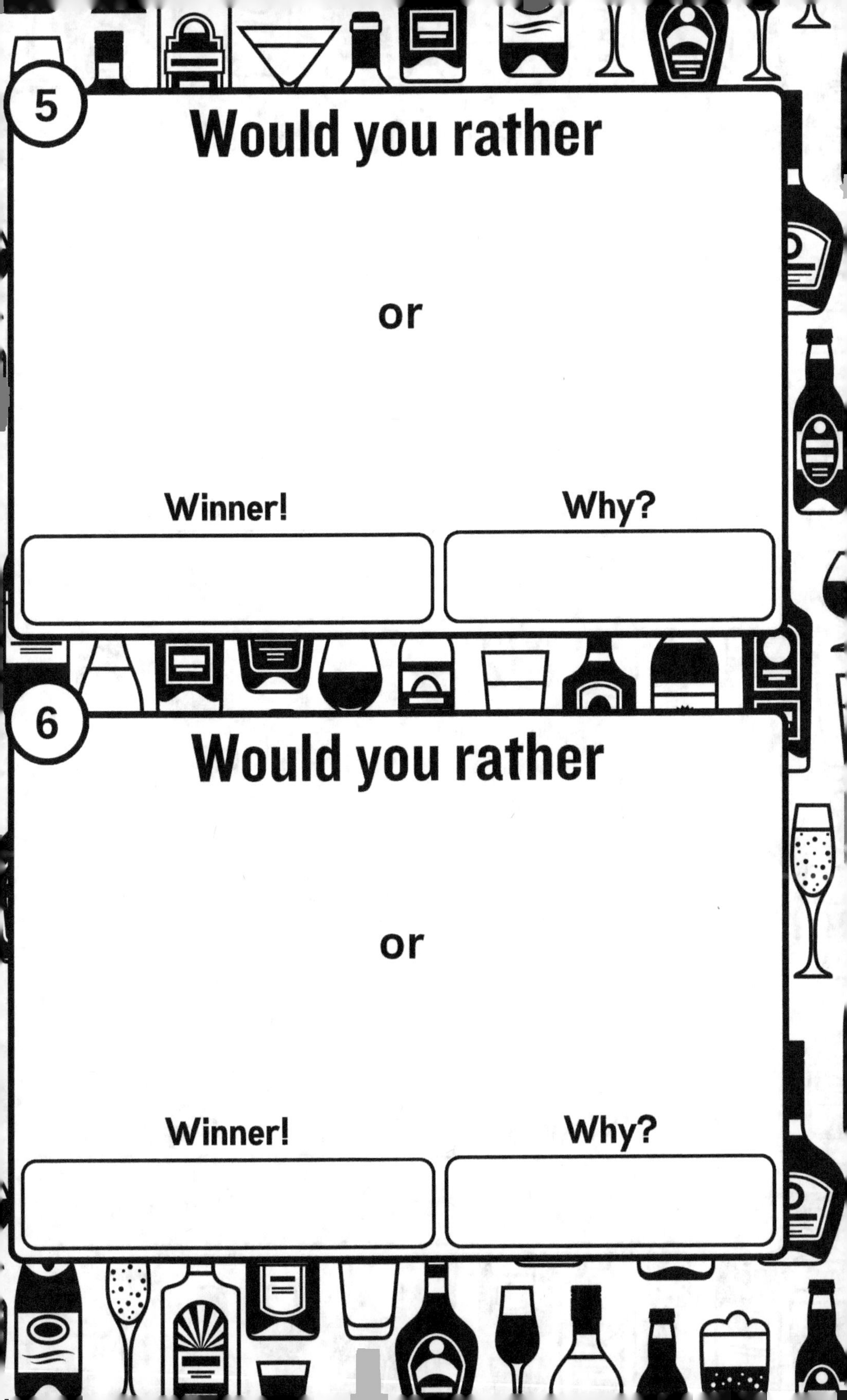

5
Would you rather

or

Winner!

Why?

6
Would you rather

or

Winner!

Why?

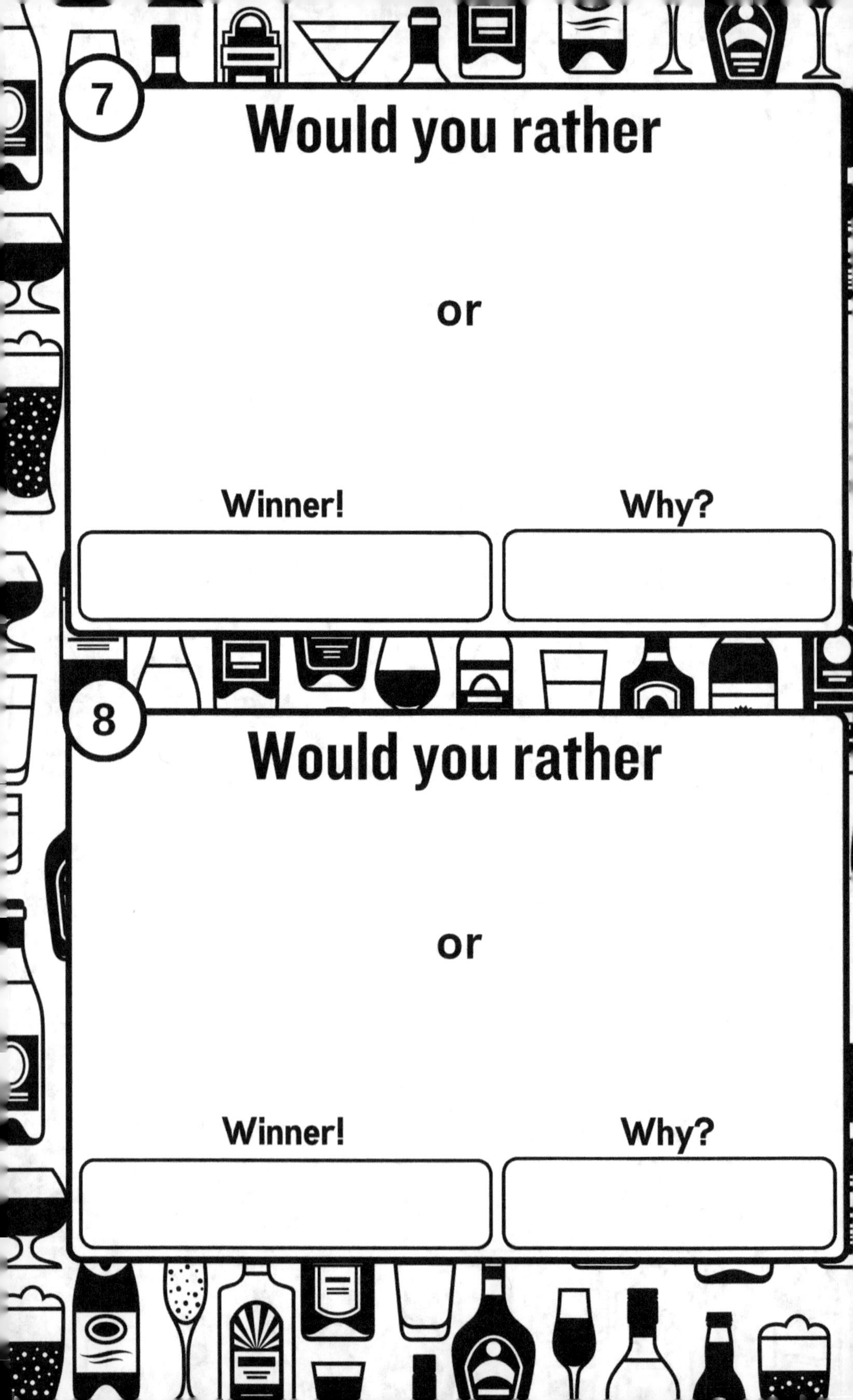

7

Would you rather

or

Winner!

Why?

8

Would you rather

or

Winner!

Why?

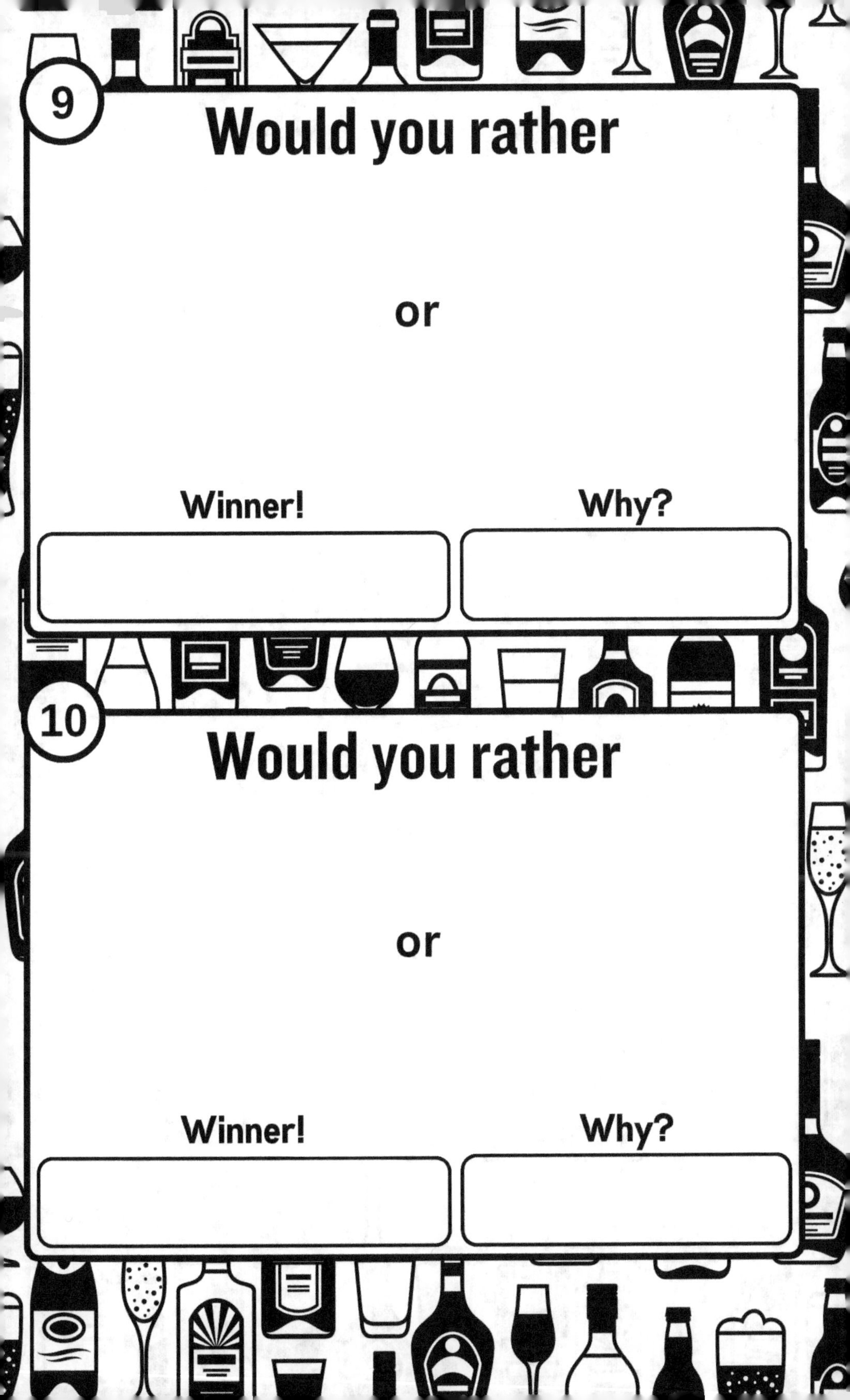

9

Would you rather

or

Winner!

Why?

10

Would you rather

or

Winner!

Why?

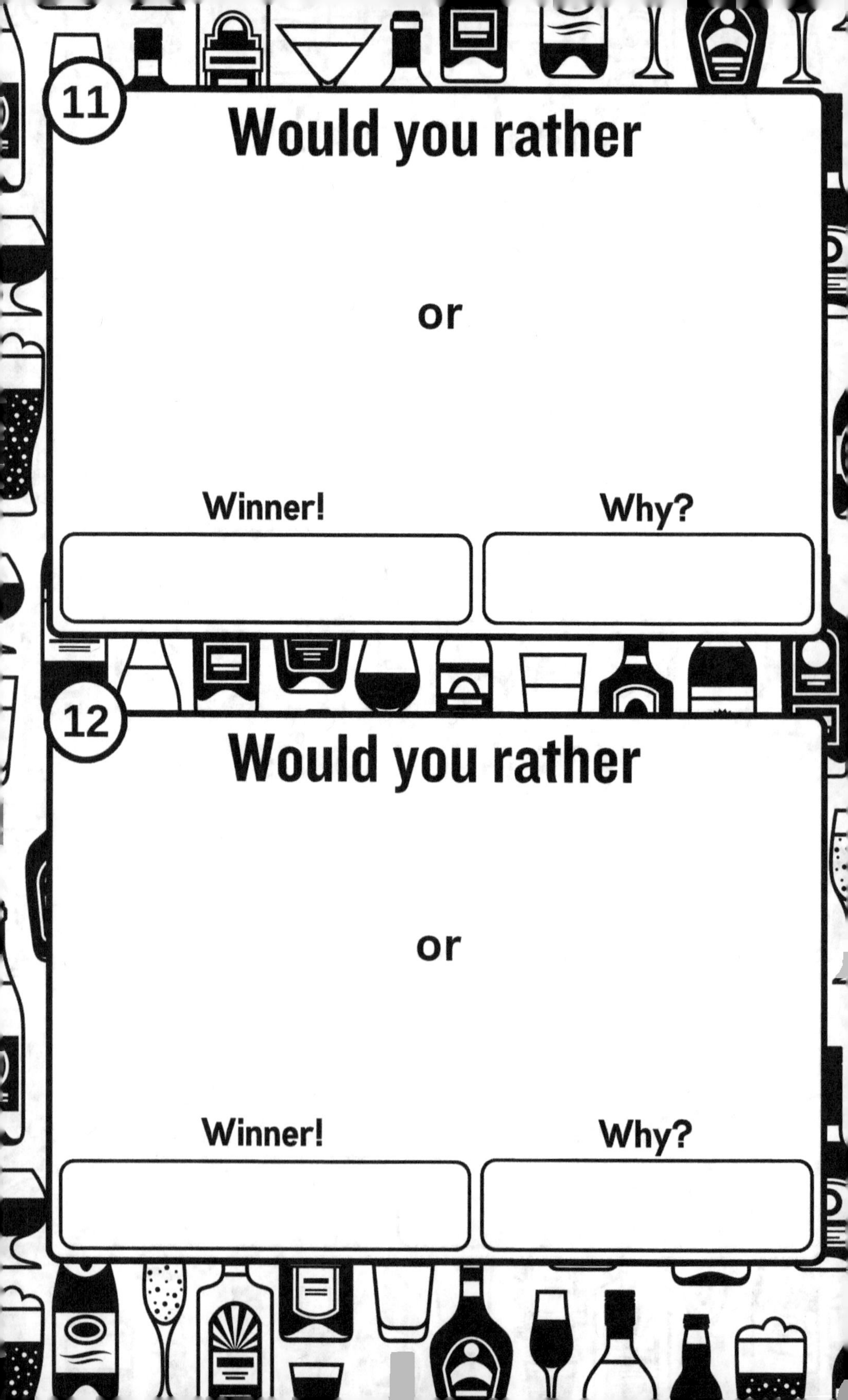

11
Would you rather
or
Winner!
Why?
12
Would you rather
or
Winner!
Why?

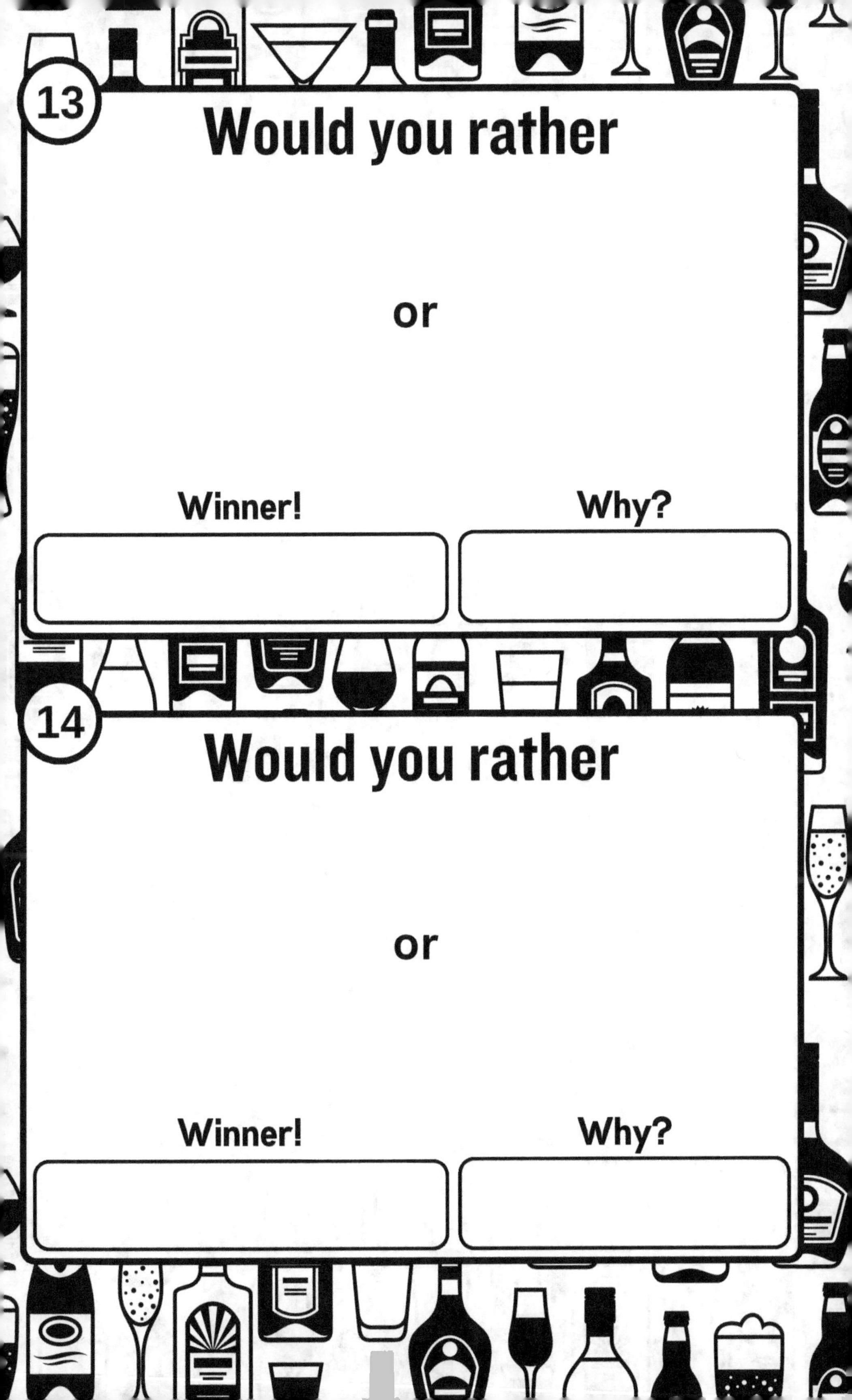
13
Would you rather

or

Winner!
Why?

14
Would you rather

or

Winner!
Why?

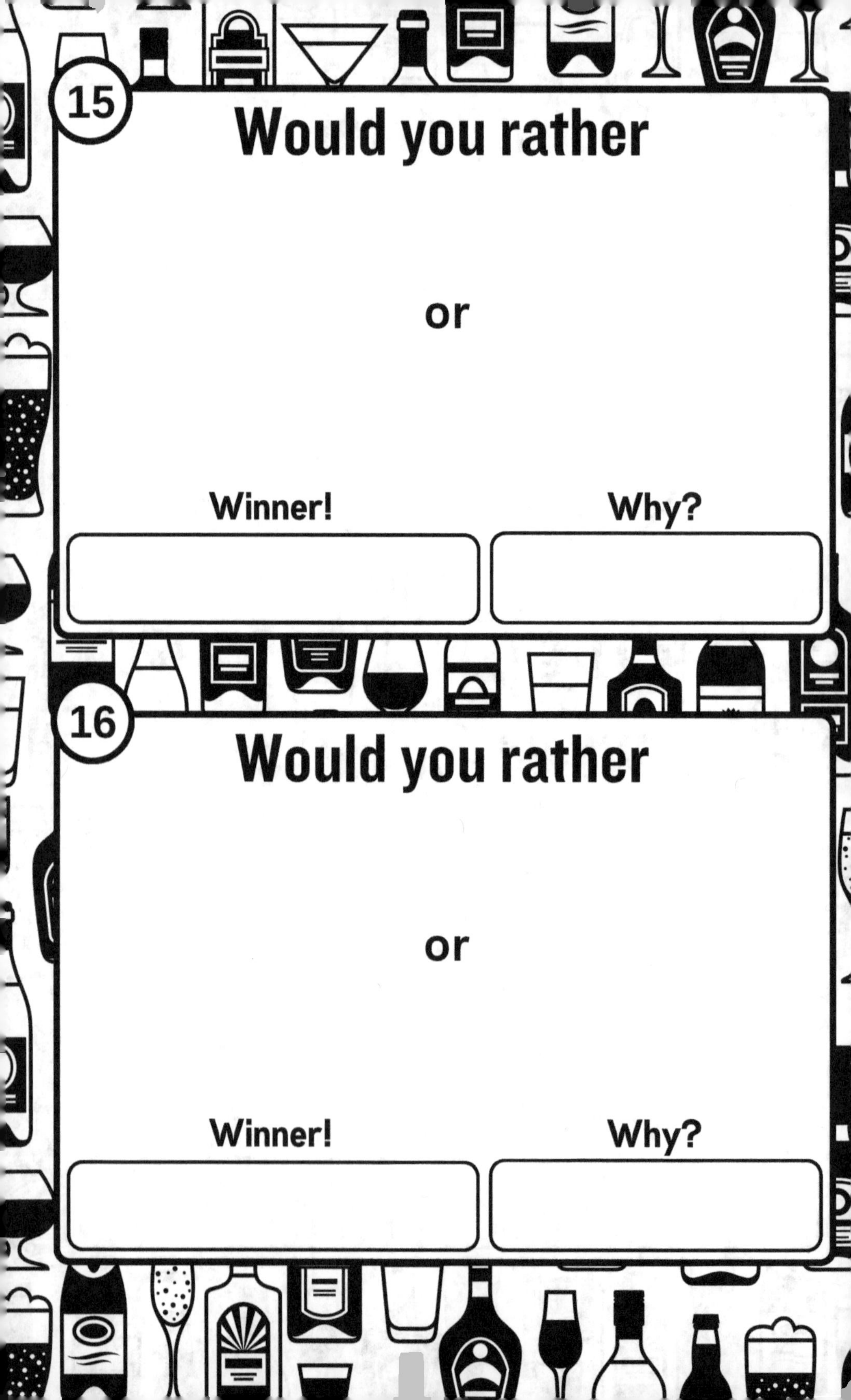
15
Would you rather
or
Winner!
Why?
16
Would you rather
or
Winner!
Why?

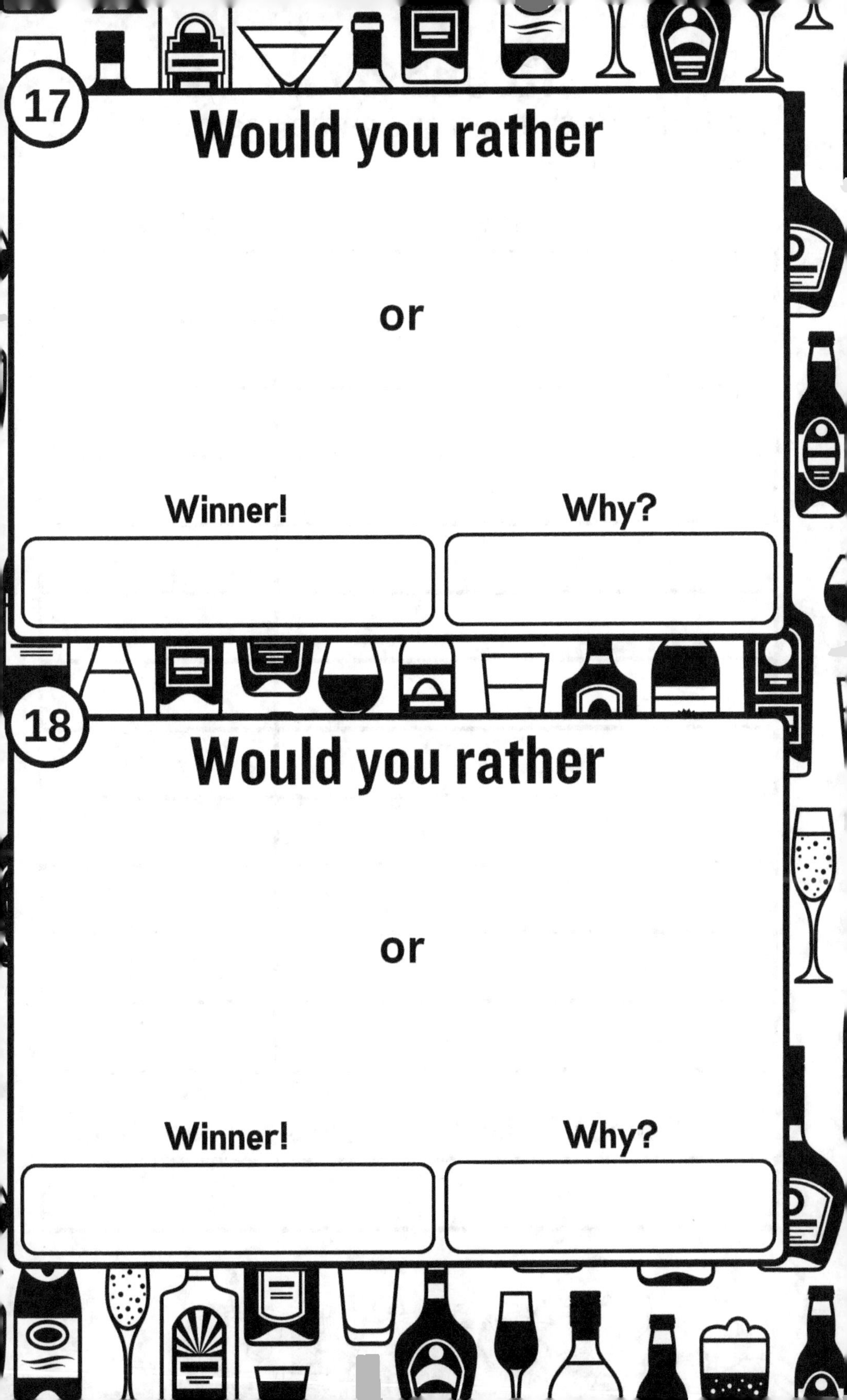
17
Would you rather
or
Winner!
Why?
18
Would you rather
or
Winner!
Why?

Round over!

It's time for the current game-master to add up the scores!

Name	Points

Round Winner	Round Winners Choice

Final Scores

Winner

www.ingramcontent.com/pod-product-compliance
Lightning Source LLC
Chambersburg PA
CBHW061045250726
48653CB00001B/260